Australasian Language Technology Association Workshop 2012

(ALTA 2012)

Dunedin, New Zealand
4 – 6 December 2012

Editors:

Paul Cook
Scott Nowson

ISBN: 978-1-62748-403-9
ISSN: 1834-7037

Printed from e-media with permission by:

Curran Associates, Inc.
57 Morehouse Lane
Red Hook, NY 12571

Some format issues inherent in the e-media version may also appear in this print version.

Printed by Curran Associates, Inc. (2013)

For permission requests, please contact the Association for Computational Linguistics at the address below.

Association for Computational Linguistics
209 N. Eighth Street
Stroudsburg, Pennsylvania 18360

Phone: 1-570-476-8006
Fax: 1-570-476-0860

acl@aclweb.org

Additional copies of this publication are available from:

Curran Associates, Inc.
57 Morehouse Lane
Red Hook, NY 12571 USA
Phone: 845-758-0400
Fax: 845-758-2634
Email: curran@proceedings.com
Web: www.proceedings.com

Australasian Language Technology Association Workshop 2012

Proceedings of the Workshop

Editors:
Paul Cook
Scott Nowson

4–6 December 2012
Otago University
Dunedin, New Zealand

Australasian Language Technology Association Workshop 2012
(ALTA 2012)

http://www.alta.asn.au/events/alta2012

Sponsors:

Volume 10, 2012
ISSN: 1834-7037

ALTA 2012 Workshop Committees

Workshop Co-Chairs

- Paul Cook (The University of Melbourne)
- Scott Nowson (Appen Butler Hill)

Workshop Local Organiser

- Alistair Knott (University of Otago)

Programme Committee

- Timothy Baldwin (University of Melbourne)
- Lawrence Cavedon (NICTA and RMIT University)
- Nathalie Colineau (CSIRO - ICT Centre)
- Rebecca Dridan (University of Oslo)
- Alex Chengyu Fang (The City University of Hong Kong)
- Nitin Indurkhya (UNSW)
- Jong-Bok Kim (Kyung Hee University)
- Alistair Knott (University of Otago)
- Oi Yee Kwong (City University of Hong Kong)
- Francois Lareau (Macquarie University)
- Jey Han Lau (University of Melbourne)
- Fang Li (Shanghai Jiao Tong University)
- Haizhou Li (Institute for Infocomm Research)
- Marco Lui (University of Melbourne)
- Ruli Manurung (Universitas Indonesia)
- David Martinez (NICTA VRL)
- Tara McIntosh (Wavii)
- Meladel Mistica (The Australian National University)
- Diego Mollá (Macquarie University)
- Su Nam Kim (Monash University)
- Luiz Augusto Pizzato (University of Sydney)
- David Powers (Flinders University)
- Stijn De Saeger (National Institute of Information and Communications Technology)
- Andrea Schalley (Griffith University)
- Rolf Schwitter (Macquarie University)
- Tony Smith (Waikato University)
- Virach Sornlertlamvanich (National Electronics and Computer Technology Center)
- Hanna Suominen (NICTA)
- Karin Verspoor (National ICT Australia)

Preface

The precious volume you are currently reading contains the papers accepted for presentation at the Australasian Language Technology Association Workshop (ALTA) 2012, held at the University of Otago in Dunedin, New Zealand on 4–6 December 2012. We are excited that this tenth anniversary edition of the ALTA Workshop sees ALTA leaving Australia for the first time, and becoming a truly Australasian workshop. Sadly we say goodbye to the Aussie bush hat on the conference webpage, but it is in the spirit of Mick "Crocodile" Dundee that we cross the Tasman.

The goals of the workshop are to:

- bring together the growing Language Technology (LT) community in the Australasian region and encourage interactions;
- encourage interactions and collaboration within this community and with the wider international LT community;
- foster interaction between academic and industrial researchers, to encourage dissemination of research results;
- provide a forum for students and young researchers to present their research;
- facilitate the discussion of new and ongoing research and projects;
- provide an opportunity for the broader artificial intelligence community to become aware of local LT research; and, finally,
- increase visibility of LT research in Australasia and overseas.

This year's ALTA Workshop presents 14 peer-reviewed papers, including eleven full and three short papers. We received a total of 18 submissions. Each paper, full and short, was reviewed by at least three members of the program committee. With the more-international flavour of the workshop, this year's program committee consisted of more members from outside of Australia and New Zealand than in past years. The reviewing for the workshop was double blind, and done in accordance with the DIISRTE requirements for E1 conference publications. Furthermore, great care was taken to avoid all conflicts of interest; in particular, no paper was assessed by a reviewer from the same institution as any of the authors. In the case of submissions by a programme co-chair, the double-blind review process was upheld, and acceptance decisions were made by the non-author co-chair.

In addition to peer-reviewed papers, the proceedings include the abstracts of the invited talks by Jen Hay (University of Canterbury) and Chris Brockett (Microsoft Research), both of whom we are honoured to welcome to ALTA. Also within, you will find an overview of the ALTA Shared Task and three system descriptions by shared task participants. These contributions were not peer-reviewed.

We would like to thank, in no particular order: all of the authors who submitted papers to ALTA; the fellowship of the program committee for the time and effort they put into maintaining the high standards of our reviewing process; our Man In Dunedin, the local organiser Alistair Knott for taking care of all the physical logistics and lining up some great social events; our invited speakers Jen Hay and Chris Brockett for agreeing to share their wisdom with us; the team from NICTA and James Curran for agreeing to host two fascinating tutorials, and; Diego Mollá and David Martinez, the program co-chairs of ALTA 2011, for their valuable help and support. We would like to acknowledge the constant support and advice of the out-going ALTA Executive Committee and in particular President Timothy Baldwin.

Finally, we gratefully recognise our sponsors: NICTA, Microsoft Research, Appen Butler Hill, and the University of Otago. Their generous support enabled us to offer travel subsidies to six students to attend and present at ALTA.

Paul Cook and Scott Nowson
Programme Co-Chairs

ALTA 2012 Programme

The proceedings are available online at `http://www.alta.asn.au/events/alta2012/proceedings/`

Tuesday 4 December 2012 Pre-workshop tutorials

Biomedical Natural Language Processing (Owheo 106)

A Crash Course in Statistical Natural Language Processing (Lab F)

Wednesday 5 December 2012

08:50–09:00	Opening remarks (Owheo 106)
09:00–10:00	Invited talk (Owheo 106; Chair: Paul Cook) Jennifer Hay *Using a large annotated historical corpus to study word-specific effects in sound change*
10:00–10:30	Coffee
Session 1 (Owheo 106; Chair: Ingrid Zukerman)	
10:30–11:00	Angrosh M.A., Stephen Cranefield and Nigel Stanger *A Citation Centric Annotation Scheme for Scientific Articles*
11:00–11:30	Michael Symonds, Guido Zuccon, Bevan Koopman, Peter Bruza and Anthony Nguyen *Semantic Judgement of Medical Concepts: Combining Syntagmatic and Paradigmatic Information with the Tensor Encoding Model*
11:30–12:00	Teresa Lynn, Jennifer Foster, Mark Dras and Elaine Uí Dhonnchadha *Active Learning and the Irish Treebank*
12:00–13:30	Lunch
Session 2 (Owheo 106; Chair: Diego Mollá)	
13:30–14:00	Marco Lui, Timothy Baldwin and Diana McCarthy *Unsupervised Estimation of Word Usage Similarity*
14:00–14:30	Mary Gardiner and Mark Dras *Valence Shifting: Is It A Valid Task?*
14:30–15:00	**ALTA 2012 best paper** Minh Duc Cao and Ingrid Zukerman *Experimental Evaluation of a Lexicon- and Corpus-based Ensemble for Multi-way Sentiment Analysis*
15:00–15:30	Coffee
Session 3 (Owheo 106; Chair: Chris Brockett)	
15:30–16:00	James Breen, Timothy Baldwin and Francis Bond *Extraction and Translation of Japanese Multi-word Loanwords*
16:00–16:30	Yvette Graham, Timothy Baldwin, Aaron Harwood, Alistair Moffat and Justin Zobel *Measurement of Progress in Machine Translation*
16:30–17:30	ALTA business meeting (Owheo 106)
19:30–	Conference dinner (Filadelfio's, 3 North Road)

Thursday 6 December 2012

09:00–10:00	Invited talk (Owheo 206; Chair: Timothy Baldwin) Chris Brockett *Diverse Words, Shared Meanings: Statistical Machine Translation for Paraphrase, Grounding, and Intent*
10:00–10:30	Coffee
Session 4: ALTA/ADCS shared session (Owheo 106; Chair: Alistair Knott)	
10:30–11:00	**ADCS paper** Lida Ghahremanloo, James Thom and Liam Magee *An Ontology Derived from Heterogeneous Sustainability Indicator Set Documents*
11:00–11:30	**ADCS paper** Bevan Koopman, Peter Bruza, Guido Zuccon, Michael John Lawley and Laurianne Sitbon *Graph-based Concept Weighting for Medical Information Retrieval*
11:30–12:00	Abeed Sarker, Diego Mollá-Aliod and Cecile Paris *Towards Two-step Multi-document Summarisation for Evidence Based Medicine: A Quantitative Analysis*
12:00–12:30	Alex G. Smith, Christopher X. S. Zee and Alexandra L. Uitdenbogerd *In Your Eyes: Identifying Clichés in Song Lyrics*
12:30–14:00	Lunch
Session 5: ALTA Shared Task and poster boasters (Owheo 206; Chair: Karin Verspoor)	
14:00–14:30	Iman Amini, David Martinez and Diego Molla *ALTA 2012 Shared Task overview*
14:30–14:50	ALTA poster boasters
	Paul Cook and Marco Lui *langid.py for better language modelling*
	Robert Fromont and Jennifer Hay *LaBB-CAT: an Annotation Store*
	Jenny Mcdonald, Alistair Knott and Richard Zeng *Free-text input vs menu selection: exploring the difference with a tutorial dialogue system.*
	Jared Willett, Timothy Baldwin, David Martinez and Angus Webb *Classification of Study Region in Environmental Science Abstracts*
	ALTA Shared Task poster boasters
	Marco Lui *Feature Stacking for Sentence Classification in Evidence-based Medicine*
	Abeed Sarker *Multi-class classification of medical sentences using SVMs*
14:50–15:00	Awards and final remarks (Owheo 206)
15:00–15:30	Coffee
15:30–17:00	Poster session with ADCS (Owheo 106)
19:30–21:30	Boat trip: Meet at 19:00 at the wharf, 20 Fryatt St.

Contents

Invited talks

Using a large annotated historical corpus to study word-specific effects in sound change

Jennifer Hay
School of Languages, Cultures and Linguistics
University of Canterbury
jen.hay@canterbury.ac.nz

Abstract

The Origins of New Zealand English Corpora (ONZE) at the University of Canterbury contain recordings spanning 150 years of New Zealand English. These have all been force-aligned at the phoneme-level, and are stored with many layers of annotation some which have been automatically generated, and some which have been manually annotated. We interact with the corpus via our custom LaBB-CAT interface (LAnguage, Brain and Behaviour Corpus Analysis Tool). I will begin the talk by describing and demonstrating the corpus, and its associated LaBB-CAT tool. I will then focus on one particular recent study which has used the corpus, which aims to understand processes of sound change.

The combination of the time-depth of the ONZE collection, and the degree of careful annotation it contains, makes it an ideal data-set for the study of mechanisms underlying sound change. In particular, we aim to address the question which has been the subject of long-standing debate in the sound-change literature do sound changes proceed uniformly through the lexicon, or are there word-specific changes, with some words more ahead in the change than others? I describe a study which aimed to investigate this question by focusing on the mechanisms underpinning the New Zealand English front short vowel shift, of the vowels in words like bat, bet and bit. We automatically extracted formant values for over 100,000 tokens of words containing these vowels, We show that this data contains good evidence for word-specific effects in sound change, and argue that these are predicted by current models of speech production and perception, in combination with well-established psycholinguistic processes.

Diverse Words, Shared Meanings: Statistical Machine Translation for Paraphrase, Grounding, and Intent

Chris Brockett
Microsoft Research
Redmond, WA
Chris.Brockett@microsoft.com

Abstract

Can two different descriptions refer to the same event or action? Recognising that dissimilar strings are equivalent in meaning for some purpose is something that humans do rather well, but it is a task at which machines often fail. In the Natural Language Processing Group at Microsoft Research, we are attempting to address this challenge at sentence scale by generating semantically equivalent rewrites that can be used in applications ranging from authoring assistance to intent mapping for search or command and control. The Microsoft Translator paraphrase engine, developed in the NLP group, is a large-scale phrasal machine translation system that generates short sentential and phrasal paraphrases in English and has a public API that is available to researchers and developers. I will present the data extraction process, architecture, issues in generating diverse outputs, applications and possible future directions, and discuss the strengths and limitations of the statistical machine translation model as it relates to paraphrasing, how paraphrase is like machine translation, and how it differs in important respects. The statistical machine translation approach also has broad applications in capturing user intent in search, conversational understanding, and the grounding of language in objects and actions, all active areas of investigation in Microsoft Research.

Full papers

A Citation Centric Annotation Scheme for Scientific Articles

Angrosh M.A. **Stephen Cranefield** **Nigel Stanger**
Department of Information Science, University of Otago, Dunedin, New Zealand
{angrosh, scranefield, nstanger}@infoscience.otago.ac.nz

Abstract

This paper presents an annotation scheme for modelling citation contexts in scientific articles. We present an argumentation framework based on the Toulmin model for scientific articles and develop an annotation scheme with different context types based on the argumentation model. We present the results of the inter-rater reliability study carried out for studying the reliability of our annotation scheme.

1 Introduction

Citations play an important role in scientific writing. However, there are not many tools that provide citation context based information services. The citation services provided by academic search engines such as Google Scholar[1] includes information about the number of citing documents and links to citing articles. Search can also be performed for keywords in citing articles. Citation focused tools such as CiteSeerX [2] and Microsoft Academic Search [3] engines go a little further in identifying the passage of citations in citing articles. The objective of such services is to facilitate quick access to citation content to aid the learning process. However, the high volume of research content renders it difficult to achieve optimum use of these services.

Identifying this need, we proposed to develop tools for providing intelligent citation context based information services. However, an annotation scheme for citation contexts is one of the key requirements of citation context based information tools. An annotation scheme providing citation contexts can help in classifying citation passages and provide better citation context based information services. Accordingly, we studied the existing annotation schemes and noted that it was difficult to use these schemes for our application and proposed to develop a new annotation scheme. Angrosh, Cranefield and Stanger (2012a) have successfully used the annotation scheme with machine learning techniques for developing intelligent citation context based tools. These included a linked data application (Angrosh, Cranefield, and Stanger, 2012b) and a Web-based application[4].

We present in this paper our annotation scheme designed to represent citation contexts based on an argumentation model, which can be used to develop citation context based information tools.

2 Related Work

Over the years, several researchers have proposed annotation schemes for scientific articles. These schemes can be classified into two categories: (a) those that consider the full text of an article; and (b) those addressing citation sentences only.

2.1 Annotation Schemes for Full Text

Conceptualizing the idea of 'argumentative zoning', Teufel (1999) proposed an annotation scheme of seven categories and called them argumentative zones for sentences. Mizuta and Collier (2004a) extended Teufel's argumentation scheme (Teufel, 1999) for zone analysis in biology texts and provided a scheme of seven categories. Langer et al. (2004) noted that newer applications in areas such as the Semantic Web required richer and more fine-grained annotation of seven topic types for documents. Motivated by the need to identify passages of reliable scientific facts, Wilbur et al. (2006) devised an annotation scheme of five categories for biomedical texts. Ibekwe-sanjuan et al. (2007) developed local grammars to annotate sentences in a rhetorical scheme consisting of eight categories. Liakata et al. (2009) presented two complementary annotation schemes for scientific papers in

[1] http://scholar.google..com
[2] http://citeseerx.ist.psu.edu
[3] http://academic.research.microsoft.com/

[4] www.applications.sciverse.com/action/appDetail/297884?zone=main&pageOrigin=appGallery&activity=display

Chemistry: the Core Scientific Concepts (CoreSC) annotation scheme and the Argumentative Zoning-II scheme (AZ-II) (Teufel, 1999).

2.2 Annotation Schemes for Citation Sentences

Researchers have also specifically focused on citation sentences. In 1965, Eugene Garfield, the creator of Science Citation Index, outlined fifteen different reasons for citations (Garfield, 1964). Lipetz (1965) explored the possibility of improving selectivity in citation indexes by including citation relationship indicators and devised a scheme of 29 citation relationship types for science literature. Claimed to be the first in-depth study on classifying citations, Moravcsik and Murugesan (1975) proposed a classification scheme for citations consisting of four categories. Chubin and Moitra (1975) redefined the four categories of Moravcsik and Murugesan as a set of six mutually exclusive categories in order to further generalize the scheme. Spiegel-Rosing (1977) analyzed the use of references in 66 articles published in *Science Studies* and proposed a classification scheme of 13 categories. Oppenheim and Renn (1978) proposed a scheme of seven categories identifying citation reasons for historical papers. Frost (1979) proposed a classification scheme of citations in literary research and applied the scheme for a sample of publications in German literary research. Peritz (1983) proposed a classification scheme of eight categories for substantive-empirical papers in social sciences.

Focusing on automatic citation identification and classification, Nanba and Okumura (1999) proposed a simplified classification scheme of three categories based on the 15 reasons identified by Garfield (1964). Pham and Hoffmann (2003) developed KAFTAN, a "Knowledge Acquisition Framework for TAsks in Natural language", which classified citations into four citation types. Teufel, Siddharthan, and Tidhar (2006) presented an annotation scheme for citations involving 12 categories, based on the categories proposed by Spiegel-Rosing (1977). Le et al. (2006) defined six categories of citations that facilitated emerging trend detection. Radoulov (2008) carried out a study for exploring automatic citation function classification and redesigned Garzone's scheme of 35 categories from the perspective of usability and usefulness.

3 Why another Annotation Scheme?

Though there already exist various annotation schemes for scientific articles, we present in this paper another annotation scheme that defines various context types for sentences. The objective of developing this annotation scheme is to provide a set of context type definitions that can be used for providing citation context based information services.

There exist several difficulties in using existing schemes across different applications. Baldi (1998) notes the older classification schemes published during the 1970s and the 1980s were developed in a completely ad hoc manner and were virtually isolated from one another during the development process. White (2004) described existing classification schemes as "idiosyncratic" and emphasized the difficulty in employing them, particularly when using them across disciplines.

Studies that have focused on the full text of the article (Teufel, 1999; Mizuta and Collier, 2004a; Langer et al., 2004; Wilbur et al., 2006; Ibekwe-sanjuan et al., 2007) have proposed a generic set of categories that would be less useful in designing citation context based services. The objective of these studies has been to achieve text summarization.

On the other hand, studies carried out with citation sentences have proposed fine-grained categories that are difficult to use. The use of these classification schemes presents challenges in defining features in order to achieve automatic citation classification. Further, a focus on citation sentences alone would result in excluding surrounding sentences of citations that can provide additional contextual knowledge about citations.

Gao, Tang and Lin (2009) recommend that the selection of an annotation scheme should be task-oriented, and that the optimal scheme for use should depend on the level of detail required by the application at hand. The key focus of our study is to identify contexts of citations and develop information systems based on this contextual knowledge. However, the use of existing schemes creates difficulties as it is either too generic or fine grained as mentioned above. Our application would require an annotation scheme that would consider both citation and non-citation sentences and provide a set of context types that can also be used for automatic context identification.

The structure of this paper is as follows. In Section 4, we describe an argumentation framework for scientific articles based on the Toulmin model. In Section 5, we present the different context type definitions for sentences in scientific articles, defined based on the argumentation model. In Section 6, we discuss the results of an inter-rater reliability study to evaluate this set of context types, and we conclude the paper in Section 7.

4 Argumentation in Scientific Articles

An important characteristic of a scientific article is its persuasive nature, and citations play an important role in developing this feature for an article. Gilbert (1977) viewed scientific papers as 'tools of persuasion' and noted that references increase the persuasiveness of a scientific paper. Brooks (1985) surveyed authors to assess their motivations for citing and concluded that persuasiveness was a major motivating factor. In another study, Brooks (1986) further confirmed his findings with a different survey, concluding that persuasiveness was the dominant reason for citing. Cozzens (1989) observed that the primary function of a document is to persuasively argue about a knowledge claim, and noted that the art of writing scientific papers consists of marshalling the available rhetorical resources such as citations to achieve this goal. Hyland (2002) observed that arguments in research articles required procedural and citation support.

Thus, it is evident that scientific papers are argumentative in nature and one of the prominent reasons for using citations is to persuade the reader about the argument presented in the paper.

4.1 Toulmin Model for Modelling Scientific Discourse

In order to develop an argumentation model for scientific articles, we make use of the well-known Toulmin model of argument (Toulmin, 1958). The Toulmin model asserts that most arguments can be modelled using six elements: claim, data, warrant, qualifier, rebuttal and backing. The first three are considered as essential components and the last three as additional components of an argument.

The Toulmin model of argument can be applied for scientific articles as shown in Figure 1. The different elements of the Toulmin model as applied to scientific articles are explained below.

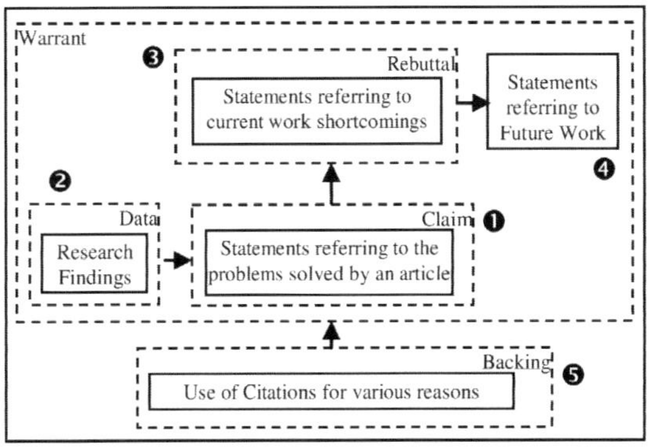

Figure 1: Argumentation Framework for Scientific Articles

A **Claim** in the Toulmin model refers to the proposition or conclusion of an argument. With respect to a scientific article, a claim therefore consists of the statements that describe the outcomes or the results of the article (block ❶ in Figure 1). In other words, these are the statements that refer to the problems solved by the article.

The **Data** in the Toulmin model refers to the factual information that supports the claim. In a scientific article, these are the research findings that are used to substantiate the claim, i.e., the results or outcomes of the article (block ❷).

A **Rebuttal** in the Toulmin model refers to exceptions to the claim. In a scientific article, these are the statements that refer to the shortcomings or gaps of the article (block ❸). These are situations where the results of the article may not hold or the problems that the article has not solved. The rebuttal statements also result in statements that refer to future work arising from the article (block ❹).

A **Warrant** in the Toulmin model forms the key of the argument process and provides the reasoning and the thinking process that binds the data to the claim. With respect to a scientific article, warrants play a crucial role as it is this reasoning aspect that is responsible for making the article presentable. These are specifically a set of sentences that relate the data and claim for making the article convincing. They also connect rebuttal sentences for making the argument clear. The dotted lines in Figure 1, surrounding blocks ❶ to ❹, indicates this aspect of warrants, bringing together the different components of the article.

A **Backing** in the Toulmin model refers to aspects that provide additional support to a warrant. The use of citations in scientific articles can be identified with *backing* as explained below.

4.2 Role of Citations in the Argumentation Model

We explained in the previous sections an argumentation model for scientific articles based on the Toulmin model. We also noted that citations play an important role in scientific writing with their persuading nature as one its prime characteristics.

In the argumentation model discussed above, citations can play various roles in different components. For example, citations can facilitate development of a good warrant. Citations can also be considered as warrants themselves as they also contribute to the reasoning process for linking data and the claim. Further, the data in the article can be developed using the outputs of the cited work.

To generalize this notion, citations can be considered as *backing* providing additional support to the different components of the argumentation model. This is indicated in Figure 1 with a link provided from block ❺ to the overall warrant block comprising different elements of the Toulmin model.

5 Context Types for Sentences based on Argumentation Model

We discussed in the previous section an argumentation framework for scientific articles based on the Toulmin model of argument and identified citations as a *backing* component for presenting the argumentation made in the paper. We also noted that one of the prominent reasons for using citations is to persuade the reader. Generally, the act of persuasion involves providing sufficient proof in order to convince the reader about a concept or an idea. In a scientific article, the use of citations to persuade the reader may focus on the following:

1. To demonstrate that others (cited work(s)) have identified a similar problem.
2. To demonstrate that others (in cited work(s)) have solved a similar problem.
3. To demonstrate how the current paper solves other problems (presented in cited paper(s))
4. To demonstrate the limitations or the shortcomings or the gaps of others (in cited work(s))
5. To compare works of others (in cited paper(s))
6. To compare the results of the current work with others (in cited work(s))

Thus, we analyzed citations against these persuading characteristics in order to examine the role of citations. To this end, we created a dataset of 1000 paragraphs that had sentences with citations. Paragraphs with citations were only considered, as the focus was to identify the contexts of sentences with citations. These paragraphs were obtained from 71 research articles. The articles were chosen from the Lecture Notes in Computer Science (LNCS) series published by Springer and accessed according to the terms of our institutional licence.

The dataset had a total of 4307 sentences, including 1274 citation sentences and 3031 non-citation sentences. We differentiated between citation and non-citation sentences and manually analyzed each of these sentences. This resulted in defining various context types for sentences as discussed below.

The Oxford English Dictionary defines the word "context" as "the parts of something written or spoken that immediately precede and follow a word or passage and clarify its meaning" (Oxford Dictionary of English, 2010). Thus, the set of words in a sentence are chosen with an intention to provide a meaning to the reader. Following this definition, we identify the context type of a sentence as 'the meaning of a sentence'. For example consider the passage shown in Figure 2. Each of the sentences in the passage has its own meaning and thus a specific context type. For instance, in Sentence 1, the authors refer to a cited work to describe a topic and in Sentences 2 and 3, the authors further describe that cited work.

1 *Razak et al. have studied the effect of MAC interactions on single chains under saturated UDP traffic [1].*
2 *They develop a systematic methodology for determining the types of interaction that are possible in chains of 3 and 4 hops and they study the effect of these interactions on chain performance.*
3 *They further extend their work to analyze chains of n hops.*
4 *These studies do not consider the effect of TCP traffic on chain performance.*
5 *TCP introduces several factors like bi-directional traffic, congestion control, round trip time estimations for timeout prediction etc. that are affected by interference interactions within a chain.*
6 *As we will show in this paper, the types of interactions within chain have a substantial effect on the performance of a network under TCP traffic.*

Source: Majeed et al. (2009)

Figure 2: Example Passage

Further, it needs to be noted that the context of a citation may not be evident from the sentence containing the citation alone and may require understanding of sentences surrounding this sentence, which necessitates the need to identify the contexts of surrounding sentences. For example, in the passage provided in Figure 2, though the authors refer to the cited work in sentence 1 and further describe it in sentences 2 and 3, it is only in sentence 4 (shaded in grey) that the authors identify gaps in the cited work(s). Thus, in order to understand the citation context of the citation in sentence 1, we need to identify the context types of surrounding sentences with and without citations.

5.1 Context Types for Citation Sentences

The analysis of citation sentences with a focus on the persuasive nature of citations described above resulted in identifying the following context types for citation sentences.

1. *Citing Works to Identify Gaps or Problems (CWIG)* – authors cite works that identify gaps to inform the reader about the existence of a problem.
2. *Citing Works that Overcome Gaps or Problems (CWOG)* – authors cite works to inform readers that other researchers are working on a similar problem and that they have solved some of the identified gaps.
3. *Using Outputs from Cited Works (UOCW)* – authors cite works to inform the reader about their outputs such as a methodology or training dataset, especially when these are used in the author's research.
4. *Comparing Cited Works (CCW)* – authors cite various related works and provide a comparison to bolster their argument.
5. *Results with Cited Works (RWCW)* – authors cite works to relate their research results to the cited work.
6. *Shortcomings in Cited Works (SCCW)* – authors cite works to identify shortcomings or gaps in them.
7. *Issue Related Cited Works (IRCW)* – authors cite works to inform readers about related research issues.

5.2 Context Types for Non-Citation Sentences

Similarly we analyzed the surrounding non-citation sentences and accordingly identified the following types of non-citation sentences:

1. *Background Sentences (BGR)* – Sentences that provide background or introduction.
2. *Gaps Sentences (GAPS)* – Sentences that identify gaps or problems. It was observed that authors identify gaps or problems in different ways. For example, authors identified gaps in the work cited earlier in the article, or related research topics addressed in the article, or could also mention the shortcomings of the current article itself.
3. *Issue Sentences (ISSUE)* – Sentences that refer to author viewpoints. These sentences are referred as issue sentences as these are the issues or points identified by the author.
4. *Current Work Outcome Sentences (CWO)* – Sentences that refer to the outcomes of the current research (the work being reported).
5. *Future Work Sentences (FW)* – Sentences that refer to future work.
6. *Descriptive Sentences (DES)* – Sentences that are descriptive in nature. For example, authors can further describe a cited work.

Thus, following this approach, we developed the annotation scheme shown in Figure 3 for sentences in full text of articles.

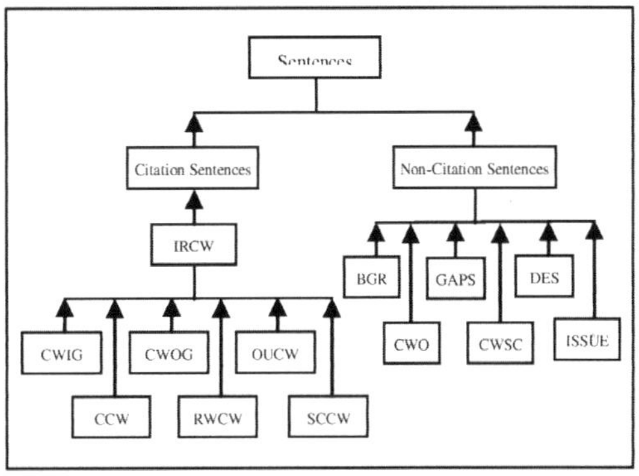

Figure 3: Our Initial Annotation Scheme

As seen in Figure 3, sentences are initially classified as citation sentences or non-citation sentences. With respect to non-citation sentences, we define six different context types that could be associated with them. However, with respect to citation sentences, we define a hierarchy of context types for sentence. We define at the top level of the hierarchy the class of IRCW (Issue Related Cited Work). Thus, if a citation sentence cannot be classified into any other class, it will have the class of IRCW. This implies that a citation in the article is made for some issue other than the context types defined in our annotation scheme. We identify six context types for citation sentences as subclasses of IRCW.

6 Reliability of Context Types

In order to study how reliably coders can interpret the context types defined above in an objective way, we carried out an inter-rater reliability (IRR) study. The approach followed during this study is as follows.

6.1 Approach of IRR Study

Researchers have adopted different strategies while carrying out inter-rater reliability studies. Teufel and Moens (2002) worked with annotations of a subset of 80 conference articles from a larger corpus of 260 articles. The articles were annotated by two annotators other than the first author herself. Wilbur et al. (2006) chose 10 articles randomly and worked with nine annotators for reporting annotation results.

With respect to the practice adopted for reporting inter-annotator agreement, Bird et al. (2009) note that double annotation of 10% of the corpus forms a good practice in such studies. Further Artstein and Poesio (2008) observe that the most common approach to infer the reliability of large-scale annotation involves each sentence being marked by one coder and measuring agreement using a smaller subset that is annotated by multiple coders. We adopted a similar approach for measuring the agreement about the context type definitions proposed in our study.

As mentioned earlier, the training dataset was created using 70 articles chosen from LNCS. We chose to annotate 10% of the corpus. Each article was annotated by at least three annotators, with one of the annotators being the first author of this paper. This facilitated deriving the following measures: (a) overall agreement between annotators (b) agreement between individual annotators, and (c) agreement for each label.

Choice of Statistic – We used Krippendorff's alpha (α) (Krippendorff, 2011) for measuring reliability as it provides a generalization of several known reliability indices. This statistic enables researchers to evaluate different kinds of data using the same reliability standard and can be used in different situations such as (a) any number of observers, (b) any number of categories, scale values or measures, (c) large and small sample sizes, and (d) incomplete or missing data. Krippendorff's alpha (α) is defined "as a reliability coefficient developed to measure the agreement among observers, coders, judges or raters" (Krippendorff, 2011). The general form of α is given by:

$$\alpha = 1 - \frac{D_o}{D_e}$$

Where D_o is the observed disagreement among values assigned to units of analysis:

$$D_o = \frac{1}{n}\sum_{c}\sum_{k} o_{ck}\delta^2_{ck}$$

and D_e is the expected disagreement due to chance rather than properties of the units:

$$D_e = \frac{1}{n(n-1)}\sum_{c}\sum_{k} n_c \cdot n_k \delta^2_{ck}$$

The arguments of the two disagreement measures, o_{ck}, n_c, n_k and n refer to frequencies of values in the coincidence matrices.

Characteristics of the annotators – The annotators in our study had considerable training in scientific writing and publishing with most of them being PhD students pursuing their doctoral research and a few of them being faculty members in the field of information science.

Choice of Articles – We provided annotatators articles chosen from their own field. This was done for the following reasons: (a) it would be easier for annotators to understand the content and hence apply the labels easily and thoughtfully; and (b) minimize the annotating time; and (c) as a motivation factor as articles were from their own field.

Guidelines for annotators – The guidelines used for annotators provided details of the context type definitions of the study along with example sentences for each definition. Each annotator was briefed about the purpose the study and the context type definitions. The briefing time spent with the annotators ranged between 15 and 30 minutes. The annotators were provided with paragraphs containing citations that were extracted from articles. The paragraphs were formatted to show individual sentences in them with the citation sentences highlighted to help annotators distinguish between citation and non-citation sentences.

Before carrying out the study, we conducted a pilot study to examine the feasibility of our approach. The pilot study resulted in making certain changes to the annotation scheme as will be discussed in the following section.

6.2 Pilot Study

We conducted a pilot study with three annotators using three articles, with each annotator annotating one article. All three articles were also annotated by the first author of this article, henceforth referred to as Annotator A. Thus, we were able to compare the annotations made by Annotator A with the annotations of the three other annotators. The paragraphs extracted from the three articles provided a total of 300 sentences and hence there were 300 cases and 600 decisions to be made. After the coding of individual articles, we had discussions with the coders about the study. The coders felt that the context type definitions were clear enough and the examples were helpful in classifying sentences. However, they said there was confusion between the classes DES and ISSUE and, it was difficult to distinguish between the two. The analysis of these experiments resulted in a Krippendorff's Alpha (α) (Krippendorff, 2011), score of 0.79 (N = 300, k = 2), where N is the number of items (sentences) and k is the number of coders. This is equivalent to 85% agreement between the Annotator A and each of the three annotators. The classification results for each label along with the confusion matrix are shown in Table 1[5].

As can be seen in Table 1, there was confusion for the classes DES and ISSUE. With respect to Description (DES) sentences, the coders classified about 10% (14 out of 144) as ISSUE sentences and 62% (18 out of 29) of ISSUE sentences as DES sentences. Thus, in order to avoid this confusion, we merged the classes of DES and ISSUE into one class of DES and removed the label ISSUE from context type definitions. The merging of these classes resulted in achieving a α value of 0.93 for the pilot data, which is 95.7% agreement between the annotators. With these changes we carried out the study with a large number of annotators, as discussed in the next section. The modified annotation scheme based on the results of the pilot study is shown in Figure 4.

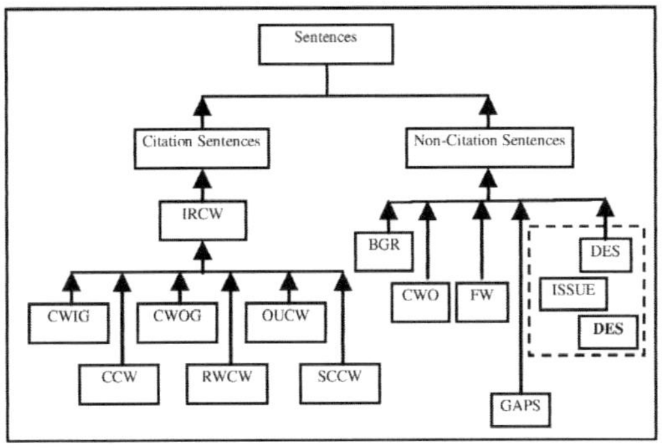

Figure 4: Modified Annotation Scheme

[5] Table 1 is provided at the end of this paper for formatting reasons.

6.3 IRR Study with Larger Sample

After conducting the pilot study and making necessary corrections to the context type definitions, we carried out a study using 11 annotators and 9 articles. This formed 12% of the training dataset. Each article was annotated by two annotators other than Annotator A, (the first author) who annotated all nine articles. The set of 9 articles provided a total of 907 sentences. The overall result achieved for α, involving nine articles and 11 annotators was 0.841 as shown in Table 2.

This is equivalent to 89.93% agreement between different pairs of annotators. The number of coders indicates that each article was annotated by three annotators. An agreement α = 0.8 or higher on Krippendorff's scale is considered as a reliable agreement, and an agreement of 0.67 to 0.8 is considered to be marginally reliable. A value lower than 0.67 for α indicates the agreement is unreliable. Therefore, the results indicate that the labels of our scheme can be reliably applied to sentences.

% Agreement	α	No. of Coders	No. of Cases	No. of Decisions
89.93	0.841	3	907	2721

Table 2: Overall Results

The details of the agreement between Annotator A and the others annotators involved in the study is shown in Table 3.

A	B	C	D	E	F	G
Annotator 4	85.3	0.760	93	16	109	218
Annotator 5	85.5	0.719	94	16	110	220
Annotator 9	87.8	0.836	72	10	82	164
Annotator 8	88.6	0.847	39	5	44	88
Annotator 10	90.5	0.831	95	10	105	210
Annotator 1	90.8	0.854	315	32	347	694
Annotator 6	91.8	0.832	101	9	110	220
Annotator 2	92.2	0.877	320	27	347	694
Annotator 7	94.4	0.930	119	7	126	252
Annotator 3	94.8	0.903	312	17	329	658
Annotator 11	95.2	0.907	100	5	105	210

A – Comparison between Annotator A and the Annotator listed below; B – Percentage Agreement; C – Krippendorff's Alpha (α); D – Number of Agreements; E – Number of Disagreements; F – Number of Cases; G – Number of Decisions

Table 3: Agreement between Annotators

As seen in Table 3, the percentage agreement with annotators varied from 85% to 95% with

Krippendorff's Alpha (α) value achieving the least value of 0.76 and a maximum value of 0.907, respectively. As seen in Table 3, the number of sentences annotated by annotators varied from a minimum of 44 to a maximum of 347. This is due to the number of articles annotated by individual annotators.

The annotators in our study were requested to annotate any number of articles depending on their availability. While some chose to annotate a single article, three of the annotators (Annotators 1, 2 and 3 – shown in grey in Table 3) annotated three articles. The α value for these annotators was of the order 0.85 to 0.90. This shows that the increase in annotated sentences resulted in better agreement indicating the ease of applying the labels to sentences by these annotators.

The agreement achieved for each article between three of the annotators is tabulated in Table 4.

7 Conclusion

We presented in this paper an annotation scheme of context types for scientific articles, considering the persuasive characteristic of citations. We described the application of the Toulmin model for developing an argumentation framework for scientific articles, which was used for defining our context types. We discussed the results of the inter-rater reliability study carried out for establishing the reliability of our scheme. As we mentioned in Section 1, studies have successfully used this annotation scheme for developing tools that provide intelligent citation context based information services, indicating the usefulness of the annotation scheme.

Our future work involves examining the application of annotation schemes across other disciplines. We also intend to focus on using our context types for analyzing sentiments associated with citation contexts.

Article	A	B	C	D	E
Article 3	82.83	82.17	90.09	76.23	0.75
Article 2	84.73	86.74	90.36	77.10	0.77
Article 6	89.09	85.45	97.27	54.54	0.78
Article 7	90.47	95.23	90.47	58.71	0.82
Article 8	87.87	88.63	93.18	81.81	0.83
Article 4	90.21	85.32	91.74	93.57	0.84
Article 9	89.43	97.80	95.12	85.36	0.85
Article 5	93.93	91.81	85.45	94.54	0.87
Article 1	95.02	96.31	96.31	92.63	0.91

A – Average Pairwise percent agreement; B – Agreement between Annotator A and Annotator 2; C – Agreement between Annotator A and Annotator 1; D – Agreement between Annotator 1 and Annotator 2; E - Krippendorff's Alpha (α)

Table 4: Agreement for Articles

Classification Results				Confusion Matrix												
Label*	P	R	F		BGR	CWIG	CWO	IRCW	CWOG	DES	GAPS	ISSUE	FW	RWCW	UOCW	TOTAL
BGR	0.50	1.00	0.66	BGR	3	0	0	0	0	0	0	0	0	0	0	3
CWIG	1.00	1.00	1.00	CWIG	0	4	0	0	0	0	0	0	0	0	0	4
CWO	0.87	1.00	0.93	CWO	0	0	14	0	0	0	0	0	0	0	0	14
IRCW	0.92	1.00	0.96	IRCW	0	0	0	52	0	0	0	0	0	0	0	52
CWOG	1.00	0.66	0.80	CWOG	0	0	0	4	8	0	0	0	0	0	0	12
DES	0.85	0.87	0.86	DES	2	0	1	0	0	126	1	14	0	0	0	144
GAPS	0.95	0.87	0.91	GAPS	0	0	0	0	0	3	21	0	0	0	0	24
ISSUE	0.39	0.31	0.34	ISSUE	1	0	1	0	0	18	0	9	0	0	0	29
FW	1.00	1.00	1.00	FW	0	0	0	0	0	0	0	0	3	0	0	3
RWCW	1.00	1.00	1.00	RWCW	0	0	0	0	0	0	0	0	0	10	0	10
UOCW	1.00	1.00	1.00	UOCW	0	0	0	0	0	0	0	0	0	0	5	5
					6	4	16	56	8	147	22	23	3	10	5	300

* Labels CCW and SCCW are not shown in the table as none of the sentences were labeled with these labels.
Captions: P – Precision; R – Recall; F – F-Score

Table 1: Results of Pilot Study for each Label

References

Angrosh, M A, Cranefield, S., and Stanger, N. (2012a). Contextual Information Retrieval in Research Articles: Semantic Publishing Tools for the Research Community. Semantic Web Journal. Accepted for publication.

Angrosh, M.A., Cranefield, S., and Stanger, N. (2012b). Context Identification of Sentences in Research Articles: Towards Developing Intelligent Tools for the Research Community. Natural Language Engineering. DOI: 10.017/S1351324912000277.

Artstein, R., and Poesio, M. (2008). Survey Article Inter-Coder Agreement for Computational Linguistics. Computational Linguistics, 34(4), 555-596.

Baldi, S. (1998). Normative versus Social Constructivist Processes in the Allocation of Citations: A Network-Analytic Model. American Sociological Review, 63(6), 829. doi:10.2307/2657504

Bird, S., Loper, E. and Klein, E. (2009). Natural Language Processing with Python. O'Reilly Media Inc.

Brooks, T. A. (1985). Private acts and public objects: An investigation of citer motivations. Journal of the American Society for Information Science, 36(4), 223-229. doi:10.1002/asi.4630360402

Brooks, T. A. (1986). Evidence of complex citer motivations. Journal of the American Society for Information Science, 37(1), 34-36. DOI:10.1002/asi.4630370106

Chubin, D. E., and Moitra, S. D. (1975). Content Analysis of References: Adjunct or Alternative to Citation Counting? Social Studies of Science, 5(4), 423-441.

Cozzens, S. E. (1989). What do citations count? The rhetoric-first model. Scientometrics, 15(5-6), 437-447. DOI:10.1007/BF02017064

Frost, C. O. (1979). The Use of Citations in Literary Research: A Preliminary Classification of Citation Functions. The Library Quarterly, 49(4), 399-414.

Gao, L., Tang, Z., and Lin, X. (2009). CEBBIP: A Parser of Bibliographic Information in Chinese Electronic Books. ACM/IEEE Joint Conference on Digital Libraries, JCDL 2009 (pp. 73-76). ACM Press.

Garfield, E. (1964). Science Citation Index - A new dimension in indexing. Science, 144(3619), 649-654.

Gilbert, G. N. (1977). Referencing as Persuasion. Social Studies of Science, 7(1), 113-122.

Hyland, K. (2002). Directives: Argument and Engagement in Academic Writing. Applied Linguistics, 23(2), 215-239. DOI:10.1093/applin/23.2.215

Ibekwe-sanjuan, F., Chen, C., and Pinho, R. (2007). Identifying Strategic Information from Scientific Articles through Sentence Classification. Journal of Applied Linguistics, 1518-1522.

Krippendorff, K. (2011). Computing Krippendorff's Alpha Reliability. Annenberg School of Communication. Departmental Papers (ASC). University of Pennsylvania. http://www.asc.upenn.edu/usr/krippendorff/mwebreliability4.pdf

Langer, H., Lüngen, H., and Bayerl, P. S. (2004). Text type structure and logical document structure. Proceedings of the 2004 ACL Workshop on Discourse Annotation - DiscAnnotation'04 (pp. 49-56). Morristown, NJ, USA: Association for Computational Linguistics. DOI:10.3115/1608938.1608945

Le, M.H., Ho, T.B., and Nakamori, Y. (2006). Detecting Citation Types Using Finite-State. PAKDD 2006, Lecture Notes in Artificial Intelligence 3918 (pp. 265-274). Springer-Verlag, Berlin Heidelberg.

Liakata, M. (2010). Zones of Conceptualisation in Scientific Papers: a Window to Negative and Speculative Statements. Proceedings of the Workshop on Negation and Speculation in Natural Language Processing (pp. 1-4).

Lipetz, B.-A. (1965). Improvement of the selectivity of citation indexes to science literature through inclusion of citation relationship indicators. American Documentation, 16(2), 81-90. DOI:10.1002/asi.5090160207

Majeed, A., Razak, S., Abu-Ghazaleh, N. B., & Harras, Kh. A. (2009). TCP over Multi-Hop Wireless Networks: The Impact of MAC Level Interactions. ADHOC-NOW 2009, Lecture Notes in Computer Science 5793 (pp. 1-15). Springer-Verlag, Berlin Heidelberg.

Mizuta, Y., and Collier, N. (2004). An Annotation Scheme for a Rhetorical Analysis of Biology Articles. Proceedings of the Fourth International Conference on Language Resource and Evaluation (LREC 2004) (pp. 1737-1740).

Moravcsik, M. J., and Murugesan, P. (1975). Some Results on the Function and Quality of Citations. Social Studies of Science, 5(1), 86-92. DOI:10.1177/030631277500500106

Nanba, H., and Okumura, M. (1999). Towards Multi-paper Summarization Retrieval of Papers Using Reference Information. In T. Dean (Ed.), IJCAI (pp. 926-931). Morgan Kaufmann.

Pham, S. B., and Hoffmann, A. (2003). A New Approach for Scientific Citation. In T. D. Gedeon and L. C. C. Fung (Eds.), Artificial Intelligence 2003 (pp. 759-771). Springer-Verlag Berlin Heidelberg.

Radoulov, R. (2008). Exploring Automatic Citation Classification. MSc. Thesis. University of Waterloo, Ontario.

Spiegel-Rosing, I. (1977). Science Studies: Bibliometric and Content Analysis. So-cial Studies of Science, 7(1), 97-113. DOI:10.1177/030631277700700111

Teufel, S. (1999). Argumentative Zoning: Information Extraction from Scientific Text. University of Edinburgh.

Teufel, S., and Moens, M. (2002). Summarizing Scientific Articles: Experiments with Relevance and Rhetorical Status. Computational Linguistics. 28(4), 409-445.

Teufel, S., Siddharthan, A., and Tidhar, D. (2006). Automatic classification of citation function. Proceedings of the 2006 Conference on Empirical Methods in Natural Language Processing (EMNLP 2006) (pp. 103-110). Association for Computational Linguistics.

Toulmin, S. (1958). The Uses of Argument. Cambridge University Press, Cambridge, England.

White, H. D. (2004). Citation Analysis and Discourse Analysis Revisited. Applied Linguistics, 25(1), 89-116. DOI:10.1093/applin/25.1.89

Wilbur, W. J., Rzhetsky, A., and Shatkay, H. (2006). New directions in biomedical text annotation: definitions, guidelines and corpus construction. BMC bioinformatics, 7, 356. DOI:10.1186/1471-2105-7-356

Semantic Judgement of Medical Concepts: Combining Syntagmatic and Paradigmatic Information with the Tensor Encoding Model

Mike Symonds[1], **Guido Zuccon**[2], **Bevan Koopman**[1,2], **Peter Bruza**[1], **Anthony Nguyen**[2]

michael.symonds@qut.edu.au, guido.zuccon@csiro.au, bevan.koopman@csiro.au
p.bruza@qut.edu.au, anthony.nguyen@csiro.au

[1] School of Information Systems, Queensland University of Technology
[2] Australian e-Health Research Centre, CSIRO

Brisbane, Australia

Abstract

This paper outlines a novel approach for modelling semantic relationships within medical documents. Medical terminologies contain a rich source of semantic information critical to a number of techniques in medical informatics, including medical information retrieval. Recent research suggests that corpus-driven approaches are effective at automatically capturing semantic similarities between medical concepts, thus making them an attractive option for accessing semantic information.

Most previous corpus-driven methods only considered *syntagmatic* associations. In this paper, we adapt a recent approach that explicitly models *both syntagmatic and paradigmatic* associations. We show that the implicit similarity between certain medical concepts can only be modelled using paradigmatic associations. In addition, the inclusion of both types of associations overcomes the sensitivity to the training corpus experienced by previous approaches, making our method both more effective and more robust. This finding may have implications for researchers in the area of medical information retrieval.

1 Introduction

Semantic similarity measures are central to several techniques used in medical informatics, including: medical search (Voorhees and Tong, 2011; Cohen and Widdows, 2009), literature-based discovery (e.g., drug discovery (Agarwal and Searls, 2009)), clustering (e.g., gene clustering (Glenisson et al., 2003)), and ontology construction or maintenance (Cederberg and Widdows, 2003).

Automatically determining the similarity between medical concepts presents a number of specific challenges, including vocabulary mismatch. For example, the phrases *heart attack* and *myocardial infarction* are synonymous, referring to the same medical concept. Beyond vocabulary mismatch are situations where semantic similarity is based on implied relationships, for example the mention of an organism (e.g. *Varicella zoster virus*) suggests the presence of a disease (e.g. *chickenpox*).

Existing approaches for measuring medical semantic similarities fall into two major categories: (i) those that utilise path-based measures between concepts in medical thesauri/ontologies, and (ii) corpus-based approaches that derive similarity judgements from the occurrence and co-occurrence of concepts within text, e.g., using Latent Semantic Analysis (LSA).

Research comparing path-based methods with corpus-based methods highlighted the ability for corpus-based methods to provide superior performance on medical concept similarity judgements (Pedersen et al., 2007). However, research evaluating eight different corpus-based approaches found that the performance was sensitive to the choice of training corpus (Koopman et al., 2012). This finding means it is difficult to apply a corpus-based approach which is both robust and effective.

It is important to note that the corpus based approaches referred to in this paper do not rely on syntactic information found in extra-linguistic resources, and use solely the co-occurrence statistics of words found in natural language to model word associations. Therefore, research modelling semantic associations using part of speech (POS) taggers, parsers or hand-coded resources are not within the scope of this work.

Within this paper we adapt a novel corpus-based approach, known as the *tensor encoding* (TE) model (Symonds et al., 2011a), for use in judging the similarity of medical concepts. The TE approach explicitly models the two types of word associations argued to give words their meaning within structural linguistic theory. These are: (i) syntagmatic and (ii) paradigmatic associations.

A syntagmatic association exists between two words if they co-occur more frequently than expected from chance. Two medical concepts that likely have a strong syntagmatic association include *bone* and *x-ray*.

A paradigmatic association exists between two words if they can substitute for one another in a sentence without affecting the grammaticality or acceptability of the sentence. Medical concepts that display synonymy, like *heart attack* and *myocardial infarction* display a strong paradigmatic association.

The TE model combines measures of syntagmatic and paradigmatic association within a single, formal framework. In this paper we demonstrate that not only does the TE model provide robust, superior performance across a wide variety of data sets when compared to past corpus-based approaches, but offers a flexible framework whose performance is not sensitive to the choice of training corpus. Our findings provide a robust and effective model for predicting semantic similarity between medical concepts, and also draws out useful statistical behavior relating to the modelling of syntagmatic and paradigmatic associations that exist within medical documents.

The remainder of this paper is set out as follows. Section 2 provides background on corpus-based approaches previously evaluated on medical concept similarity judgements. In Section 3 we describe the TE model and outline our novel variant for use in judging the similarity of medical concepts. Section 4 details the experiments to be used in evaluating the performance of the TE approach, with the results and their discussion following in Section 5. Concluding remarks and suggestions for future work are presented in Section 6.

2 Background

Corpus-based models that learn the relationships between words based on their distribution in natural language have a strong history in the field of natural language processing. Some of the most well-known include LSA (Latent Semantic Analysis (Landauer and Dumais, 1997)) and HAL (Hyperspace to Analogue of Language (Lund and Burgess, 1996)).

A rigorous evaluation of eight different corpus-based approaches on the task of judging medical concept similarity found that the best performance was achieved using a positive point-wise mutual information (PPMI) measure. This measure had an average correlation of ≈ 0.7 with judgements made by expert human assessors (Koopman et al., 2012).

PPMI is a variation of PMI where negative values are substituted by zero-values. The strength of PMI between word q and w within a stream of text can be expressed as:

$$S_{\text{ppmi}}(q, w) = \begin{cases} \log\left[\frac{p(q,w)}{p(q)p(w)}\right] & \text{if } \log\left[\frac{p(q,w)}{p(q)p(w)}\right] > 0 \\ 0 & \text{otherwise,} \end{cases} \tag{1}$$

where $p(q, w)$ is the joint probability of q and w, and $p(q)$, $p(w)$ are the expected probabilities of q and w respectively. In practice, these probabilities are computed as:

$$p(q, w) = \frac{|D_q \cap D_w|}{|D|},$$

$$p(q) = \frac{|D_q|}{|D|}, \quad p(w) = \frac{|D_w|}{|D|},$$

where D_q is the set of documents containing term q and D is the set of documents in the collection.

Although the PPMI measure achieved the best average performance across a number of test sets, it displayed a high degree of sensitivity when the training corpus was changed, thus reducing its overall utility.

Next, we introduce the tensor encoding model as a robust and effective alternative to previous proposed measures.

3 The Tensor Encoding Model

A recent corpus-based approach, known as the *tensor encoding* (TE) model, was originally presented as a model of word meaning (Symonds et al., 2011a), and later used to provide a flexible approach to semantic categorisation (Symonds et al.,

2012). The TE model provides a formal framework for combining two measures that explicitly model syntagmatic and paradigmatic associations between words.

As the TE model has a strong theoretical basis in linguistics, it has potential applications in other areas that deal with natural language, including e.g. information retrieval. To demonstrate, the TE model was used to perform similarity judgements within the query expansion process of an ad-hoc information retrieval task (Symonds et al., 2011b). This method, known as *tensor query expansion* achieved robust and significant performance improvements over a strong benchmark model. This result was attributed to the inclusion of information about paradigmatic associations, which are not effectively modelled in existing information retrieval systems. Similarly, these paradigmatic associations are not explicitly modelled in previous corpus-based measures of medical concept similarity. We hypothesise that the inclusion of paradigmatic associations in semantic similarity measures would better capture similarities between medical concepts.

To support this insight, consider how the PPMI measure in Equation (1) is oblivious to paradigmatic associations that may exist between two words. If word q and word w do not co-occur in any documents (i.e., $|D_q \cap D_w| = 0$) then $S_{\text{ppmi}}(q, w) = 0$. This result suggests q and w are unrelated. However, consider a toy example using *heart attack*(q) and *myocardial infarction*(w). One clinician may use the first concept exclusively in a document, while another may use the second term exclusively. If the PPMI score between *heart attack* and *myocardial infarction* was calculated using these two example documents, the score would be zero and the two concepts considered unrelated.

From a structural linguistic viewpoint, one might say there are no syntagmatic associations between the two concepts, as they do not co-occur in the same context (i.e., medical report). Therefore, PPMI only captures syntagmatic associations, and hence fails to model any paradigmatic information that may exist.

However, consider the same example using the TE model's paradigmatic measure, and hence a pure paradigmatic perspective. Within the TE model, the strength of paradigmatic associations between two medical concepts, q and w can be defined as:

$$S_{\text{par}}(q, w) = \sum_{i=1}^{N} \frac{f_{\overline{iq}} \cdot f_{\overline{iw}}}{\max(f_{\overline{iq}}, f_{\overline{iw}}, f_{\overline{wq}})^2}, \quad (2)$$

where $f_{\overline{iq}}$ is the unordered co-occurrence frequency of concepts i and q, $f_{\overline{iw}}$ is the unordered co-occurrence frequency of concepts i and w, and N is the number of concepts in the vocabulary.

Intuitively, Equation (2) enhances the score for concept w if q and w co-occur with the same concepts, independent of whether q and w occur within the same document. In fact this measure has a factor, $\frac{1}{f_{\overline{wq}}}$, that reduces the paradigmatic score if concepts q and w occur within the same document often. In our simple example, this would mean that if *heart attack* and *myocardial infarction* co-occurred with any of the same terms (e.g., CPR, chest pain, etc.) then they would have a paradigmatic score greater than 0.

The fact that pure paradigmatic information is not currently utilised within most corpus-based approaches leads us to hypothesise that more robust performance on medical concept similarity judgements can be achieved by adding paradigmatic information to the similarity estimate. In the remainder of this paper the measure in Equation (2) will be referred to as **PARA**.

The TE model uses a Markov random field to formalise the estimate of observing one concept w given a second concept q:

$$P(w|q) = \frac{1}{Z}\left[\gamma S_{\text{par}}(q, w) + (1 - \gamma) S_{\text{ppmi}}(q, w)\right], \quad (3)$$

where $\gamma \in [0, 1]$ mixes the paradigmatic $S_{\text{par}}()$ and syntagmatic $S_{\text{ppmi}}()$ measures, and Z normalises the resulting distribution. We refer the interested reader to Symonds et al. (2012) for details.

The estimate in Equation (3) can be reduced to the following rank equivalent measure of semantic similarity between q and w:

$$S_{\text{TE}}(q, w) \propto \gamma S_{\text{par}}(q, w) + (1 - \gamma) S_{\text{ppmi}}(q, w). \quad (4)$$

In the remainder of this paper the model defined in Equation (4) will be referred to as **TE**.

It is worth noting that the TE model formally supports the combining of any measure of syntagmatic and paradigmatic information. Therefore, if a more effective measure of syntagmatic or paradigmatic information is developed, it can be applied within the TE framework.

Corpus	# Docs	Avg. doc. len.	Vocab Size
TREC'11 MedTrack	17,198	5,010	54,546
OHSUMED	293,856	100	55,390

Table 1: Document collections (corpora) used.

Test: Corpus (data set)	Training: Corpus (data set)	γ	TE	PPMI
MedTrack (Ped)	OHSUMED (Ped)	0.5	$r = 0.6706$	$r = 0.4674$
MedTrack (Cav)	MedTrack (Ped)	0.5	$r = 0.6857$	$r = 0.6154$
OHSUMED (Ped)	OHSUMED (Cav)	0.2	$r = 0.7698$	$r = 0.7427$
OHSUMED (Cav)	MedTrack (Cav)	0.4	$r = 0.8297$	$r = 0.8242$

Table 2: Performance of TE using the γ produced by the specified train/test splits; performance of PPMI included for comparison.

4 Experimental Setup

In this section we outline the experimental setup used to evaluate the performance of the TE approach on two separate medical concept similarity judgement data sets. The first data set involves judging the similarity of 29[1] UMLS medical concept pairs. These were first developed by Pedersen et al. (Pedersen et al., 2007) and human assessments of semantic similarity were produced by 9 clinical terminologists (coders) and 3 physicians, with inter-coded relatedness equal to 0.85. Assessors scored each pair between 1 and 4, with 1 being unrelated and 4 being highly synonymous. This data set is indicated as **Ped** in the remainder of this paper.

The second data set is comprised of 45 UMLS concept pairs, developed by Caviedes and Cimino (2004), for which semantic similarity assessments were performed by three physicians. Similarities were scored between 1 and 10, with higher scores indicating a stronger similarity between concepts. This data set is indicated as **Cav** in the remainder of this paper.

Two separate corpora were used as data to prime all models; corpus statistics are shown in Table 1. The TREC MedTrack collection consists of documents created from concatenating clinical patient records for a single visit, while the OHSUMED collection is based on MEDLINE journal abstracts.

Following the procedure outlined by Koopman et al. (2012) the original textual documents for both corpora were translated into UMLS medical concept identifiers using MetaMap, a biomedical concept identification system (Aronson and Lang, 2010). After processing, the individual documents contained only UMLS concept ids. For example, the phrase *Congestive heart failure* in the original document will be replaced with `C0018802` in the new document. Both data sets (Ped and Cav) contained UMLS concept pairs (which may actually represent term phrases rather than single terms); converting the corpora to concepts thus allows direct comparison of the single concept pairs contained in the two data sets.

When modelling paradigmatic associations it is common to consider only those terms close to the target term, i.e. within a window of text centred around the target term. However, here we used the whole document as the context window. In this way we aim to capture in MedTrack the associations that exists within the context of a single patient record and in OHSUMED the associations that exists within the context of a single medical abstract.

As the TE model in Equation (4) is parameterized over γ, i.e. the mix between paradigmatic and syntagmatic information, this parameter was tuned to maximise the correlation with human similarity judgements (gold standard/ground truth labels). To fairly tune γ and also provide insight into the robustness of the TE model, a split train/test methodology was used. This was done by training on one data set and corpus to find the best value of γ and then testing on another data set/corpus, ensuring a cross corpus and cross data set combination was done for each.

Table 2 summarises the results obtained following this methodology and also reports the per-

[1]The pair *Lymphoid hyperplasia* was removed from the original set of 30 as neither concept existed in the test collections shown in table 1.

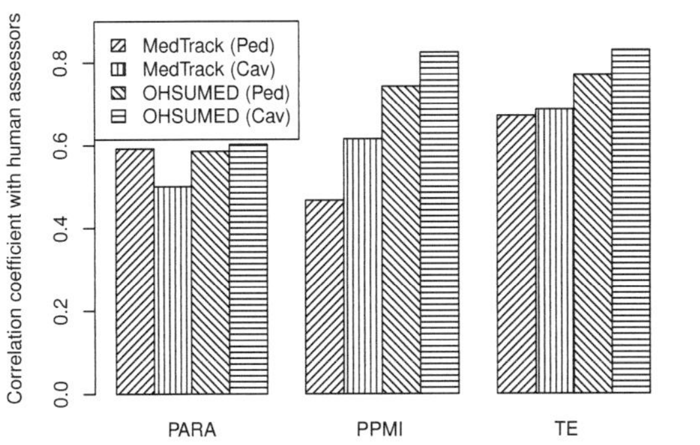

Figure 1: Correlation of medical concept judgements produced by PARA, PPMI and TE with those produced by human assessors.

formance of PPMI for comparison. Note that PPMI was shown to be the strongest performing measure when compared to thirteen other corpus based measures (Koopman et al., 2012).

5 Experimental Results

The effect of explicitly modelling both syntagmatic and paradigmatic information when estimating the similarity of medical concepts is shown in Figure 1. This graph shows that the TE model achieves a much higher correlation with human judged similarity scores (with an average correlation of 0.74 over all datasets and corpora) than both the paradigmatic (PARA: 0.57) and syntagmatic (PPMI: 0.66) approaches alone. To gain a broader understanding of how each of these measures compares to our TE variant, an updated graph showing the average performance of each across all data sets is provided in Figure 2. We refer the reader to Koopman et. al., (Koopman et al., 2012) for more details on the settings used for each of the other measures.

5.1 Sensitivity to the Mixing Parameter γ

The sensitivity to the mixing parameter γ of the TE approach is shown in Figure 3. This illustrates that for all datasets the best performance is achieved by some mix of both syntagmatic (PPMI) and paradigmatic (PARA) information.

The robustness of the PPMI and PAR measures across datasets and corpora can be inferred by comparing the distance between the end points of the TE lines drawn in Figure 3. The left hand side of the graph (where $\gamma = 0$) illustrates the performance of TE when only syntagmatic associations are considered, i.e. when TE uses only the PPMI

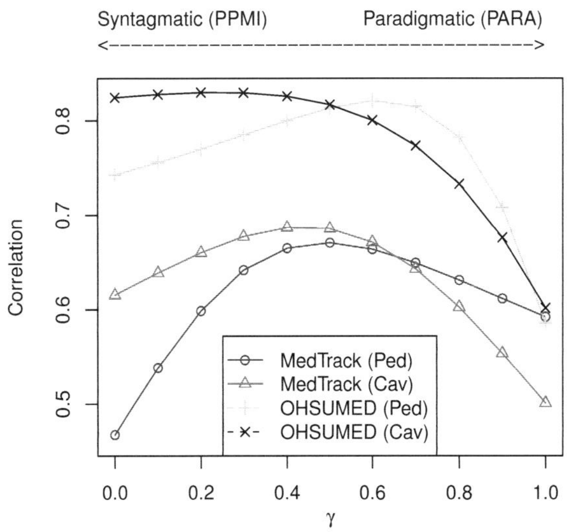

Figure 3: TE sensitivity to the mixing parameter γ. Results show that the TE model is robust across datasets and corpora.

measure (as Equation (4) reduces to only $S_{\text{ppmi}}()$ when $\gamma = 0$).

The right hand side of the graph ($\gamma = 1$) shows the performance of TE when considering only paradigmatic information, i.e. when only the PARA measure is used. With most lines converging to the same point on the right hand side, this demonstrates the increased robustness the PARA measure (and therefore paradigmatic associations) brings to the overall model.

5.2 Analysis of Paradigmatic and Syntagmatic Behaviour

To illustrate why the combination of both paradigmatic and syntagmatic measures can achieve such robust results across all datasets and corpora we compare the correlation of PPMI, PAR and TE against human assessments on a per concept-pair basis.

Figure 4 illustrates the normalised similarity scores (on log scale) of human assessors, PPMI, PARA and TE on the Caviedes and Cimino (Cav) dataset when using the OHSUMED corpora. The concept-pairs are placed in descending order of similarity as assessed by human judges, i.e. from the most similar human judged pairs to the least from left to right. The performance of a measure can be visualised by comparing its trend line with that of the descending human judged trend line. If the measure's trend line is parallel to that of the

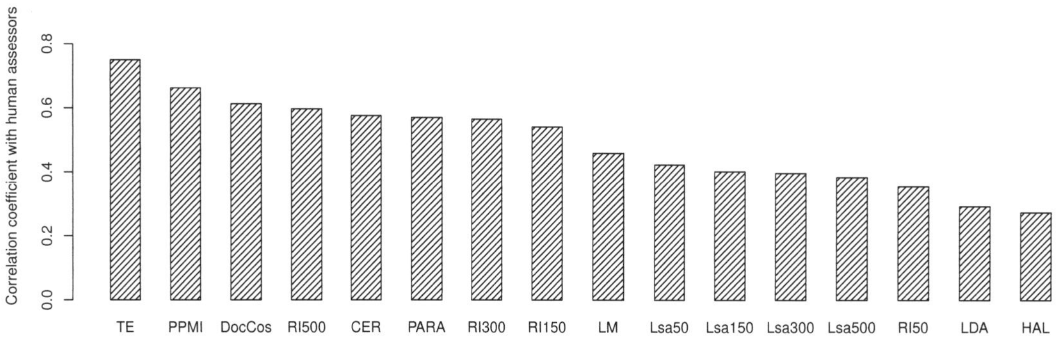

Figure 2: Comparison of all corpus-based measures (from Koopman et al., 2012), including TE and PARA; correlations averaged across datasets and corpora.

Pair #	Concept 1	Doc. Freq.	Concept 2	Doc. Freq.
11	Arrhythmia	2,298	Cardiomyopathy, Alcoholic	13
16	Angina Pectoris	1,725	Cardiomyopathy, Alcoholic	13
21	Abdominal pain	690	Respiratory System Abnormalities	1
34	Cardiomyopathy, Alcoholic	13	Respiratory System Abnormalities	1
36	Heart Diseases	1,872	Respiratory System Abnormalities	1
37	Heart Failure, Congestive	1,192	Respiratory System Abnormalities	1
38	Heartburn	104	Respiratory System Abnormalities	1

Table 3: Example concept pairs for which the PARA measure diverges from the human judgements on the OHSUMED corpus. Document frequencies showing the prevalence of the concepts in the corpus are reported. We conclude that the PARA measure is unable to estimate accurate semantic similarity when insufficient occurrence statistics are available for either concept.

human judges, then this indicates a strong correlation.

To better understand why the paradigmatic based measure differs from human assessors in Figure 4, the document frequencies of concept pairs 11, 16, 21, 34, 36, 37 and 38 from the Cav data set are reported in Table 3.

This table shows that for these concept pairs at least one concept occurs in a very small number of documents. This provides little evidence for the accurate estimation of paradigmatic associations between the concept pairs. We therefore conclude that the PARA measure requires that concepts occur in a sufficient number of documents for an effective semantic similarity estimation.

Similar observations are valid across datasets and corpora. For example, consider the correlation of PARA with human judgements for the Pedersen et al. (Ped) data set and the MedTrack corpus, as shown in Figure 5. The document frequencies for a number of concept pairs that show divergence from the Ped data set are shown in Table 4.

For these concept pairs where PARA is inconsistent with human judges, the PPMI measure effectively estimates semantic similarity. Thus the TE model, which mixes the two form of associations, is still effective even when the PARA measure is unreliable. This further supports the inclusion of both paradigmatic and syntagmatic associations for assessing semantic similarity between medical concepts.

Figure 4 also illustrates a large number of discontinuities in the PPMI graph. A discontinuity, i.e. the absence of the data-point within the plot, is due to a PPMI score of zero for the concept pair[2].

In practice, these discontinuities represent instances where the concept pair never co-occurs within any document. The same situation applies across other datasets and corpora, for example the

[2] As the graph is in log scale, $\log(0) = -\infty$ cannot be plotted.

Pair #	Concept 1	Doc. Freq.	Concept 2	Doc. Freq.
9	Diarrhea	6,184	Stomach cramps	14
23	Rectal polyp	26	Aorta	3,555

Table 4: Example concept pairs for which the PARA measure diverges from the human judgements on the MedTrack corpus. Document frequencies showing the prevalence of the concepts in the corpus are reported. We conclude that the PARA measure is unable to estimate accurate semantic similarity when insufficient occurrence statistics are available for either concept.

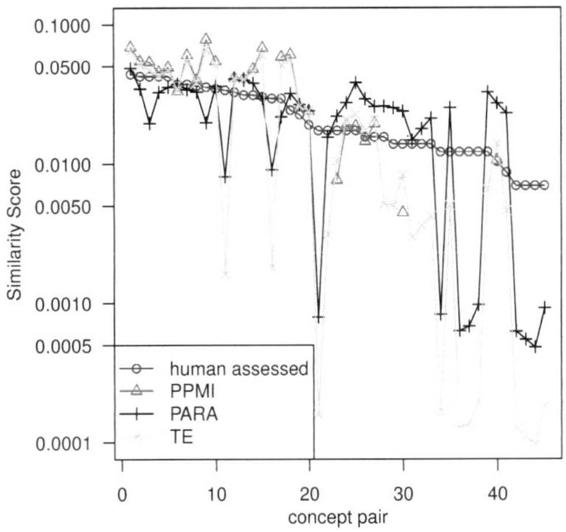

Figure 4: Normalised similarity scores (on log scale) of human assessors, PPMI, PARA and TE on Caviedes and Cimino dataset (Cav) when using the OHSUMED corpus for priming.

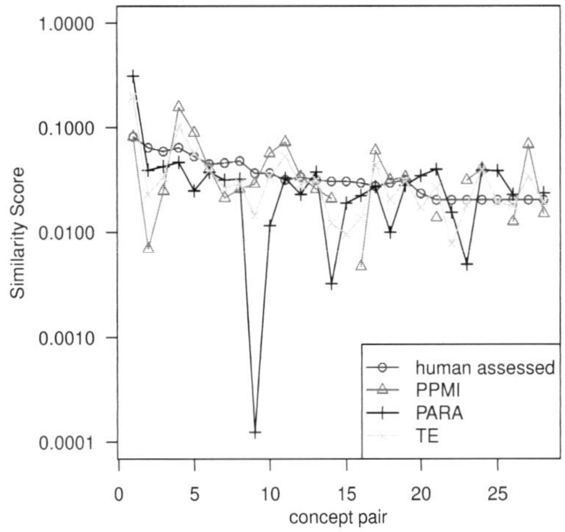

Figure 5: Normalised similarity scores (on log scale) of human assessors, PPMI, PARA and TE on Pedersen et al dataset (Ped) when using the Medtrack corpus for priming.

Ped data set on MedTrack corpus shown in Figure 5.

While PPMI discontinuities for concept pairs judged as unrelated by human assessors are correct estimates (as PPMI$=0$ implies unrelatedness), discontinuities for concept pairs judged similar (e.g. pairs 11, 16, etc. in Figure 4) indicate a failure of the PPMI measure. These situations may provide the reason why the performance of PPMI, and indeed of many existing corpus-based approaches (Koopman et al., 2012), are sensitive to the choice of priming corpus. This may indicate that the ability to successfully model syntagmatic associations is sensitive to the corpus used for priming. However, because of the results obtained by the TE model we can conclude that appropriately mixing both syntagmatic and paradigmatic associations overcomes corpus sensitivity issues.

In summary, the performance (both in terms of robustness and effectiveness) of the TE model is achieved by including both syntagmatic and paradigmatic associations between medical concepts; this is due to the diversification of the type of information used to underpin the semantic similarity estimation process.

6 Conclusion

This paper has presented a novel variant of a robust and effective corpus-based approach that estimates similarity between medical concepts that strongly correlates with human judges. This approach is based on the *tensor encoding* (TE) model. By explicitly modelling syntagmatic and paradigmatic associations the TE model is able to outperform state of the art corpus-based approaches. Furthermore, the TE model is robust across corpora and datasets, in particular overcoming corpus sensitivity issues experienced by previous approaches.

A significant contribution of this paper is to highlight the important role of paradigmatic associations. Our results suggest that paradigmatic information provides an alternative source of evidence from which semantic similarity judgements can be drawn. It is this diversity of both syntagmatic and paradigmatic information that allows the TE model to be robust and effective.

A possible area of future work is the development of an adaptive TE approach. An adaptive approach would determine the best mix of syntagmatic and paradigmatic information on a case-by-case basis, using corpus statistic features. Our analysis in fact has shown that paradigmatic associations require a minimum number of *occurrences of concepts* within documents. While, syntagmatic associations require a minimum number of *co-occurrences of concept pairs* within documents. These corpus statistics could represent features for a machine learning approach that predicts the optimal mix of syntagmatic and paradigmatic information for the TE model.

Finally, because of its effectiveness and robustness, the TE model has other potential applications beyond semantic similarity measures. One relevant application may include using the TE model within query expansion tasks in ad-hoc medical information retrieval (as this process already relies heavily on similarity judgements).

References

Pankaj Agarwal and David B Searls. 2009. Can literature analysis identify innovation drivers in drug discovery? *Nature reviews. Drug discovery*, 8(11):865–78, November.

Alan R Aronson and François-Michel Lang. 2010. An overview of MetaMap: historical perspective and recent advances. *JAMIA*, 17(3):229–236.

Jorge E Caviedes and James J Cimino. 2004. Towards the development of a conceptual distance metric for the UMLS. *Journal of biomedical informatics*, 37(2):77–85, April.

Scott Cederberg and Dominic Widdows. 2003. Using LSA and noun coordination information to improve the precision and recall of automatic hyponymy extraction. In *Proc of CoNLL'03*, pages 111–118, NJ, USA.

Trevor Cohen and Dominic Widdows. 2009. Empirical distributional semantics: Methods and biomedical applications. *Journal of Biomedical Informatics*, 42(2):390–405.

P Glenisson, P Antal, J Mathys, Y Moreau, and B De Moor. 2003. Evaluation Of The Vector Space Representation In Text-Based Gene Clustering. In *Proc Pacific Symposium of Biocomputing*, pages 391–402.

Bevan Koopman, Guido Zuccon, Peter Bruza, Laurianne Sitbon, and Michael Lawley. 2012. An Evaluation of Corpus-driven Measures of Medical Concept Similarity for Information Retrieval. In *The 21st ACM International Conference on Information Knowledge Management 2012*, pages 2439–2442.

Thomas K. Landauer and Susan T. Dumais. 1997. Solution to Plato's Problem: The Latent Semantic Analysis Theory of Acquisition, Induction and Representation of Knowledge. *Psychological Review*, 104(2):211–240.

Kevin Lund and Curt Burgess. 1996. Producing high-dimensional semantic spaces from lexical co-occurrence. *Behavior research methods, instruments and computers*, 28:203–208.

Ted Pedersen, Sarguei Pakhomov, Siddharth Patwardhan, and Christopher Chute. 2007. Measures of semantic similarity and relatedness in the biomedical domain. *Journal of Biomedical Informatics*, 40(3):288–299.

Michael Symonds, Peter Bruza, Laurianne Sitbon, and Ian Turner. 2011a. Modelling Word Meaning using Efficient Tensor Representations. In *Pacific Asia Conference on Language, Information and Computation 2011*, pages 313–322.

Michael Symonds, Peter Bruza, Laurianne Sitbon, and Ian Turner. 2011b. Tensor Query Expansion: a cognitive based relevance model. In *Australasian Document Computing Symposium 2011*, pages 87–94.

Michael Symonds, Peter Bruza, Laurianne Sitbon, and Ian Turner. 2012. A Tensor Encoding Model for Semantic Processing. In *The 21st ACM International Conference on Information Knowledge Management 2012*, pages 2267–2270.

Ellen Voorhees and Richard Tong. 2011. Overview of the TREC Medical Records Track. In *Proc of TREC'11*, MD, USA.

Active Learning and the Irish Treebank

Teresa Lynn[1,2], **Jennifer Foster**[1], **Mark Dras**[2] and **Elaine Uí Dhonnchadha**[3]
[1]NCLT/CNGL, Dublin City University, Ireland
[2]Department of Computing, Macquarie University, Sydney, Australia
[3]Centre for Language and Communication Studies, Trinity College, Dublin, Ireland
[1]{tlynn,jfoster}@computing.dcu.ie
[2]{teresa.lynn,mark.dras}@mq.edu.au, [3]uidhonne@tcd.ie

Abstract

We report on our ongoing work in developing the Irish Dependency Treebank, describe the results of two Inter-annotator Agreement (IAA) studies, demonstrate improvements in annotation consistency which have a knock-on effect on parsing accuracy, and present the final set of dependency labels. We then go on to investigate the extent to which active learning can play a role in treebank and parser development by comparing an active learning bootstrapping approach to a passive approach in which sentences are chosen at random for manual revision. We show that active learning outperforms passive learning, but when annotation effort is taken into account, it is not clear how much of an advantage the active learning approach has. Finally, we present results which suggest that adding automatic parses to the training data along with manually revised parses in an active learning setup does not greatly affect parsing accuracy.

1 Introduction

The Irish language is an official language of the European Union and is the first national language of the Republic of Ireland. It is a Verb-Subject-Object language, belonging to the Celtic language group. Irish is considered a low-density language, lacking in sufficient resources for various natural language processing (NLP) applications. The development of a dependency treebank is part of a recent initiative to address this lack of resources, as has been the case for, for example, Danish (Kromann, 2003), Slovene (Džeroski et al., 2006) and Finnish (Haverinen et al., 2010). Statistical parsers are data-driven and require a sufficient number of parsed sentences to learn from. One of the expected uses of a treebank for Irish is to provide training data for the first Irish statistical dependency parser which will form the basis of useful NLP applications such as Machine Translation or Computer Aided Language Learning.

What counts as a sufficient number of trees for training an Irish statistical dependency parser remains an open question. However, what is clear is that the parser needs to have encountered a linguistic phenomenon in training in order to learn how to accurately analyse it. Creating a treebank is a resource-intensive process which requires extensive linguistic research in order to design an appropriate labelling scheme, as well as considerable manual annotation (parsing). In general, manual annotation is desired to ensure high quality treebank data. Yet, as is often encountered when working with language, the task of manually annotating text can become repetitive, involving frequent encounters with similar linguistic structures.

In an effort to speed up the creation of treebanks, there has been an increased focus towards automating, or at least, semi-automating the process using various bootstrapping techniques. A basic bootstrapping approach such as that outlined by Judge et al. (2006) involves several steps. Firstly a parser is trained on a set of gold standard trees. This parser is then used to parse a new set of unseen sentences. When these new trees are reviewed and corrected, they are combined with the first set of trees and used to train a new parsing model. These steps are repeated until all sentences are parsed. By adding to the training data on each iteration, the parser is expected to improve progressively. The process of correcting the trees should become, in turn, less onerous. An *active learning* bootstrapping approach, also referred to as selective sampling, focuses on selecting 'informative' sentences on which to train the parser on each iteration. Sentences are regarded as informative if their inclusion in the training data is expected to fill gaps in the parser's knowledge.

This paper is divided into two parts. In Part One, we report on our ongoing work in developing the Irish Dependency Treebank, we describe the results of two Inter-annotator Agreement (IAA) studies and we present the finalised annotation scheme. In Part Two, we assess the extent to which active learning can play a role in treebank and parser development. We compare an active learning bootstrapping approach to a passive one in which sentences are chosen at random for manual revision. We show that we can reach a certain level of parsing accuracy with a smaller training set using active learning but the advantage over passive learning is relatively modest and may not be enough to warrant the extra annotation effort involved.

2 The Irish Dependency Treebank

The work discussed in this paper builds upon previous work on the Irish Dependency Treebank by Lynn et al. (2012). The treebank consists of randomly selected sentences from the National Corpus for Ireland (NCII) (Kilgarriff et al., 2006). This 30 million word corpus comprises text from news sources, books, government legislative acts, websites and other media. A 3,000 sentence gold-standard part-of-speech (POS) tagged corpus was produced by Uí Dhonnchadha et al. (2003). Another 225 hand-crafted Irish sentences are also available as a result of work by Uí Dhonnchadha (2009). These 3,225 sentences, subsequently randomised, formed the starting point for the treebank.

2.1 Inter-annotator agreement experiments

Inter-annotator agreement (IAA) experiments are used to assess the consistency of annotation within a treebank when more than one annotator is involved. As discussed by Artstein and Poesio (2008), an IAA result not only reveals information about the annotators, i.e. consistency and reliability, but it can also identify shortcomings in the annotation scheme or gaps in the annotation guide. The analysis of IAA results can also provide insight as to the types of disagreements involved and their sources.

	Kappa (labels)	**LAS**	**UAS**
IAA-1	0.7902	74.37%	85.16%
IAA-2	0.8463	79.17%	87.75%

Table 1: IAA results. LAS or Labelled Attachment Score is the percentage of words for which the two annotators have assigned the same head and label. UAS or Unlabelled Attachment Score is the percentage of words for which the two annotators have assigned the same head.

In previous work (Lynn et al., 2012) , an inter-annotator agreement assessment was conducted by selecting 50 sentences at random from the Irish POS-tagged corpus. Two nominated annotators (Irish-speaking linguists) annotated the sentences individually, according to the protocol set out in the annotation guide, without consultation. The results are shown in the first row of Table 1. For this present study, we held three workshops with the same two annotators and one other fluent Irish speaker/linguist to analyse the results of IAA-1. We took both annotators' files from IAA-1 to assess the types of disagreements that were involved. The analysis highlighted many gaps in the annotation guide along with the requirement for additional labels or new analyses. Thus, we updated the scheme and the annotation guide to address these issues. We then carried out a second IAA assessment (IAA-2) on a set of 50 randomly selected sentences. The results are shown in the second row of Table 1. A notable improvement in IAA-2 results demonstrates that the post-IAA-1 analysis, the resulting workshop discussions and the subsequent updates to the annotation scheme and guidelines were highly beneficial steps towards improving the quality of the treebank.

We have reviewed and updated the already annotated trees (300 sentences) to ensure consistency throughout the treebank. In total, 450 gold standard trees are now available. 150 of these sentences have been doubly annotated: prior to IAA-1, we used a set of 30 sentences for discussion/ training purposes to ensure the annotation guide was comprehensible to both annotators. A set of 20 sentences were used for the same purposes prior to IAA-2.

2.2 Sources of annotator disagreements

The analysis of IAA results provided information valuable for the improvement of the annotation scheme. This analysis involved the comparison of both annotators' files of 50 sentences to see where they disagreed and the types of disagreements involved. Close examination of the disagreements allowed us to categorise them as: (i) Interpretation disagreements (ii) Errors (iii) Gaps in annotation guide (iv) Outstanding issues with the dependency scheme.

2.2.1 Interpretation disagreements

The treebank data was extracted from the NCII which contains many examples of Irish legislative text. Some of these sentences are over 200 tokens in length and use obscure terminology or syntactic structures. Both annotators encountered difficulties in (i) interpreting the intended meaning of these sentences and (ii) analysing their structures. Sources of disagreement included long distance dependencies and coordinated structures.

2.2.2 Errors

Human error played a relatively small role as both annotators carried out careful reviews of their annotations. Nevertheless, some discrepancies were due to an annotator applying the wrong label even though they were aware of the correct one.

2.2.3 Gaps in the annotation guide

Gaps relate to a lack of sufficient examples in the annotation guide or lack of coverage for certain structures. For example, our analysis of IAA-1 confusions revealed that differences between the labels `padjunct` (prepositional modifier) and `obl` (oblique) were not described clearly enough.

2.2.4 Outstanding issues in the dependency scheme

We also noted during the workshops that there were still some issues we had yet to resolve. For example, in the earlier labelling scheme, we used the Sulger (2009) analysis to label as `adjunct` the relationship between predicates and prepositional phrases in a copula construction. An example is *Is maith liom tae* 'I like tea' (lit. 'tea is good with me'). However, in such a construction, the prepositional phrase – *liom* 'with me' in this case – is not optional. We choose instead to label them as `obl`. Other outstanding issues involved linguistic phenomena that had not arisen during earlier annotations and thus required discussion at this stage.

The annotation scheme defined by Lynn et al. (2012) is inspired by Lexical Functional Grammar (Bresnan, 2001) and similar to that of Çetinoğlu et al. (2010). As a result of IAA-2, we have extended the scheme by adding a hierarchical structure where appropriate and updating some analyses. The final scheme is presented in Table 2. In what follows we briefly discuss some updates to the scheme.

Labelling of predicates Our prior labelling scheme (Lynn et al., 2012) regarded predicates of both the copula *is* and the substantive verb *bí* as `xcomp` - as inspired by discussions in the LFG literature e.g. Dalrymple et al. (2004), Sulger (2009). However, open complement verbs (infinitive verbs and progressive verb phrases) were also labelled as `xcomp`. In order to differentiate these different kinds of functions, we have adopted a `pred` hierarchy of `npred`, `ppred`, `adjpred` and `advpred`. While a more fine-grained labelling scheme could result in more data sparsity, it also results in a more precise description of Irish syntax. Examples are provided in Figure 1 and Figure 2.

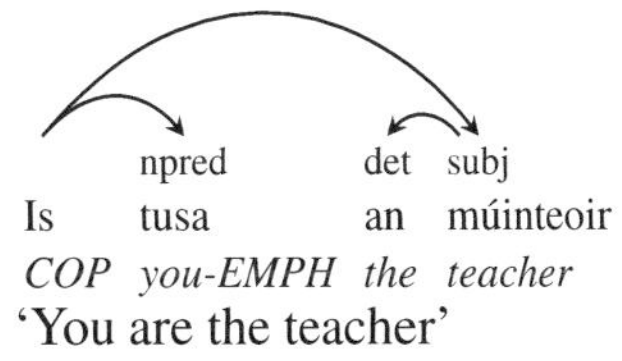

Figure 1: Dependency structure with new nominal predicate labelling (identity copular construction)

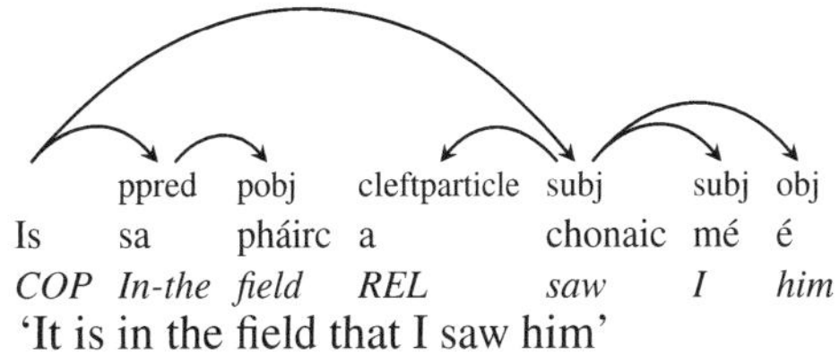

Figure 2: Dependency structure with new prepositional predicate labelling (cleft copular construction)

Cleft constructions - cleft particle Clefting or fronting is a commonly used structure in the Irish

dependency label	function
top	root
punctuation	internal and final punctuation
subj	subject
csubj	clausal subject
obj	object
pobj	object of preposition
vnobj	object of verbal noun
obl	oblique object
obl2	second oblique object
obl_ag	oblique agent
det	determiner
det2	post or pre-determiner
dem	demonstrative pronoun
poss	possessive pronoun
aug	augment pronoun
quant	quantifier
coord	coordinate
relmod	relative modifier
particle	particle
relparticle	relative particle
cleftparticle	cleft particle
advparticle	adverbial particle
nparticle	noun particle
vparticle	verb particle
particlehead	particle head
qparticle	quantifier particle
vocparticle	vocative particle
addr	addressee
adjunct	adjunct
adjadjunct	adjectival modifier
advadjunct	adverbial modifier
nadjunct	nominal modifier
padjunct	prepositional modifier
subadjunct	subordinate conjunction
toinfinitive	infinitive verb marker
app	noun in apposition
xcomp	open complement
comp	closed complement
pred	predicate
ppred	prepositional predicate
npred	nominal predicate
adjpred	adjectival predicate
advpred	adverbial predicate
subj_q	subject (question)
obj_q	object (question)
advadjunct_q	adverbial adjunct (question)
for	foreign (non-Irish) word

Table 2: The Irish Dependency Treebank labels: sublabels are indicated in bold and their parents in italics

language. Elements are fronted to predicate position to create emphasis. Irish clefts differ to English clefts in that there is more freedom with regards to the type of sentence element that can be fronted (Stenson, 1981). In Irish the structure is as follows: Copula (*is*), followed by the fronted element (Predicate), followed by the rest of the sentence (Relative Clause). The predicate can take

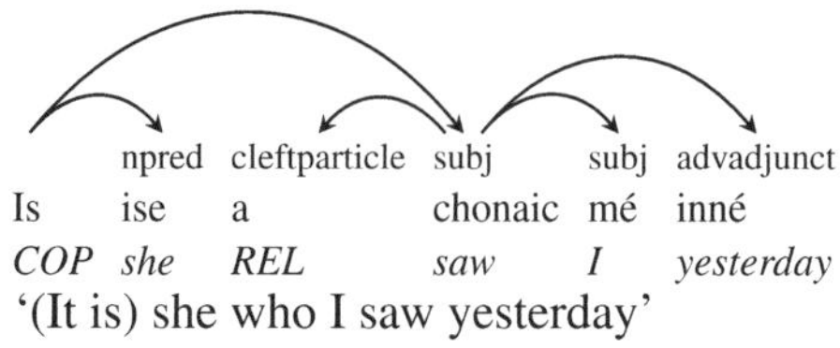

Figure 3: Dependency structure for cleft construction

the form of a pronoun, noun, verbal noun, adverb, adjective, prepositional or adverbial phrase. For example:

- Adverbial Fronting:
  Is ***laistigh de bhliain*** *a déanfar é*: "It's **within a year** that it will be done"
- Pronoun Fronting:
  Is ***ise*** *a chonaic mé inné*: "It is **she** who I saw yesterday"

Stenson (1981) describes the cleft construction as being similar to copular identity structures with the order of elements as Copula, Predicate, Subject. This is the basis for the cleft analysis provided by Sulger (2009) in Irish LFG literature. We follow this analysis but with a slight difference in the way we handle the *'a'*. According to Stenson, the *'a'* is a relative particle which forms part of the relative clause. However, there is no surface head noun in the relative clause – it is missing a NP. Stenson refers to these structures as having an 'understood' nominal head such as *an rud* "the thing" or *an té* "the person/the one". e.g. *Is ise* ***[an té]*** *a chonaic mé inné*". When the nominal head is present, it becomes a copular identity construction: *She is the one who I saw yesterday*[1]. To distinguish the *'a'* in these cleft sentences from those that occur in relative clauses with surface head nouns, we introduce a new dependency label `cleftparticle` and we attach *'a'* to the verb *chonaic* using this relation. This is shown in Figure 3.

Subject complements In copular constructions, the grammatical subject may take the form of a finite verb clause. In the labelling scheme of Lynn et al. (2012), the verb, being the head of the clause is labelled as a subject (`subj`). We choose to highlight these finite verb clauses as more specific types of grammatical subjects, i.e. subject

[1]Note that this sentence is ambiguous, and can also translate as *She was the one who saw me yesterday*.

complement (`csubj`)[2]. See Figure 4 for an example.

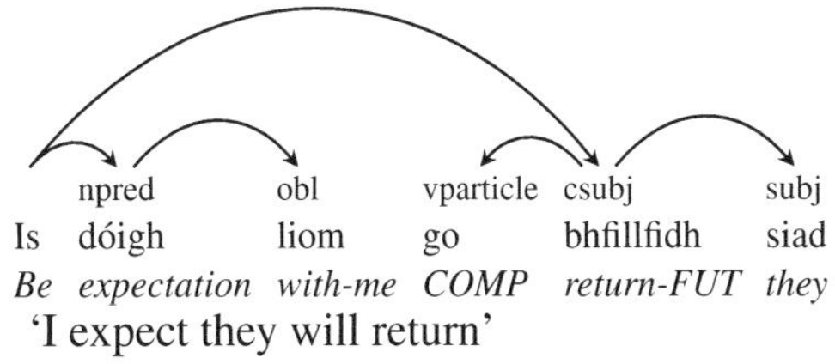

Figure 4: Dependency structure with new subject complement labelling

Wh-questions Notwithstanding Stenson's observation that WH-questions are syntactically similar to cleft sentences, we choose to treat them differently so that their predicate-argument structure is obvious and easily recoverable. Instead of regarding the WH-word as the head (just as the copula is the head in a cleft sentence), we instead regard the verb as the sentential head and mark the WH-element as a dependent of that, labelled as `subj_q`, `obj_q` or `advadjunct_q`. An example of `obj_q` is in Figure 5.

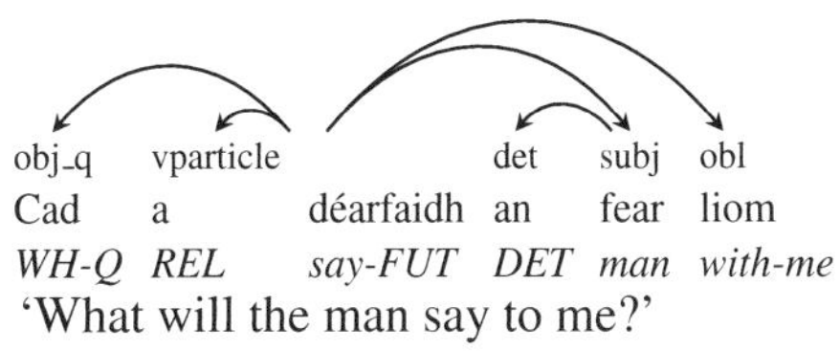

Figure 5: Dependency structure for question construction

2.3 Comparison of Parsing experiments

Lynn et al. (2012) carried out preliminary parsing experiments with MaltParser (Nivre et al., 2006) on their original treebank of 300 sentences. Following the changes we made to the labelling scheme as a result of the second IAA study, we re-ran the same parsing experiments on the newly updated seed set of 300 sentences. We used 10-fold cross-validation on the same feature sets (various combinations of form, lemma, fine-grained POS and coarse-grained POS). The improved results, as shown in the final two columns of Table 3, reflect the value of undertaking an analysis of IAA-1 results.

[2]This label is also used in the English Stanford Dependency Scheme (de Marneffe and Manning, 2008)

3 Active Learning Experiments

Now that the annotation scheme and guide have reached a stable state, we turn our attention to the role of active learning in parser and treebank development. Before describing our preliminary work in this area, we discuss related work .

3.1 Related Work

Active learning is a general technique applicable to many tasks involving machine learning. Two broad approaches are Query By Uncertainty (QBU) (Cohn et al., 1994), where examples about which the learner is least confident are selected for manual annotation; and Query By Committee (QBC) (Seung et al., 1992), where disagreement among a committee of learners is the criterion for selecting examples for annotation. Active learning has been used in a number of areas of NLP such as information extraction (Scheffer et al., 2001), text categorisation (Lewis and Gale, 1994; Hoi et al., 2006) and word sense disambiguation (Chen et al., 2006). Olsson (2009) provides a survey of various approaches to active learning in NLP.

For our work, the most relevant application of active learning to NLP is in parsing, for example, Thompson et al. (1999), Hwa et al. (2003), Osborne and Baldridge (2004) and Reichart and Rappoport (2007). Taking Osborne and Baldridge (2004) as an illustration, the goal of that work was to improve parse selection for HPSG: for all the analyses licensed by the HPSG English Resource Grammar (Baldwin et al., 2004) for a particular sentence, the task is to choose the best one using a log-linear model with features derived from the HPSG structure. The supervised framework requires sentences annotated with parses, which is where active learning can play a role. Osborne and Baldridge (2004) apply both QBU with an ensemble of models, and QBC, and show that this decreases annotation cost, measured both in number of sentences to achieve a particular level of parse selection accuracy, and in a measure of sentence complexity, with respect to random selection.

However, this differs from the task of constructing a resource that is intended to be reused in a number of ways. First, as Baldridge and Osborne (2004) show, when "creating labelled training material (specifically, for them, for HPSG parse se-

Model	LAS-1	UAS-1	LAS-2	UAS-2
Form+POS:	60.6	70.3	64.4	74.2
Lemma+POS:	61.3	70.8	64.6	74.3
Form+Lemma+POS:	61.5	70.8	64.6	74.5
Form+CPOS:	62.1	72.5	65.0	76.1
Form+Lemma+CPOS:	62.9	72.6	66.1	76.2
Form+CPOS+POS:	63.0	72.9	66.0	76.0
Lemma+CPOS+POS:	63.1	72.4	66.0	76.2
Lemma+CPOS:	63.3	72.7	65.1	75.7
Form+Lemma+CPOS+POS:	63.3	73.1	66.5	76.3

Table 3: Preliminary MaltParser experiments with the Irish Dependency Treebank: Pre- and post-IAA-2 results

lection) and later reusing it with other models, gains from active learning may be negligible or even negative": the simulation of active learning on an existing treebank under a particular model, with the goal of improving parser accuracy, may not correspond to a useful approach to constructing a treebank. Second, in the actual task of constructing a resource — interlinearized glossed text — Baldridge and Palmer (2009) show that the usefulness of particular example selection techniques in active learning varies with factors such as annotation expertise. They also note the importance of measures that are sensitive to the cost of annotation: the sentences that active learning methods select are often difficult to annotate as well, and may result in no effective savings in time or other measures. To our knowledge, active learning has not yet been applied to the actual construction of a treebank: that is one of our goals.

Further, most active learning work in NLP has used variants of QBU and QBC where instances with the *most* uncertainty or disagreement (respectively) are selected for annotation. Some work by Sokolovska (2011) in the context of phonetisation and named entity recognition has suggested that a distribution over degrees of uncertainty or disagreement may work better: the idea is that examples on which the learners are more certain or in greater agreement might be more straightforwardly added to the training set. This may be a particularly suitable idea in the context of treebank construction, so that examples selected by active learning for annotation are a mix of easier and more complex.

3.2 Setup

The basic treebank/parser bootstrapping algorithm is given in Figure 6. In an initialisation step, a parsing model is trained on a seed set of gold standard trees. In each iterative step, a new batch of unseen sentences is retrieved, the parsing model is used to parse these sentences, a subset of these automatically parsed sentences is selected, the parse trees for the sentences in this subset are manually corrected, the corrected trees are added to the training set and a new parsing model is trained. This process is repeated, ideally until parsing accuracy converges.

$t \leftarrow$ seed training set
Train a parsing model, p, using the trees in t
repeat
  $u \leftarrow$ a set of X unlabelled sentences
  Parse u with p to yield u_p
  $u\prime \leftarrow$a subset of Y sentences from u
  Hand-correct $u\prime_p$ to yield $u\prime_{gold}$
  $t \leftarrow t + u\prime_{gold}$ {Add $u\prime_{gold}$ to t}
  Train a parsing model, p, using the trees in t
until convergence

Figure 6: The basic bootstrapping algorithm

We experiment with two versions of this basic bootstrapping algorithm. In the *passive learning* variant, the Y trees that are added to the training data on each iteration are chosen at random from the batch of X unseen sentences. In the *active learning* variant, we select these trees based on a notion of how informative they are, i.e. how much the parser might be improved if it knew how to parse them correctly. We approximate informativeness based on QBC, specifically, disagreement between a committee of two parsers Thus, we rank the set of X trees (u_p) based on their disagreement with a second reference parser.[3] The

[3]This assessment of disagreement between two trees is based on the number of dependency relations they disagree on, which is the fundamental idea of the F-complement measure of Ngai and Yarowsky (2000). Disagreement between

top Y trees from this ordered set are manually revised and added to the training set for the next iteration.

We use MaltParser as the only parser in the passive learning setup and the main parser in the active learning setup. We use another dependency parser Mate (Bohnet, 2010) as our second parser in the active learning setup. Since we have 450 gold trees, we split them into a seed training set of 150 trees, a development set of 150 and a test set of 150. Due to time constraints we run the two versions of the algorithm for four iterations, and on each iteration 50 (Y) parse trees are hand-corrected from a set of 200 (X). This means that the final training set size for both setups is 350 trees (150 + (4*50)). However, the 4*50 training trees added to the seed training set of 150 are not the same for both setups. The set of 200 unseen sentences in each iteration is the same but, crucially, the subsets of 50 chosen for manual correction and added to the training set on each iteration are different — in the active learning setup, QBC is used to choose the subset and in the passive learning setup, the subset is chosen at random. Only one annotator carried out all the manual correction.

3.3 Results

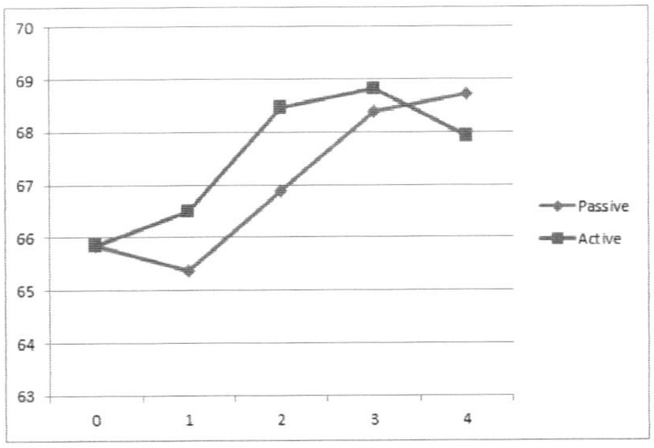

Figure 7: Passive versus Active Learning: **Labelled Attachment Accuracy**. The x-axis represents the number of training iterations and the y-axis the labelled attachment score.

The results of our bootstrapping experiments are shown in Figures 7 and 8. Figure 7 graphs the labelled attachment accuracy for both the passive and active setups over the four training iterations.

two trees, t_1 and t_2 is defined as $1 - LAS(t_1, t_2)$.

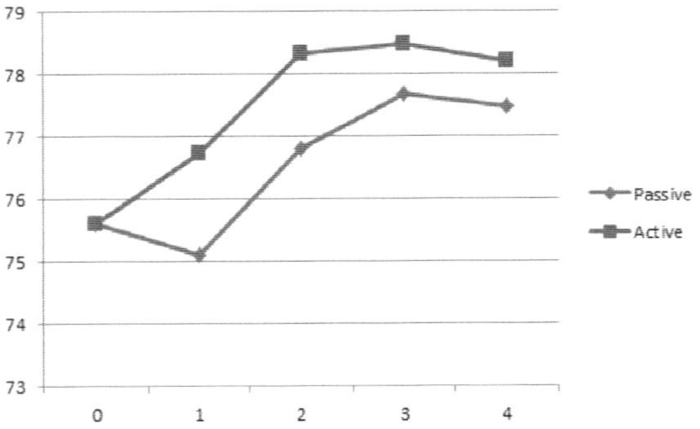

Figure 8: Passive versus Active Learning: **Unlabelled Attachment Accuracy**. The x-axis represents the number of training iterations and the y-axis the unlabelled attachment score.

	It. 1	It.2	It.3	It.4
	Average Sentence Length			
Passive	18.6	28.6	23.9	24.5
Active	18.8	25.5	24.8	35.9
	Correction Effort			
Passive	23.8	30.2	27.0	23.8
Active	36.7	37.6	32.4	32.8

Table 4: Differences between active and passive training sentences. Correction effort is the level of disagreement between the automatic parse and its correction (1-LAS)

Figure 8 depicts the unlabelled attachment accuracy. All results are on our development set.

3.4 Analysis

On the whole, the results in Figures 7 and 8 confirm that adding training data to our baseline model is useful and that the active learning results are superior to the passive learning results (particularly for unlabelled attachment accuracy). However, the drop in labelled attachment accuracy from the penultimate to the final iteration in the active learning setup is curious.

We measure the difference between the passive and active learning training sentences in terms of sentence length as a way of ascertaining the difference in annotation difficulty between the two sets. Since the training sentences were manually corrected before adding them to the training sets, this means that we can also measure how much correction was involved by measuring the level of disagreement between the automatic parses and their gold-standard corrected versions. This represents another approximation of annotation difficulty.

The results are shown in Table 4. We can see that there is no significant difference in average sentence length between the active and passive learning sets (apart from the final iteration). However, the correction effort figures confirm that the active learning sentences require more correction than the passive learning sentences. This demonstrates that the QBC metric is successful in predicting whether a sentence is hard to parse but it also calls into doubt the benefits of active learning over passive learning, especially when resources are limited. Do the modest gains in parsing accuracy warrant the extra annotation effort involved?

It is interesting that the biggest difference in sentence length is in iteration 4 where there is also a drop in active learning performance on the development set when adding them to the parser. If we examine the 50 trees that are corrected, we find one that has a length of 308 tokens. If this is omitted from the training data, labelled attachment accuracy rises from 67.92 to 69.13 and unlabelled attachment accuracy rises from 78.20 to 78.49. It is risky to conclude too much from just one example but this appears to suggest that if sentences above a certain length are selected by the QBC measure, they should not be revised and added to the training set since the correction process is more likely to be lengthy and error-prone.

The test set shows similar trends to the development set. The baseline model obtains a LAS of 63.4%, the final passive model a LAS of 67.2% and the final active model a LAS of 68.0%, (increasing to 68.1% when the 308-token sentence is removed from the training set). The difference between the active and passive learning results is not, however, statistically significant.

3.5 Making Use of Unlabelled Data

One criticism of the active learning approach to parser/treebank bootstrapping is that it can result in a set of trees which is an unrepresentative sample of the language since it is skewed in favour of the type of sentences chosen by the active learning informative measure. One possible way to mitigate this is to add automatically labelled data in addition to hand-corrected data. Taking the third active learning iteration with a training set of 300 sentences as our starting point, we add automatic parses from the remaining sentences in the unlabelled set for that iteration. The unlabelled set is ordered by disagreement with the reference parser and so we keep adding from the bottom of this set until we reach the subset of 50 trees which were manually corrected, i.e. we prioritise those parses that show the highest agreement with the reference parser first because we assume these to be more accurate. The results, shown in Figure 9, demonstrate that the addition of the automatic parses makes little difference to the parsing accuracy. This is not necessarily a negative result since it demonstrates that the training sentence bias can be adjusted without additional annotation effort and without adversely affecting parsing accuracy (at least with this limited training set size).

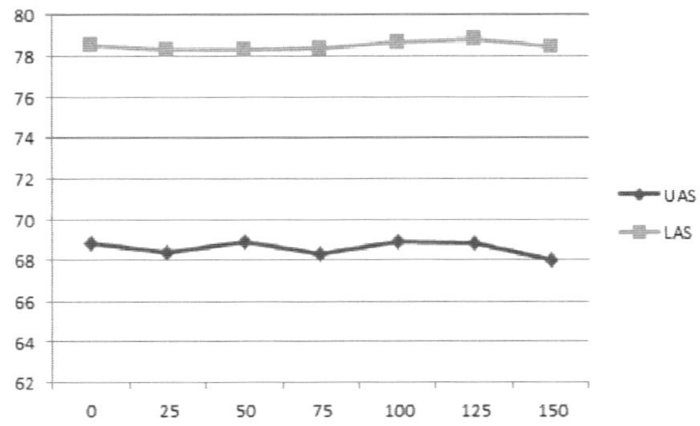

Figure 9: Adding Automatically Parsed Data to the Training set: the x-axis shows the number of automatically parsed trees that are added to the training set and the y-axis shows the unlabelled and labelled attachment accuracy on the development set.

4 Conclusion

We have presented the finalised annotation scheme for the Irish Dependency Treebank and shown how we arrived at this using inter-annotator agreement experiments, analysis and discussion. We also presented the results of preliminary parsing experiments exploring the use of active learning. Future work involves determining the length threshold above which manual annotation should be avoided during bootstrapping, experimenting with more active learning configurations, and, of course, further manual annotation.

5 Acknowledgements

The authors would like to thank Josef van Genabith and the three anonymous reviewers for their insightful comments and suggestions.

References

Ron Artstein and Massimo Poesio. 2008. Inter-coder agreement for computational linguistics. *Computational Linguistics*, 34(4):555–596, December.

Jason Baldridge and Miles Osborne. 2004. Active Learning and the Total Cost of Annotation . In *Proceedings of EMNLP 2004*, pages 9–16, Barcelona, Spain.

Jason Baldridge and Alexis Palmer. 2009. How well does active learning *actually* work? Time-based evaluation of cost-reduction strategies for language documentation. In *Proceedings of the 2009 Conference on Empirical Methods in Natural Language Processing*, pages 296–305, Singapore.

Timothy Baldwin, Emily M. Bender, Dan Flickinger, Ara Kim, and Stephan Oepen. 2004. Road testing the English Resource Grammar over the British National Corpus. In *Proceedings of LREC*.

Bernd Bohnet. 2010. Top accuracy and fast dependency parsing is not a contradiction. In *In Proceedings of COLING*.

Joan Bresnan. 2001. *Lexical Functional Syntax*. Oxford: Blackwell.

Özlem Çetinoğlu, Jennifer Foster, Joakim Nivre, Deirdre Hogan, Aoife Cahill, and Josef van Genabith. 2010. LFG without c-structures. In *Proceedings of the 9th International Workshop on Treebanks and Linguistic Theories (TLT9)*.

Jinying Chen, Andrew Schein, Lyle Ungar, and Martha Palmer. 2006. An Empirical Study of the Behavior of Active Learning for Word Sense Disambiguation. In *Proceedings of the Human Language Technology Conference of the NAACL*, pages 120–127, New York City, USA, June.

David Cohn, Les Atlas, and Richard Ladner. 1994. Improving generalization with active learning. *Machine Learning*, 15(2):201–221.

Mary Dalrymple, Helge Dyvik, and Tracy Holloway King. 2004. Copular complements: Closed or open? In Miriam Butt and Tracy Holloway King, editors, *The Proceedings of the LFG '04 Conference*.

Marie-Catherine de Marneffe and Christopher D. Manning. 2008. The Stanford typed dependencies representation. In *Workshop on Crossframework and Cross-domain Parser Evaluation (COLING2008)*.

Sašo Džeroski, Tomaž Erjavec, Nina Ledinek, Petr Pajas, Zdenek Žabokrtsky, and Andreja Žele. 2006. Towards a Slovene dependency treebank. In *Proceedings of the 5th International Conference on Language Resources and Evaluation (LREC 2006)*.

Katri Haverinen, Timo Viljanen, Veronika Laippala, Samuel Kohonen, Filip Ginter, and Tapio Salakoski. 2010. Treebanking Finnish. In *Proceedings of The Ninth International Workshop on Treebanks and Linguistic Theories (TLT9)*, pages 79–90.

Steven C. H. Hoi, Rong Jin, and Michael Lyu. 2006. Large-scale text categorization by batch mode active learning. In *Proceedings of the 15th International World Wide Web Conference (WWW 2006)*, pages 633–642, Edinburgh, UK.

Rebecca Hwa, Miles Osborne, Anoop Sarkar, and Mark Steedman. 2003. Corrected co-training for statistical parsers. In *Proceedings of the Workshop on the Continuum from Labeled to Unlabeled Data in Machine Learning and Data Mining*, Washington DC, US.

John Judge, Aoife Cahill, and Josef van Genabith. 2006. Questionbank: Creating a corpus of parse-annotated questions. In *In Proceedings of the 21st International Conference on Computational Linguitics and 44th Annual Meeting of the ACL*.

Adam Kilgarriff, Michael Rundell, and Elain Uí Dhonnchadha. 2006. Efficient corpus creation for lexicography. *Language Resources and Evaluation*, 18(2).

Matthias Kromann. 2003. The Danish Dependency Treebank and the DTAG Treebank Tool. In *Proceedings from the 2nd Workshop on Treebanks and Linguistic Theories (TLT 2003)*.

David Lewis and William Gale. 1994. A Sequential Algorithm for Training Text Classifiers. In *Proceedings of the 17th Annual International ACL-SIGIR Conference on Research and Development of Information Retrieval*, pages 3–12, Dublin, Ireland.

Teresa Lynn, Ozlem Cetinoglu, Jennifer Foster, Elaine Uí Dhonnchadha, Mark Dras, and Josef van Genabith. 2012. Irish treebanking and parsing: A preliminary evaluation. In *Proceedings of the Eight International Conference on Language Resources and Evaluation (LREC'12)*.

Grace Ngai and David Yarowsky. 2000. Rule writing or annotation: Cost-efficient resource usage for base noun phrase chunking. In *Proceedings of ACL*.

Joakim Nivre, Johan Hall, and Jens Nilsson. 2006. Maltparser: A data-driven parser-generator for dependency parsing. In *Proceedings of the 5th International Conference on Language Resources and Evaluation (LREC 2006)*.

Fredrik Olsson. 2009. A literature survey of active machine learning in the context of natural language processing. Technical Report T2009:06, SICS.

Miles Osborne and Jason Baldridge. 2004. Ensemble-based Active Learning for Parse Selection. In *HLT-NAACL 2004: Main Proceedings*, pages 89–96, Boston, MA, USA.

Roi Reichart and Ari Rappoport. 2007. An Ensemble Method for Selection of High Quality Parses. In *Proceedings of the 45th Annual Meeting of the Association of Computational Linguistics*, pages 408–415, Prague, Czech Republic.

Tobias Scheffer, Christian Decomain, and Stefan Wrobel. 2001. Active hidden Markov models for information extraction. In *Proceedings of the 4th International Conference on Advances in Intelligent Data Analysis (IDA-2001)*, pages 309–318.

Sebastian Seung, Manfred Opper, and Haim Sompolinsky. 1992. Query by committee. In *Proceedings of the Fifth Annual ACM Workshop on Computational Learning Theory*, pages 287–295, Pittsburgh, PA, US.

Nataliya Sokolovska. 2011. Aspects of Semi-Supervised and Active Learning in Conditional Random Fields. In *Proceedings of the European Conference on Machine Learning (ECML PKDD) 2011*, pages 273–288.

Nancy Stenson. 1981. *Studies in Irish Syntax*. Gunter Narr Verlag Tübingen.

Sebastian Sulger. 2009. Irish clefting and information-structure. In *Proceedings of the LFG '09 Conference*.

Cynthia Thompson, Mary Elaine Califf, and Raymond Mooney. 1999. Active learning for natural language parsing and information extraction. In *Proceedings of the Sixteenth International Machine Learning Conference (ICML-99)*, pages 406–414, Bled, Slovenia.

Elaine Uí Dhonnchadha, Caoilfhionn Nic Pháidín, and Josef van Genabith. 2003. Design, implementation and evaluation of an inflectional morphology finite state transducer for Irish. *Machine Translation*, 18:173–193.

Elaine Uí Dhonnchadha. 2009. *Part-of-Speech Tagging and Partial Parsing for Irish using Finite-State Transducers and Constraint Grammar*. Ph.D. thesis, Dublin City University.

Unsupervised Estimation of Word Usage Similarity

Marco Lui,[♠♡] **Timothy Baldwin,**[♠♡] and **Diana McCarthy** [♣]
♠ NICTA Victoria Research Laboratory
♡ Dept of Computing and Information Systems, The University of Melbourne
♣ Dept of Theoretical and Applied Linguistics, University of Cambridge
mhlui@unimelb.edu.au, tb@ldwin.net, diana@dianamccarthy.co.uk

Abstract

We present a method to estimate word use similarity independent of an external sense inventory. This method utilizes a topic-modelling approach to compute the similarity in usage of a single word across a pair of sentences, and we evaluate our method in terms of its ability to reproduce a human-annotated ranking over sentence pairs. We find that our method outperforms a bag-of-words baseline, and that for certain words there is very strong correlation between our method and human annotators. We also find that lemma-specific models do not outperform general topic models, despite the fact that results with the general model vary substantially by lemma. We provide a detailed analysis of the result, and identify open issues for future research.

1 Introduction

Automated Word Usage Similarity (Usim) is the task of determining the similarity in use of a particular word across a pair of sentences. It is related to the tasks of word sense disambiguation (WSD) and word sense induction (WSI), but differs in that Usim does not pre-suppose a predefined sense inventory. It also captures the fact that word senses may not always be distinct, and that the applicability of word senses is not necessarily mutually exclusive. In Usim, we consider pairs of sentences at a time, and quantify the similarity of the sense of the target word being used in each sentence. An example of a sentence pair (SPAIR) using similar but not identical senses of the word *dry* is given in Figure 1.

Usim is a relatively new NLP task, partly due to the lack of resources for its evaluation. Erk et al. (2009) recently produced a corpus of sentence pairs annotated for usage similarity judgments, allowing Usim to be formulated as a distinct task from the related tasks of word sense disambiguation and word sense induction.

Part c) All this has been a little dry so far: now for some fun.
For people who knew him, it was typical of his dry humor, but some in the audience thought he was tipsy.

Figure 1: Example of an SPAIR judged by annotators to use similar but not identical senses of the word *dry*.

In this work, we propose a method to estimate word usage similarity in an entirely unsupervised fashion through the use of a topic model. We make use of the well-known Latent Dirichlet Allocation (LDA) model (Blei et al., 2003) to model the distribution of topics in a sentence, then examine the similarity between sentences on the basis of the similarity between their topic distributions.

Our main contributions in this work are: (1) we introduce a method to compute word usage similarity in an unsupervised setting based on topic modelling; (2) we show that our method performs better than the bag-of-words modelling approach; (3) we find that each lemma has a distinct optimum parametrization of the approach that does not generalize across parts of speech; and (4) we demonstrate empirically that per-lemma topic models do not perform differently from global topic models.

2 Background

Polysemy is a linguistic phenomenon whereby the same word has different meaning depending on the context it is used it. For example, the use of the word *charge* in the phrase *charge a battery* is different from its use in the phrase *charge a hill*, and also distinct from its use in *charge in court*.

Word sense disambiguation (WSD) is the task of distinguishing between different senses of a word given a particular usage (Agirre and Edmonds, 2006; Navigli, 2009). Word sense disambiguation presupposes the existence of a *sense inventory*, enumerating all possible senses of a word. WSD is the task of selecting the sense of a word being used from the sense inventory given the context of its use. In contrast, word sense induction (WSI) is the task of partitioning uses of a word according to different senses, producing a sense inventory. In most research to date, the applicability of senses has been regarded as binary, in that a sense either entirely applies or entirely does not apply to a particular use of a word, and senses are regarded as mutually exclusive. This does not take into account situations where a word has different but related senses where more than one sense can apply at a time.

WSI research to date has been evaluated against fixed sense inventories from resources such as dictionaries or WordNet, since they are the primary resources available. However, WSI is a two-part task, where the first part is to determine the similarity between uses of a word, and the second is to partition the uses based on this similarity. The partitions derived thus divide the usages of a particular word according to its distinct senses. Use of a fixed sense inventory in evaluation makes it impossible to evaluate the similarity comparison independently of the partitioning technique. Furthermore, it prevents us from evaluating a WSI technique's ability to detect novel senses of a word or unusual distributions over common senses, because divergence from the fixed sense inventory is usually penalized.

2.1 Usim

Usim was introduced by Erk et al. (2009) to build a case for a graded notion of word meaning, eschewing the traditional reliance on predefined sense inventories and annotation schemas where words are tagged with the best-fitting sense. They found that the human annotations of word usage similarity correlated with the overlap of paraphrases from the English lexical substitution task. In their study, three annotators were asked to rate the similarity of pairs of usages of a lemma on a 5-point scale, where 1 indicated that the uses were completely different and 5 indicated they were identical. The SPAIRS annotated were drawn from LEXSUB (McCarthy and Navigli, 2007), which comprises open class words with token instances of each word appearing in the context of one sentence taken from the English Internet Corpus (EIC) (Sharoff, 2006). Usim annotations were produced for 34 lemmas spanning nouns, verbs, adjectives and adverbs. Each lemma is the target in 10 LEXSUB sentences, and all pairwise comparisons were presented for annotation, resulting in 45 SPAIRS per lemma, for a total of 1530 comparisons per annotator overall. Erk et al. (2009) provide a detailed analysis of the annotations collected, but do not propose an automated approach to word usage similarity, which is the subject of this work.

2.2 Topic Modelling

Topic models are probabilistic models of latent document structure. In contrast to a standard bag-of-words model, a topic model posits an additional intermediate layer of structure, termed the "topics". Each topic is a distribution over words, and a document is modeled as a finite mixture over topics.

The model that we will be using in this work is the Latent Dirichlet Allocation (LDA) model (Blei et al., 2003). In the LDA model, each document is modelled as a mixture of topics. Each topic is a multinomial distribution over words, and LDA places a Dirichlet prior on word distributions in topics. Although exact inference of LDA parameters is intractable, the model has gained prominence due to the availability of computationally efficient approximations, the most popular being based on Gibbs sampling (Griffiths and Steyvers, 2004). For brevity, we do not give a detailed description of the LDA model.

2.3 Related Work

Stevenson (2011) experimented with the use of LDA topic modelling in word sense disambiguation, where he used topic models to provide context for a graph-based WSD system (Agirre and Soroa, 2009), replacing a local context derived from adjacent words. This approach is of limited relevance to our work, as the graph-based approach considered state-of-the-art in unsupervised WSD (De Cao et al., 2010) maps senses to individual nodes in a graph. This presupposes the existence of a fixed sense inventory, and thus does not lend itself to determining unsupervised word usage similarity.

Brody and Lapata (2009) proposed an LDA topic modelling approach to WSI which combines feature sets such as unigram tokens and dependency relations, using a layered feature representation. Yao and Van Durme (2011) extended this work in applying a Hierarchical Dirichlet Process (HDP: Teh et al. (2006)) to the WSI task, whereby the topic model dynamically determines how many topics to model the data with, rather than relying on a preset topic number. Recently, Lau et al. (2012) further extended this work and applied it to the task of novel sense detection.

More broadly, this work is related to the study of distributional semantics of words *in context* (Erk and Padó, 2008). Dinu and Lapata (2010) propose a probabilistic framework for representing word meaning and measuring similarity of words in context. One of the parametrizations of their framework uses LDA to automatically induce latent senses, which is conceptually very similar to our approach. One key difference is that Dinu and Lapata focus on inferring the similarity in use of *different* words given their context, whereas in this work we focus on estimating the similarity of use of a *single* word in a number of different contexts.

3 Methodology

Our basic framework is to produce a vector representation for each item in a LEXSUB sentence pair (SPAIR), and then compare the two vectors using a distance measure (Section 3.2). Evaluation is carried out by comparing the per-SPAIR predictions of word usage similarity to the average rating given by human annotators to each SPAIR. The use of the average rating as the goldstandard is consistent with the use of leave-one-out resampling in estimating inter-annotator agreement (Erk et al., 2009). Our evaluation metric is Spearman's ρ with tie-breaking, also consistent with Erk et al. (2009). We compute ρ over the set of all SPAIRS, as well as broken down by part-of-speech and by individual lemma. Positive correlation (higher positive values of ρ) indicates better agreement.

3.1 Background Collections

The data used to learn the parameters of the topic model (henceforth referred to as the *background collection*) has a strong influence on the nature of the topics derived. We investigated learning topic model parameters from 3 global background collections:

SENTENCE The set of 340 sentences used in the Usim annotation

PAGE The set of 340 pages in the EIC from which SENTENCE was extracted

CORPUS The full English Internet Corpus (EIC)

A global background collection is expected to learn word associations ('topics') that are representative of the content of the corpus. Our intuition is that the distribution over topics for similar senses of a word should also be similar, and thus that the distribution over topics can be used to represent a particular use of a word. We discuss how to derive this distribution in Section 3.2.

Prior to learning topic models, we lemmatized the text and eliminated stopwords. In this work, we do not investigate the LDA hyperparameters α and β. We use the common default values of $\alpha = 0.1$ and $\beta = 0.01$.

3.2 Vector-based Representation

Our representation for each usage (each item in an SPAIR) consists of a distribution over topics. We obtain this distribution by mapping each word in the usage context onto a single latent topic using the LDA model. We denote the context in terms of a tuple CONTEXT(*a*,*b*). CONTEXT(0,0) indicates that only the annotated sentence was used, whereas CONTEXT(3,3) indicates that three sentences before and three sentences after the annotated sentence were used. Note that in the Usim annotations of Erk et al. (2009), the annotators' judgments were based solely on the sentence pairs, without any additional context. This corresponds exactly to CONTEXT(0,0).

For comparing the vector-based representations of two sentences, we used cosine similarity (`Cosine`). Since the topic vectors can be interpreted as a probability distribution over topics, we also experimented with a similarity metric based on Jensen-Shannon Divergence. We found that cosine similarity provided marginally better results, though the differences were usually minimal.

We also investigated the topic distribution of specific words in the sentence, such as the words

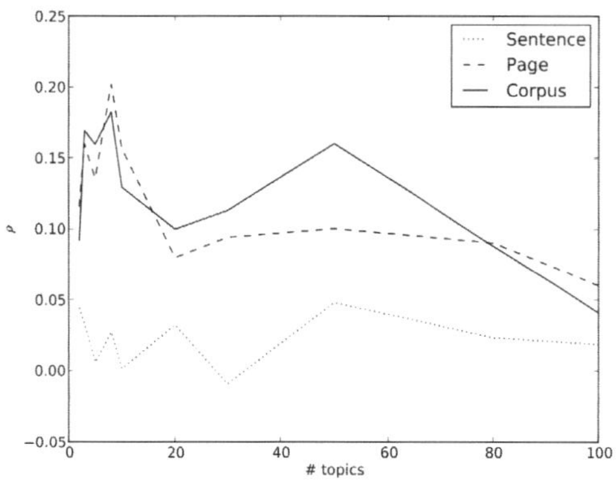

Figure 2: Plot of number of topics against Spearman's ρ per background collection

T_0: ⟨water, plant, area, small, large, fire, tree, tea, food, high⟩
T_1: ⟨quot, http, text, count, amp, book, review, page, language, film⟩
T_2: ⟨war, American, country, force, miltary, government, Iraq, political, United, church⟩
T_3: ⟨service, provide, business, school, cost, need, pay, include, market, information⟩
T_4: ⟨information, system, site, need, computer, number, datum, test, program, find⟩
T_5: ⟨think, question, thing, point, give, want, fact, find, idea, need⟩
T_6: ⟨PM, post, think, Comment, March, Bush, want, thing, write, June⟩
T_7: ⟨look, think, want, find, tell, thing, give, feel⟩

Figure 3: Characteristic terms per topic in the 8-topic model of PAGE

before and after the annotated word, but found that the whole-sentence model outperformed the per-word models, and thus omit the results on per-word models for brevity.

As a baseline for comparison, we use a standard bag-of-words representation where frequency vectors of words in context are compared. We use the same contexts for the bag-of-word-model that we used to infer topic distributions, thus allowing for a direct evaluation of topic modelling in contrast to a more conventional text representation. Our baseline results are thus derived by using `Cosine` to quantify the similarity between the bag-of-words of the context of different uses of the same lemma.

4 Results

For each of the three background collections SENTENCE, PAGE and CORPUS, we considered topic counts between 2 and 100 in pseudo-logarithmic increments. We computed Spearman's ρ between the average human annotator rating for each SPAIR and the output of our method for each combination of background collection and topic count. We analyzed the results in terms of an aggregation of SPAIRs across all lemmas, as well as broken down by lemma and part-of-speech.

We found that the best overall result was obtained using an 8-topic model of PAGE, where the overall Spearman's ρ between the human annota-

		8-topic	T-topic	
Lemma/POS	IAA	ρ	T	ρ
bar(n)	0.410	0.244	30	0.306
charge(n)	0.836	**0.394**	10	**0.667**
charge(v)	0.658	**0.342**	30	**0.429**
check(v)	0.448	0.233	8	0.233
clear(v)	0.715	0.224	8	0.224
draw(v)	0.570	0.192	10	**0.606**
dry(a)	0.563	**0.608**	5	**0.756**
execution(n)	0.813	0.174	30	0.277
field(n)	0.267	0.118	3	**0.375**
figure(n)	0.554	0.158	3	**0.356**
flat(a)	0.871	**0.444**	50	**0.684**
fresh(a)	0.260	-0.002	20	**0.408**
function(n)	0.121	0.234	30	0.292
hard(r)	0.432	0.138	5	**0.309**
heavy(a)	0.652	-0.014	5	0.261
investigator(n)	0.299	**0.364**	10	**0.583**
light(a)	0.549	-0.078	20	0.180
match(n)	0.694	-0.228	80	0.227
order(v)	0.740	0.153	10	0.287
paper(n)	0.701	-0.026	3	**0.330**
poor(a)	0.537	0.210	10	**0.353**
post(n)	0.719	**0.482**	8	**0.482**
put(v)	0.414	**0.544**	8	**0.544**
raw(a)	0.386	**0.387**	2	**0.392**
right(r)	0.707	**0.436**	8	**0.436**
rude(a)	0.669	**0.449**	8	**0.449**
softly(r)	0.610	**0.604**	8	**0.604**
solid(a)	0.603	**0.364**	3	**0.417**
special(a)	0.438	0.140	30	**0.393**
stiff(a)	0.386	0.289	8	0.289
strong(a)	0.439	0.163	2	0.292
tap(v)	0.773	0.233	30	0.272
throw(v)	0.401	**0.334**	8	**0.334**
work(v)	0.322	-0.063	80	0.132
adverb	0.585	**0.418**	8	**0.418**
verb	0.634	**0.268**	8	**0.268**
adjective	0.601	**0.171**	50	**0.219**
noun	0.687	**0.109**	3	**0.261**
overall	0.630	**0.202**	8	**0.202**

Table 1: Comparison of mean Spearman's ρ of inter-annotator agreement (IAA), Spearman's ρ for best overall parameter combination for CONTEXT(0,0), and Spearman's ρ for the optimal number of topics, using PAGE as the background collection. ρ values significant at the 0.05 level are presented in **bold**.

T_0: ⟨think, want, thing, look, tell, write, text, find, try, book⟩
T_1: ⟨information, system, need, government, provide, include, service, case, country, number⟩
T_2: ⟨find, give, child, water, place, woman, hand, look, leave, small⟩

Figure 4: Characteristic terms per topic in the 3-topic model of PAGE

Mowing The way that you mow your lawn will also affect how well it survives hot, dry conditions.
Surprisingly in such a dry continent as Australia, salt becomes a problem when there is too much water.
If the mixture is too dry, add some water ; if it is too soft, add some flour.

Figure 5: Sentences for *dry(a)* with a strong component of Topic 0 given the 8-topic model illustrated in figure 3

tor averages and the automated word usage similarity computation was a statistically significant 0.202.

A detailed breakdown of the best overall result is given in Table 1. Alongside this breakdown, we also provide: (1) the average inter-annotator agreement (IAA); and (2) the Spearman's ρ for the optimal number of topics for the given lemma.

The IAA is computed using leave-one-out resampling (Lapata, 2006), and is a detailed breakdown of the result reported by Erk et al. (2009). In brief, the IAA reported is the mean Spearman's ρ between the ratings given by each annotator and the average rating given by all other annotators. We also present the Spearman's ρ for the best number of topics in order to illustrate the impact of the number of topics parameter for the model of the background collection. We find that for some lemmas, a lower topic count is optimal, whereas for other lemmas, a higher topic count is preferred. In aggregate terms, we found that verbs, adverbs and nouns performed better with a low topic count, whereas adjectives performed best with a much higher topic count.

On the basis of the best overall result, we examined the effect of the topic count and training collection. These results are shown in Figure 2. We found that aggregated over all lemmas, the topic models learned from the full-page contexts (PAGE) and the whole English Internet Corpus (CORPUS) always do better than those learned from just the single-sentence training collection (SENTENCE). This observation is also true

The software is the program that sifts through the millions of pages recorded in the index to find match to a search and rank them in order of what it believes is most relevant.
The tag consists of a tiny chip, about the size of a match head that serves as a portable database.

Figure 6: Sentences for *match(n)* with a high concentration of Topic 4

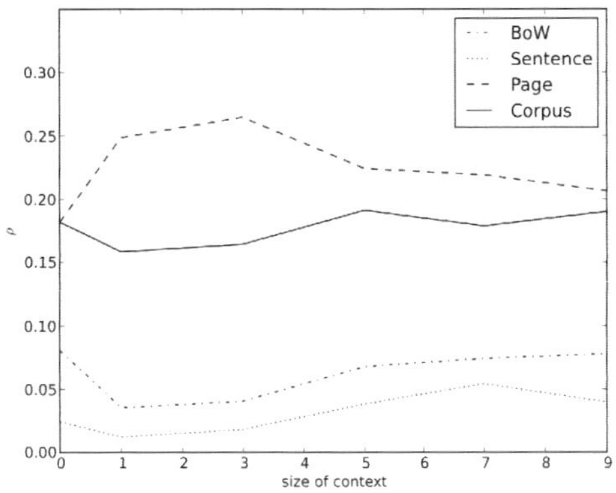

Figure 7: Plot of SPAIR context size against Spearman's ρ (8-topic background collection)

when we examine the aggregation over individual parts-of-speech. In general, the results obtained with topic models of PAGE tend to be similar to those obtained with topics models of CORPUS, and across all lemmas the optimum number of topics is about 8.

Finally, we also examined our results at a per-lemma level, identifying the optimal topic count for each individual lemma. We found that for all lemmas, there existed a topic count that resulted in a ρ of > 0.4, with the exception of *light(a)*. For some lemmas, their optimal topic count resulted in $\rho > 0.8$ (*check(v)*, *draw(v)*, *softly(r)*). However, the best choice of parameters varied greatly between lemmas, and did not show any observable consistency overall, or between lemmas for a given part-of-speech.

4.1 Topic Modelling vs. Bag-of-words

We computed a baseline result for Usim by using a bag-of-words model for each item in an SPAIR. We examined using only the annotated sentence (CONTEXT(0,0)), as well as varying amounts of context drawn symmetrically around the sentence (CONTEXT(a,b) for $a = b \in \{1, 3, 5, 7, 9\}$).

Figure 7 shows the result of varying the size

of the context used. On the x-axis, a value of 0 indicates no additional context was used (i.e. only the annotated sentence was used). A value of 3 indicates that CONTEXT(3,3) was used (i.e. 3 sentences before and after, in addition to the annotated sentence). Based on earlier results, we only considered 8-topic models for each background collection. In general, we found that the page-level(PAGE) and corpus-level(CORPUS) topic models perform better than the bag-of-words (BoW) model and the sentence-level topic model(SENTENCE).

For each context, we used Welch's t-test to determine if the difference between background collections was statistically significant. We found that at the 5% level, for all contexts, CORPUS and PAGE are different from BoW. We also found that at the 5% level, for all contexts, CORPUS and PAGE are different. Overall, the best performance was observed on the 8-topic PAGE model, using CONTEXT(3,3). This yielded a Spearman's ρ of 0.264 with respect to the gold standard annotations.

4.2 Global vs. Per-lemma Topic Models

We have already demonstrated that the topic modelling approach yields improvements over the bag of words model for estimating word usage similarity, provided that that PAGE or CORPUS background collections are used. However, performance on individual lemmas varies widely. [1] One possible reason for this is that the topics being learned are too general, and thus the latent semantics that they capture are not useful for estimating the similarity in word use. To address this issue, we experiment with learning topic models *per-lemma*, learning topics that are specific to each target lemma.[2]

In the per-lemma approach, instead of a single global topic model, we learn a distinct set of topics for each lemma. The per-lemma models use only sentences in which the target lemma occurs, plus one sentence before and one sentence after (CONTEXT(1,1)). Thus, the background collections for each lemma are a (small) subset of CORPUS, and have some overlap with PAGE, although they also include uses of the lemmas that were not annotated and therefore not present in PAGE. We assembled the background collection for each lemma before part-of-speech tagging, so for *charge(n)* and *charge(v)* a single topic model was used. This gave us 33 different topic models for the set of 34 lemmas.

We compare the use of a global topic model to the use of per-lemma topic models in estimating the similarity in word usage of a given lemma L in each sentence in an SPAIR. Given a topic count T and a symmetric usage context CONTEXT(k, k), we map each word in the context into the corresponding topic space. For the global model, we use a topic space of T topics in PAGE, and for the per-lemma model we use the T topic model of all the occurrences of L in CORPUS. Note that the context extracted for each occurrence of L in CORPUS is kept constant (CONTEXT(1,1)); it is the context k used to represent each sentence in the annotated SPAIR that is varied. Thus, the overall result we compute for the global topic models is based on inference on a single global topic model, whereas the overall result reported for the per-lemma approach is based on inference in each of the per-lemma topic models.

Disappointingly, the per-lemma topic models fail to improve on the performance of the global topic models. Across a range of context sizes k and number of topics T in the topic model, we find that the global PAGE model and the per-lemma topic models have nearly indistinguishable performance. The per-lemma models are actually worse than the global model at a high topic count ($T = 50$ and beyond). The overall best result remains the 8-topic PAGE model using CONTEXT(3,3), which a Spearman's ρ of 0.264 with respect to the gold standard annotations. The best result for the per-lemma topic models is 0.209, obtained with an 8-topic model using CONTEXT(5,5).

5 Discussion & Future Work

From the breakdown given in Table 1, we observe that the effectiveness of our approach varies significantly between parts-of-speech and between individual lemmas. For example, for *dry(a)*, we see a fairly strong correlation between the calculated similarity and the human annotations. This

[1]Human performance also varies by lemma as shown by the range in IAA scores. System performance would be increased if we could focus on those lemmas with higher IAA but since we would have no way of predicting IAA in advance we include all lemmas in our overall figures.

[2]This also addresses the unlikely situation where an SPAIR shares two target lemmas, where the uses of one are very similar and the uses of the other are very different.

correlation is much stronger than that observed across all the adjectives.

For the lemmas *dry(a)*, *investigator(n)* and *put(v)*, the correlation between our method and the human annotations exceeds the average inter-annotator agreement. This is due to variation in the inter-annotator agreement by lemma. Often, two annotators produce rankings that are similar, with the third being very different. In this case our system output may be more similar to the average of the three annotators than the mean similarity of each annotator to the average of the other two. In absence of additional annotations,[3] it may be possible to correct for systematic differences in the annotators use of the gradings to achieve a more consistent ordering over SPAIRS. We leave this investigation to future work.

For part-of-speech aggregation, the highest correlation is seen in adverbs, which is somewhat surprising since adverbs are not normally thought of as being strongly topical in nature. In order to gain further insight into the sources of the correlations, we examined the data in greater detail. In particular, we manually inspected the characteristic terms of each topic learned by the topic model. These terms are reproduced in Figure 3. For contrast, we include the best terms for each topic in the 3-topic model of PAGE, which was the best overall for nouns (Figure 4).

We examined the topic distribution for all the sentences for *dry(a)*. We found that in the 8-topic model of PAGE, Topic 0 clusters terms associated with water, food and plants. The sentences with a strong component of Topic 0 are reproduced in Figure 5. We found that sentences with strong components of Topic 0 were likely to use *dry* in the sense of "lacking in water", thus this particular topic was well suited to measuring the similarity in the use of the word *dry*; uses of *dry* in relation to water had a strong component of Topic 0, whereas uses of *dry* not related to water did not.

Although a topic count of 2 is unusually low for LDA modelling of text, we found that for some lemmas this was the optimum topic count, and for *raw(a)* the correlation between annotations and our usage similarity estimation was statistically significant. A possible explanation is that the topics in the 2-topic model aligned with variation in the senses of raw found in different genres of text.[4]

The use of topic distribution is not a panacea for usage similarity. An example of how topic modelling can be misleading is given in Figure 6. Here, we find two sentences with a high concentration of Topic 4, which is related to computers. Both sentences do indeed talk about concepts related to computers; however the use of *match(n)* in the two sentences is completely different. In the first instance, the use of match is topical to the concepts of searching and ranking, whereas in the second instance the term match is used for an analogy about size, and thus this usage of match has little to no topical relation with the rest of the sentence.

Overall, we find that the use of topic models provides a statistically significant improvement in estimating word usage similarity with respect to a bag-of-words model. We observe that for both BoW and topic-modelling approaches, modelling a usage using only the sentence that it occurs in provides inferior results to using a larger context. For the BoW model, the results kept improving as the context was increased, though at larger contexts the comparison essentially becomes one of word distributions in the entire document rather than in the particular usage of a word. This illustrates a key issue with a bag-of-words model of a single sentence: the resulting vectors are very sparse, which makes judging their similarity very difficult.[5]

We observed that the per-lemma topic models did not perform any better than the global topic models, which suggests that the performance increase of automated estimation of word usage similarity may be simply due to dimensionality reduction rather than the latent semantic properties of the topic model. However, we found that the PAGE models outperformed the CORPUS models. This indicates that the actual data used for topic modelling has an impact on per-

[3]In more recent work (Erk et al., 2012) judgments are collected from eight annotators which increases inter-annotator agreement overall, although agreement per-lemma will still vary depending on the semantics of the lemma in question.

[4]Inspection of the top terms for each of the two topics suggested a rough division between "news" and "lay language", but it is not clear exactly how these align with the uses or *raw(a)*. We leave further analysis of this for future work.

[5]It may be possible to use second order co-occurrences to alleviate this to some extent by using the centroid of vectors of the words in context where those vectors are taken from a whole corpus.

formance, suggesting that some latent semantic properties are being recovered. CORPUS is a very much larger background collection than PAGE. In this respect we would expect a much larger diversity of topics in CORPUS than in PAGE, and to some extent this is supported by the results presented in Figure 2. Here, we see a peak in performance at $T = 50$ topics for the CORPUS model that is not present in the PAGE model. However, this is a local optimum. The best topic count for both PAGE and CORPUS was at $T = 8$ topics. The reasons for this are not fully clear, but perhaps may be again attributable to sparsity. Where a large number of topics is used, only a very small number of words may be assigned to each topic. This is supported by the results in Figure 7, where we see an initial increase in performance as we increase the size of the context. However, this increase due to increased context is counteracted by a decreased topical coherence in the larger context, thus for the PAGE model we see that performance decreases after CONTEXT(3,3). Interestingly, for the CORPUS model there is no corresponding decrease in performance. However, at larger context sizes we are reaching a limit in the context in that the entire document is being used, and thus this increase cannot be extended indefinitely.

Overall, this work has shown promising results for a topic modelling approach to estimating word usage similarity. We have found that topic distributions under a topic model can be effective in determining similarity between word usages with respect to those determined by human annotators. One problem that we faced was that the optimal parameters varied for each lemma, and there was no obvious way of predicting them in an unsupervised context. We found that although the globally-optimal approach produced a statistically significant correlation with human annotators for many of the lemmas, most lemmas had a different locally-optimal parametrization. This suggests that a promising avenue for future research is a semi-supervised approach to estimating word usage similarity. Given a small amount of training data, it may be possible to determine the optimal parameters for topic-modelling-based estimation of word usage similarity, which can then be applied to word usage similarity estimation in much larger text collections. The HDP model of Teh et al. (2006) would be an alternative approach to resolving this issue.

We also have not fully explored the effect of the background collection. We found that topic models of background collections drawn at the document level performed better than those drawn at the corpus level, but that those drawn at the per-lemma sentence level were not measurably different from those drawn at the document level. Two additional background collections could be investigated: (1) at the per-lemma document level, where entire documents containing a given lemma are used; and (2) at a cross-corpus level. The former would give insight on whether there is an issue of data sparsity at the parameter estimation phase, since we found that for global models, the document-level background collection outperformed the sentence-level background collection. For the latter, including data from additional corpora may result in a better correspondence between topics and senses, allowing for better estimation of word usage similarity.

6 Conclusion

In this work, we examined automated estimation of word usage similarity via vector similarity over topic vectors inferred from LDA topic models. We found that such topic vectors outperform a bag-of-words baseline, with the globally optimal parametrization attaining Spearman's ρ of 0.264 with the average annotation given by 3 human annotators across 1530 SPAIRs. We also found that each lemma has a different optimum topic count. In some cases, the correlation between our method and the average of human annotations exceeds the inter-annotator agreement. However, the optimum topic count is difficult to predict, and is not consistent within parts of speech. Finally, we found that per-lemma topic models do not significantly improve results with respect to global topic models. Overall, we have shown that a topic modelling approach has potential for automated estimation of word usage similarity, but there remain a number of open issues to investigate which may lead to even better performance.

Acknowledgments

NICTA is funded by the Australian Government as represented by the Department of Broadband, Communications and the Digital Economy and the Australian Research Council through the ICT Centre of Excellence program.

References

Eneko Agirre and Philip Edmonds. 2006. *Word Sense Disambiguation: Algorithms and Applications*. Springer, Dordrecht, Netherlands.

Eneko Agirre and Aitor Soroa. 2009. Personalizing PageRank for word sense disambiguation. *Proceedings of the 12th Conference of the European Chapter of the Association for Computational Linguistics on - EACL '09*, (April):33–41.

David M Blei, Andrew Y Ng, and Michael I Jordan. 2003. Latent Dirichlet Allocation. *The Journal of Machine Learning Research*, 3:993–1022.

Samuel Brody and Mirella Lapata. 2009. Bayesian word sense induction. In *Proceedings of the 12th Conference of the EACL (EACL 2009)*, pages 103–111, Athens, Greece.

Diego De Cao, Roberto Basili, Matteo Luciani, Francesco Mesiano, and Riccardo Rossi. 2010. Robust and efficient page rank for word sense disambiguation. In *Proceedings of TextGraphs-5 - 2010 Workshop on Graph-based Methods for Natural Language Processing*, pages 24–32, Uppsala, Sweden, July. Association for Computational Linguistics.

Georgiana Dinu and Mirella Lapata. 2010. Measuring distributional similarity in context. In *Proceedings of the 2010 Conference on Empirical Methods in Natural Language Processing*, pages 1162–1172, Cambridge, MA, October. Association for Computational Linguistics.

Katrin Erk and Sebastian Padó. 2008. A structured vector space model for word meaning in context. In *Proceedings of the 2008 Conference on Empirical Methods in Natural Language Processing*, pages 897–906, Honolulu, Hawaii, October. Association for Computational Linguistics.

Katrin Erk, Diana McCarthy, and Nicholas Gaylord. 2009. Investigations on word senses and word usages. In *Proceedings of the Joint Conference of the 47th Annual Meeting of the ACL and the 4th International Joint Conference on Natural Language Processing of the AFNLP: Volume 1 - ACL-IJCNLP '09*, page 10, Morristown, NJ, USA. Association for Computational Linguistics.

Katrin Erk, Diana McCarthy, and Nick Gaylord. 2012. Measuring word meaning in context. *to appear in Computational Linguistics*.

Thomas L. Griffiths and Mark Steyvers. 2004. Finding scientific topics. *PNAS*.

Mirella Lapata. 2006. Automatic evaluation of information ordering: Kendall's tau. *Computational Linguistics*, 32(4):471–484.

Jey Han Lau, Paul Cook, Diana McCarthy, David Newman, and Timothy Baldwin. 2012. Word sense induction for novel sense detection. In *Proceedings of the 13th Conference of the EACL (EACL 2012)*, pages 591–601, Avignon, France.

Diana McCarthy and Roberto Navigli. 2007. SemEval-2007 task 10: English lexical substitution task. In *Proceedings of the 4th International Workshop on Semantic Evaluations (SemEval-2007)*, pages 48–53.

Roberto Navigli. 2009. Word sense disambiguation: A survey. *ACM Computing Surveys*, 41(2).

Serge Sharoff. 2006. Open-source Corpora Using the net to fish for linguistic data. *International Journal of Corpus Linguistics*, 4:435–462.

Mark Stevenson. 2011. Disambiguation of medline abstracts using topic models. In *Proceedings of the ACM fifth international workshop on Data and text mining in biomedical informatics*, pages 59–62. ACM.

Y.W. Teh, M.I. Jordan, M.J. Beal, and D.M. Blei. 2006. Hierarchical Dirichlet processes. *Journal of the American Statistical Association*, 101:1566–1581.

Xuchen Yao and Benjamin Van Durme. 2011. Nonparametric bayesian word sense induction. In *Proceedings of TextGraphs-6: Graph-based Methods for Natural Language Processing*, pages 10–14, Portland, USA.

Valence Shifting: Is It A Valid Task?

Mary Gardiner
Centre for Language Technology
Macquarie University
mary@mary.gardiner.id.au

Mark Dras
Centre for Language Technology
Macquarie University
mark.dras@mq.edu.au

Abstract

This paper looks at the problem of valence shifting, rewriting a text to preserve much of its meaning but alter its sentiment characteristics. There has only been a small amount of previous work on the task, which appears to be more difficult than researchers anticipated, not least in agreement between human judges regarding whether a text had indeed had its valence shifted in the intended direction. We therefore take a simpler version of the task, and show that sentiment-based lexical paraphrases do consistently change the sentiment for readers. We then also show that the Kullback-Leibler divergence makes a useful preliminary measure of valence that corresponds to human judgements.

1 Introduction

This paper looks at the problem of VALENCE SHIFTING, rewriting a text to preserve much of its meaning but alter its sentiment characteristics. For example, starting with the sentence *If we have to have another parody of a post-apocalyptic America, does it have to be this bad?*, we could make it more negative by changing *bad* to *abominable*. Guerini et al. (2008) say about valence shifting that

> it would be conceivable to exploit NLP techniques to slant original writings toward specific biased orientation, keeping as much as possible the same meaning … as an element of a persuasive system. For instance a strategic planner may decide to intervene on a draft text with the goal of "coloring" it emotionally.

There is only a relatively small amount of work on this topic, which we review in Section 2. From this work, the task appears more difficult than researchers originally anticipated, with many factors making assessment difficult, not least the requirement to be successful at a number of different NLG tasks, such as producing grammatical output, in order to properly evaluate success. One of the fundamental difficulties is that it is difficult to know whether a particular approach has been successful: researchers have typically had some trouble with inter-judge agreement when evaluating whether their approach has altered the sentiment of a text. This casts doubt on valence shifting as a well-defined task, although intuitively it should be, given that writing affective text has a very long history, computational treatment of sentiment-infused text has recently been quite effective.

This encourages us to start with a simpler task, and show that this simpler version of valence shifting achieves agreement between judges on the direction of the change. Consequently, in this paper we limit ourselves to exploring valence shifting by lexical substitution rather than exploring richer paraphrasing techniques, and testing this on manually constructed sentences. We then explore two questions:

1. Is it in fact true that altering a single lexical item in a sentence noticeably changes its sentiment for readers?
2. Is there a quantitative measure of relative lexical valence within near-synonym sets that corresponds with human-detectable differences in valence?

We investigate these questions for negative words by means of a human experiment, presenting readers with sentences with a negative lexical item replaced by a different lexical item, having them evaluate the comparative negativity of the two sentences. We then investigate the correspondence of the human evaluations to certain metrics based on the similarity of the distribution of sentiment words to the distribution of sentiment in a corpus as a whole.

2 Related work

2.1 Valence-shifting existing text

Existing approaches to valence shifting most often draw upon lexical knowledge bases of some kind, whether custom-designed for the task or adapted to it. Existing results do not yet suggest a definitively successful approach to the task.

Inkpen et al. (2006) used several lexical knowledge bases, primarily the near-synonym usage guide *Choose the Right Word* (CtRW) (Hayakawa, 1994) and the General Inquirer word lists (Stone et al., 1966) to compile information about attitudinal words in order to shift the valence of text in a particular direction which they referred to as making "more-negative" or "more-positive". They estimated the original valence of the text simply by summing over individual words it contained, and modified it by changing near synonyms in it allowing for certain other constraints, notably collocational ones. Only a very small evaluation was performed involving three paragraphs of changed text, the results of which suggested that agreement between human judges on this task might not be high. They generated more-positive and more-negative versions of paragraphs from the British National corpus and performed a test asking human judges to compare the two paragraphs, with the result that the system's more-positive paragraphs were agreed to be so three times out of nine tests (with a further four found to be equal in positivity), and the more-negative paragraphs found to be so only twice in nine tests (with a further three found to be equal).

The VALENTINO tool (Guerini et al., 2008; Guerini et al., 2011) is designed as a pluggable component of a natural language generation system which provides valence shifting. In its initial implementation it employs three strategies, based on strategies employed by human subjects: modifying single wordings; paraphrasing, and deleting or inserting sentiment charged modifiers. VALENTINO's strategies are based on part-of-speech matching and are fairly simple, but the authors are convinced by its performance. VALENTINO relies on a knowledge base of Ordered Vectors of Valenced Terms (OVVTs), with graduated sentiment within an OVVT. Substitutions in the desired direction are then made from the OVVTs, together with other strategies such as inserting or removing modifiers. Example output given input of (1a) is shown in the more positive (1b) and the less positive (1c):

(1) a. We ate *a very good dish.*
    b. We ate *an incredibly delicious dish.*
    c. We ate *a good dish.*

Guerini et al. (2008) are presenting preliminary results and appear to be relying on inspection for evaluation: certainly figures for the findings of external human judges are not supplied. In addition, some examples of output they supply have poor fluency:

(2) a. * Bob *openly admitted* that John is *highly* the *redeemingest signor.*
    b. * Bob *admitted* that John is *highly a well-behaved sir.*

Whitehead and Cavedon (2010) reimplement the lexical substitution, as opposed to paraphrasing, ideas in the VALENTINO implementation, noting and attempting to address two problems with it: the use of unconventional or rare words (*beau*), and the use of grammatically incorrect substitutions.

Even when introducing grammatical relation-based and several bigram-based measures of acceptability, they found that a large number of unacceptable sentences were generated. Categories of remaining error they discuss are: large shifts in meaning (for example by substituting *sleeper* for *winner*, accounting for 49% of identified errors); incorrect word sense disambiguation (accounting for 27% of identified errors); incorrect substitution into phrases or metaphors (such as *long term* and *stepping stone*, accounting for 20% of identified errors); and grammatical errors (such as those shown in (3a) and (3b), accounting for 4% of identified errors).

(3) a. Williams was not *interested* (in) girls.
    b. Williams was not *fascinated* (by) girls.

Whitehead and Cavedon (2010) also found that their system did not perform well when evaluated. Human judges had low, although significant, agreement with each other about the sentiment of a sentence but not significant agreement with their system's output: that is, they did not agree if sentiment shifted in the intended way.

3 Human evaluation of valence shifting

We first describe the construction of our test data, followed by the process for eliciting human judgements on the test data.

3.1 Test data

3.1.1 Selection of negativity word pairs

Quite a number of lexical resources related to sentiment have been developed, and it may seem likely that there would be an appropriate one for choosing pairs of near-synonyms where one is more negative and the other less. However, none are really suitable.

- Several resources based on WordNet contain synsets annotated with sentiment information in some fashion: these include SentiWordNet (Esuli and Sebastiani, 2006), MicroWNOP (Cerini et al., 2007) and WordNet Affect (Strapparava and Valitutti, 2004), and a dataset of subjectivity- and polarity-annotated WordNet senses by Su and Markert (2008). Individual words within a synset are not, however, given individual scores, which is what we need.
- The General Inquirer word list (Stone et al., 1966), which contains unscored words in certain categories including positive (1915 words) and negative (2291 words), does not group words into sets of near-synonyms.
- The subjectivity lexicon that is part of the MPQA Opinion Corpus does assign terms to categories, in this case positive, negative, both or neutral, but does not score the strength of their affective meaning, although this corpus does rate their effectiveness as a cue for subjectivity analysis (Wiebe et al., 2005; Wilson et al., 2005).

The closest work to that described here is that of Mohammad and Turney (2010) and Mohammad and Turney (forthcoming), who describe in detail the creation of EmoLex, a large polarity lexicon, using Mechanical Turk. Mohammad and Turney (forthcoming), rather than asking annotators to evaluate words in context as we are proposing here, instead ask them directly for their analysis of the word, first using a synonym-finding task in order to give the worker the correct word sense to evaluate. Part of a sample annotation question given by Mohammad and Turney (forthcoming) is given in Table 1. The word source used is the *Macquarie Thesaurus* (Bernard, 1986).

Our work differs from that of Mohammad and Turney (forthcoming) in that we rely on substitution evaluations, that is, having human judges rate specific contexts rather than supply their intuitions about the meaning of a word. Callison-Burch (2007) argued for this evaluation of paraphrases, that the most natural way is through substitution, and evaluate both meaning and grammaticality.

In our case, we are attempting to assess the effectiveness of valence-shifting, and we cannot presuppose that intuitions by the raters along the lines of feeling that the meaning of a word is more negative than that of another word translates into perceiving the desired effect when a word is used in context.

We therefore turn to hand-crafted data to test our hypotheses: words chosen so as to be noticeably negative, with a neutral or slightly negative near synonym. We chose 20 such word pairs, shown in Table 2. The more negative word of the pair is from the sentiment lists developed by Nielsen (2011),[1] typically rated about 3 for negativity on his scale (where 5 is reserved for obscenities) and the less negative chosen by us.

3.1.2 Selection of sentences

Our corpus for sentence selection is the SCALE dataset v1.0 movie review data set (SCALE 1.0) (Pang and Lee, 2005), a set of 5000 short movie reviews by four authors on the World Wide Web, and widely used in sentiment classification tasks. Each movie review is accompanied by both a three and four degree sentiment rating (that is, a rating on a scale of 0 to 2, and on a scale of 0 to 3) together with original rating assigned by the author to their own review on a scale of 0 to 10.

[1] Available from http://www2.imm.dtu.dk/pubdb/views/publication_details.php?id=6010

Question	Possible answers
Which word is closest in meaning (most related) to startle?	{*automobile*, *shake*, *honesty*, *entertain*}
How positive (good, praising) is the word *startle*?	*startle* is {not, weakly, moderately, strongly} positive
How negative (bad, criticizing) is the word *startle*?	*startle* is {not, weakly, moderately, strongly} negative
How much is *startle* associated with the emotion {joy,sadness,...}?	*startle* is {not, weakly, moderately, strongly} associated with {joy,sadness,...}

Table 1: Sample annotation question posed to Mechanical Turk workers by Mohammad and Turney (forthcoming).

We selected two sentences for each word pair from the SCALE 1.0 corpus. Sentences were initially selected by a random number generator: each sentence originally contained the more negative word. Since we are constructing an idealised system here, evaluating the possibility of valence shifting by changing a single word, we manually eliminated sentences where the part of speech didn't match the intended part of speech of the word pair, where the word was part of a proper name (usually a movie title) and where the fluency of the resulting sentence otherwise appeared terribly bad to us. Where a sentence was rejected another sentence was randomly chosen to take its place until each word pair had two accepted sentences for a total of 40 sentences. We then made changes to capitalisation where necessary for clarity (for example, capitalising movie titles, as the corpus is normalised to lower case).

Since each subject is being presented with multiple sentences (40 in this experiment), rather than coming to the task untrained, it is possible that there are ordering effects between sentences, in which a subject's answers to previous questions influence their answers to following questions. Therefore we used a Latin square design to ensure that the order of presentation was not the same across subjects, but rather varied in a systematic way to eliminate the possibility of multiple subjects seeing questions in the same order. In addition, the square is balanced, so that there is no cyclical ordering effect (i.e. if one row of a Latin square is A-B-C and the next B-C-A, there is still an undesirable effect where C is tending to follow B). The presentation word order to subjects was also randomised at the time of generating each subject's questions.

3.2 Elicitation of judgements

Having constructed the set of test sentences (Section 3.1), we ask human subjects to analyse the sentences on two axes: ACCEPTABILITY and NEGATIVITY. This is loosely equivalent to the FLUENCY and FIDELITY axes that are used to evaluate machine translation (Jurafsky and Martin, 2009). As in the case of machine translation, a valence-shifted sentence needs to be fluent, that is to be a sentence that is acceptable in its grammar, semantics and so on, to listeners or readers. While some notion of fidelity to the original is also important in valence shifting, it is rather difficult to capture without knowing the intent of the valence shifting, since unlike in translation a part of the meaning is being deliberately altered. We therefore confine ourselves in this work to confirming that the valence shifting did in fact take place, by asking subjects to rate sentences.

In order to obtain a clear answer, we specifically evaluate valence shifting with sentences as close to ideal as possible, choosing words we strongly believe to have large valence differences, and manually selecting sentences where the subjects' assessment of the valence of these words is unlikely to be led astray by very poor substitutions such as replacing part of a proper name. (For example, consider the band name *Panic! at the Disco*: asking whether an otherwise identical sentence about a band named *Concern! at the Disco* is less negative is unlikely to get a good evaluation of lexical valence shifting.) We then ask human subjects to evaluate these pairs of sentences for their relative fluency and negativity.

Mechanical Turk Our subjects were recruited through Amazon Mechanical Turk.[2] Mechanical Turk is a web service providing cheap de-

[2]http://www.mturk.com/

centralised work units called Human Intelligence Tasks (HITs), which have been used by computational linguistics research for experimentation. Snow et al. (2008) cite a number of studies at that time which used Mechanical Turk as an annotation tool, including several which used Mechanical Turk rather than expert annotators to produce a gold standard annotation to evaluate their systems.

Callison-Burch and Dredze (2010) provide guidelines in appropriate design of tasks for Mechanical Turk, which we broadly follow. We ameliorate potential risks of using Mechanical Turk by confining ourselves to asking workers for numerical ratings of sentences, rather than any more complex tasks, well within the type of tasks which Snow et al. (2008) reported success with; and like Molla and Santiago-Martinez (2011), giving all subjects two elimination questions in which the sentences within each pair were identical, that is, in which there was no lexical substitution. These, being identical, should receive identical scores—we also explicitly pointed this out in the instructions—and therefore we could easily eliminate workers who did not read the instructions from the pool.

Eliciting subjects' responses We considered both categorical responses (e.g. Is sentence variant A more or less negative than sentence variant B, or are A and B equally negative?) and Magnitude Estimation (ME). Categorical responses of the sort exemplified ignore magnitude, and are prone to "can't decide" option choices.

ME is a technique proposed by Bard et al. (1996) for adapting to grammaticality judgements. In this experimental modality, subjects are asked evaluate stimuli based not on a fixed rating scale, but on an arbitrary rating scale in comparison with an initial stimulus. For example, subjects might initially be asked to judge the acceptability of *The cat by chased the dog*. Assuming that the subject gives this an acceptability score of N, they will be asked to assign a multiplicative score to other sentences, that is, $2N$ to a sentence that is twice as acceptable and $\frac{N}{2}$ to one half as acceptable.

This same experimental modality was used by Lapata (2001) in which subjects evaluated the acceptability of paraphrases of adjectival phrases, for example, considering the acceptability of each of (4b) and (4c) as paraphrases of (4a):

(4) a. a *difficult* customer
b. a customer that is *difficult* to *satisfy*
c. a customer that is *difficult* to *drive*

In a standard design and analysis of a ME experiment (Marks, 1974), all the stimuli given to the subjects have known relationships (for example, in the original psychophysics context, that the power level for one heat stimulus was half that of another stimulus), and the experimenter is careful to provide subjects with stimuli ranging over the known spectrum of strength under investigation. In our case, we do not have a single spectrum of stimuli such as a heat source varying in power, or even the varying degrees of fluency given by Bard et al. (1996) or the hypothesised three levels of paraphrase acceptability (low, medium, high) that Lapata (2001) is testing that her subjects can detect. Instead, we have distinct sets of stimuli, each a pair of words, in which we hypothesise a reliable detectable difference within the pair of words, but not between a member of one pair and a member of any other pair. Thus, asking subjects to rate stimuli across the pairs of words on the same scale, as ME requires, is not the correct experimental design for our task.

We therefore use an 11 point (0 to 10) rating scale. This allows subjects to rate two sentences as identical if they really perceive the sentences to be so, while allowing fairly subtle differences to be captured. This is similar to the assessment of machine translation performance used by NIST. For our fluency guidelines, we essentially use the ones given as NIST guidelines (Linguistic Data Consortium, 2005); we also model our negativity guidelines on these.

For each translation of each segment of each selected story, judges make the fluency judgement before the adequacy judgement. We provide similar questions to NIST, although with more context in the actual instructions. The precise wording of one of our questions is shown in Figure 1.

3.3 Results

3.3.1 Number of participants

A total of 48 workers did the experiment. 8 were excluded from the analysis, for these reasons:

1. 6 workers failed to rate the identical sentence pairs in the elimination questions described in Section 3.2 identically, contrary to explicit

Acceptability and negativity: concern/panic
Evaluate these two sentences for acceptability and negativity:

- Sentence 1: As they do throughout the film the acting of CONCERN and fear by Gibson and Russo is genuine and touching.
- Sentence 2: As they do throughout the film the acting of PANIC and fear by Gibson and Russo is genuine and touching.

Acceptability: first sentence of concern/panic pair
Give sentence 1 immediately above a score from 0 to 10 for its acceptability, where higher scores are more acceptable. The primary criterion for acceptability is reading like fluent English written by a native speaker.
Acceptability: second sentence of concern/panic pair
Give sentence 2 immediately above a score from 0 to 10 inclusive for its acceptability, where higher scores are more acceptable.
Negativity: first sentence of concern/panic pair
Give sentence 1 immediately above a score from 0 to 10 inclusive its negativity, where higher scores are more negative.
Negativity: second sentence of concern/panic pair
Give sentence 2 immediately above a score from 0 to 10 inclusive its negativity, where higher scores are more negative.

Figure 1: One of the acceptability and negativity questions posed to Mechanical Turk workers.

instructions.

2. 1 worker confined themselves only to the numbers 5 and 10 in their ratings.
3. 1 worker awarded every sentence 10 for both acceptability and negativity.

Each of the 8 Latin square rows were re-submitted to Mechanical Turk for another worker to complete.[3]

3.3.2 Analysing scaled responses

We consider two hypotheses:

1. that subjects will perceive a difference in *acceptability* between the original sentence and that containing a hypothesised less negative near synonym; and
2. that subjects will perceive a difference in *negativity* between the original sentence and that containing a hypothesised less negative near synonym.

We thus require hypothesis testing in order to determine if the means of the scores of the original sentences and those containing hypothesised less negative near synonyms differ significantly. In this situation, we can use a single-factor within-subject analysis of variance (ANOVA), also known as a single-factor repeated-measures ANOVA, which allows us to account for the fact that subjects are not being exposed to a single experimental condition each, but are exposed to all the experimental conditions. In this experiment we do not have any between-subjects factors—known differences between the subjects (such as gender, age, and so on)—which we wish to explore. A within-subjects ANOVA accounts for the lesser variance that can be expected by the subject remaining identical over repeated measurements, and thus has more sensitivity than an ANOVA without repeated measures (Keppel and Wickens, 2004). Our use of an ANOVA is similar to that of Lapata (2001), although we have only one factor. Specifically, we will test whether the *mean* scores of the more negative sample are higher than the less negative sample.

Acceptability results The mean acceptability rating of sentences containing the MORE NEGATIVE words from Table 2 was 6.61. The mean acceptability rating of sentences containing the LESS NEGATIVE words was 6.41. An ANOVA does not find this difference to be statistically significant. ($F(1, 39) = 1.5975, p = 0.2138$). This is what we would expect: we manually selected sentences whose less negative versions were ac-

[3]In addition, one worker returned a single score of 610 for the negativity of one of the LESS NEGATIVE sentences: we assume this was a data entry error and the worker intended either 6 or 10 as the value. In our analysis we set this value to 10, since it is the worse (i.e. most conservative) assumption for our hypothesis that sentences containing LESS NEGATIVE words will have a lower negativity score than those containing MORE NEGATIVE words.

ceptable to us.

Negativity results The mean negativity rating of sentences containing the MORE NEGATIVE words from Table 2 was 6.11. The mean negativity rating of sentences containing the LESS NEGATIVE words was 4.82. An ANOVA finds this difference to be highly statistically significant. ($F(1, 39) = 29.324, p = 3.365 \times 10^{-6}$). In Table 2 we see that the effect is not only statistically significant overall, but very consistent: sentences in the LESS NEGATIVE group *always* have a lower mean rating than their pair in the MORE NEGATIVE group.

4 Predicting the raters' decisions

We now investigate to what extent we can predict the correct choice of near synonym so as to achieve the correct level of negativity in output. In the preceding section our data suggests that this can be accomplished with lexical substitution. However, this leaves the problem of determining the negativity of words automatically, rather than relying on hand-crafted data.

4.1 Measures of distribution

Our intuition is that words that make text more negative will tend to disproportionately be found in more negative documents, likewise words that make text less negative will tend to be found in less negative documents.

In order to quantify this, consider this as a problem of distribution. Among a set of affective documents divided into sentiment-score categories such as SCALE 1.0 (see Section 3.1), there is a certain, not necessarily even, distribution of words: for example, a corpus might be 15% negative, 40% neutral and 45% positive by total word count. However, our intuition leads us to hypothesise that the distribution of occurrences of the word *terrible*, say, might be shifted towards negative documents, with some larger percentage occurring in negative documents.

We then might further intuit that words could be compared by their relative difference from the standard distribution: a larger difference from the distribution implies a stronger skew towards some particular affective value, compared to word frequencies as a whole. (However, it should be noted that this skew could have any direction, including a word being found disproportionately among the neutral or mid-range sentiment documents.)

We thus consider two measures of differences of distribution, Information Gain (IG) and Kullback-Leibler divergence (KL). We calculate the value of our distribution measure for each MORE NEGATIVE and LESS NEGATIVE word pair, and subtract the former from the latter. If each word in the pair is distributed across sentiment categories in the same way, the difference will be zero; if the measure corresponds in some way to the human view of the word pair elements, the difference will be non-zero and have a consistent sign.

Information gain The IG $G(Y|X)$ associated with a distribution Y given the distribution X is the number of bits saving in transmitting information from Y if X is known. A high IG value thus suggests a strong predictive relationship between X and Y. We use the formulation of Yang and Pedersen (1997), who found it one of the more effective metrics for feature selection for text classification:

$$\begin{aligned} IG(r) = & -\textstyle\sum_{i=1}^{m} \Pr(c_i) \log \Pr(c_i) \\ & + \Pr(r) \textstyle\sum_{i=1}^{m} \Pr(c_i|r) \log \Pr(c_i|r) \\ & + \Pr(\bar{r}) \textstyle\sum_{i=1}^{m} \Pr(c_i|\bar{r}) \log \Pr(c_i|\bar{r}) \quad (1) \end{aligned}$$

where $P_r(c_i)$ is the relative probability of category c_i, $P_r(c_i|t)$ the relative probability of c_i given term t and $P_r(c_i|\bar{t})$ the relative probability of c_i when term t is absent.

Kullback-Leibler Cover and Thomas (1991) describe the KL divergence (Kullback and Leibler, 1951) as a measure of "the inefficiency of assuming that the distribution is q when the true distribution is p". Weeds (2003) gives the formula for KL as:

$$D(p||q) = \sum_x p(x) \log \frac{p(x)}{q(x)} \quad (2)$$

Weeds (2003) evaluated measures similar to KL for their usefulness in the distributional similarity task of finding words that share similar contexts. Our task is not an exact parallel: we seek the relative skewness of words.

4.2 Results

Information Gain The results of the IG metric given in (1) on the test data are shown in the second column from the right in Table 2. No pattern

MORE NEGATIVE / LESS NEGATIVE	MR	ΔMR	ΔIG $\times 10^{-3}$	ΔKL
ignored / overlooked	5.7/5.0	0.7	-1.48	0.12
cowardly / cautious	6.1/4.9	1.2	0.06	-0.04
toothless / ineffective	6.1/5.1	1.0	0.35	-0.39
stubborn / persistent	5.3/4.3	1.0	0.19	-0.31
frightening / concerning	6.2/5.5	0.7	-0.02	0.10
assassination / death	6.2/6.0	0.2	-0.99	-0.04
fad / trend	5.5/3.5	2.0	-0.09	0.00
idiotic / misguided	6.3/5.6	0.7	2.25	-0.27
war / conflict	6.5/5.4	1.1	2.03	-0.01
accusation / claim	6.3/4.5	1.8	0.35	-0.23
heartbreaking / upsetting	5.8/5.7	0.1	0.97	0.22
conspiracy / arrangement	5.6/4.1	1.5	-0.21	-0.02
dread / anticipate	6.6/3.9	2.7	1.58	-0.02
threat / warning	6.6/5.1	1.6	0.46	-0.10
despair / concern	6.2/4.5	1.7	0.21	-0.03
aggravating / irritating	6.2/5.7	0.5	-2.00	-0.09
scandal / event	6.9/3.8	3.1	-0.29	-0.09
panic / concern	6.5/4.5	2.0	0.56	-0.27
tragedy / incident	5.9/4.6	1.3	6.02	-0.08
worry / concern	5.3/4.5	0.7	0.31	-0.02

Table 2: MORE NEGATIVE / LESS NEGATIVE word pairs; mean negativity ratings (MR); difference in mean negativity ratings (ΔMR); difference in Information Gain (ΔIG $\times 10^{-3}$); difference in Kullback-Leibler score (ΔKL)

in the data is immediately obvious, and in particular the ordering of MORE NEGATIVE and LESS NEGATIVE is not maintained well by the metric.

Kullback-Leibler The results of the KL metric given in (2) on the test data are shown in the rightmost column of Table 2. Here we see a much stronger pattern, that the word from MORE NEGATIVE tends to have a lesser KL value than the word from LESS NEGATIVE (16 out of 20 word pairs).

Preliminary indications are thus that the KL may be a more useful metric for predicting the raters' scores most accurately, and thus perhaps for predicting negativity in usage more generally.

5 Conclusion

In this paper, we have shown that lexical substitution, as we hoped, can achieve valence shifting on its own, as judged by human raters with a substitution task. In addition, we have shown that at least one measure of the distribution of a word in a corpus, the KL divergence, is a potentially promising feature for modelling the ability of a lexical substitution to achieve a valence shift. Valence shifting then, at least in this simplified form, would appear to be a well-founded task. However, successfully implementing a fuller version of valence shifting would face several challenges. A significant one is that no existing lexical resources are suitable as is. The use of the KL metric as a way of automatically scoring elements of near-synonym sets is preliminary, and would likely need further metrics, perhaps combined in a machine learner, to be able to accurately predict human judges' scores of negativity.

Acknowledgements

We acknowledge the support of ARC Discovery grant DP0558852.

References

Ellen Gurman Bard, Dan Robertson, and Antonella Sorace. 1996. Magnitude estimation of linguistic acceptability. *Language*, 72(1):32–68, March.

John R. L. Bernard, editor. 1986. *The Macquarie Thesaurus*. Macquarie Library, Sydney, Australia.

2010. Los Angeles, California.

Chris Callison-Burch and Mark Dredze. 2010. Creating speech and language data with Amazon's Mechanical Turk. In *Proceedings of the NAACL HLT 2010 Workshop on Creating Speech and Language Data with Amazon's Mechanical Turk*, pages 1–12, Los Angeles, June. Association for Computational Linguistics.

Chris Callison-Burch. 2007. *Paraphrasing and Translation*. Ph.D. thesis, University of Edinburgh.

Sabrina Cerini, Valentina Compagnoni, Alice Demontis, Maicol Formentelli, and Caterina Gandi. 2007. Micro-WNOp: A gold standard for the evaluation of automatically compiled lexical resources for opinion mining. In *Language resources and linguistic theory: Typology, second language acquisition, English linguistics*. Franco Angeli, Milan, Italy.

Thomas M. Cover and Joy A. Thomas. 1991. *Elements of Information Theory*. Wiley, New York, USA.

Andrea Esuli and Fabrizio Sebastiani. 2006. SentiWordNet: A publicly available lexical resource for opinion mining. In *Proceedings of the fifth international conference on Language Resources and Evaluation (LREC 2006)*, pages 417–422, Genova, Italy.

Marco Guerini, Carlo Strapparava, and Oliviero Stock. 2008. Valentino: A tool for valence shifting of natural language texts. In *Proceedings of the 6th International Conference on Language Resources and Evaluation (LREC 2008)*, Marrakesh, Morocco, May.

Marco Guerini, Carlo Strapparava, and Oliviero Stock. 2011. Slanting existing text with Valentino. In *Proceedings of the 16th International Conference on Intelligent User Interfaces (IUI '11)*, pages 439–440, Palo Alto, CA, USA, February.

Samuel I. Hayakawa, editor. 1994. *Choose the Right Word*. Harper Collins Publishers, 2nd edition. revised by Eugene Ehrlich.

Diana Zaiu Inkpen, Ol'ga Feiguina, and Graeme Hirst. 2006. Generating more-positive or more-negative text. In James G. Shanahan, Yan Qu, and Janyce Wiebe, editors, *Computing Attitude and Affect in Text (Selected papers from the Proceedings of the Workshop on Attitude and Affect in Text, AAAI 2004 Spring Symposium)*, pages 187–196. Springer, Dordrecht, The Netherlands.

Daniel Jurafsky and James H. Martin. 2009. *Speech and Language Processing: An Introduction to Natural Language Processing, Speech Recognition, and Computational Linguistics*. Prentice-Hall, 2nd edition.

Geoffrey Keppel and Thomas D. Wickens. 2004. *Design and Analysis: A Researcher's Handbook*. Pearson Prentice Hall, Upper Saddle River, New Jersey, USA, fourth edition.

Solomon Kullback and Richard A. Leibler. 1951. On information and sufficiency. *The Annals of Mathematical Statistics*, 22:79–86.

Maria Lapata. 2001. A corpus-based account of regular polysemy: The case of context-sensitive adjectives. In *Proceedings of the 2nd Meeting of the North American Chapter of the Association for Computational Linguistics*, pages 63–70, Pittsburgh, PA.

Linguistic Data Consortium. 2005. Linguistic data annotation specification: Assessment of fluency and adequacy in translations. Technical report.

Lawrence E. Marks. 1974. *Sensory Processes: The New Psychophysics*. Academic Press, New York.

Saif M. Mohammad and Peter D. Turney. 2010. Emotions evoked by common words and phrases: Using Mechanical Turk to create an emotion lexicon. In *Proceedings of the NAACL-HLT 2010 Workshop on Computational Approaches to Analysis and Generation of Emotion in Text* (caa, 2010), pages 26–34.

Saif M. Mohammad and Peter D. Turney. forthcoming. Crowdsourcing a wordemotion association lexicon. *Computational Intelligence*.

Diego Molla and Maria Elena Santiago-Martinez. 2011. Development of a corpus for evidence based medicine summarisation. In *Proceedings of the Australasian Language Technology Association Workshop 2011*, pages 86–94, Canberra, Australia, December.

Finn rup Nielsen. 2011. A new ANEW: Evaluation of a word list for sentiment analysis in microblogs. In Matthew Rowe, Milan Stankovic, Aba-Sah Dadzie, and Mariann Hardey, editors, *Proceedings, 1st Workshop on Making Sense of Microposts (#MSM2011): Big things come in small packages*, pages 93–98, Heraklion, Crete, Greece, May.

Bo Pang and Lillian Lee. 2005. Seeing stars: Exploiting class relationships for sentiment categorization with respect to rating scales. In *Proceedings of the 43rd Annual Meeting of the Association for Computational Linguistics (ACL05)*, pages 115–124.

Rion Snow, Brendan O'Connor, Daniel Jurafsky, and Andrew Ng. 2008. Cheap and fast – but is it good? evaluating non-expert annotations for natural language tasks. In *Proceedings of the 2008 Conference on Empirical Methods in Natural Language Processing*, pages 254–263, Honolulu, Hawaii, October. Association for Computational Linguistics.

Philip J. Stone, Dexter C. Dunphy, Marshall S. Smith, and Daniel M. Ogilvie. 1966. *General Inquirer: A Computer Approach to Content Analysis*. The MIT Press.

Carlo Strapparava and Alessandro Valitutti. 2004. WordNet-Affect: an affective extension of WordNet. In *Proceedings of the fourth international conference on Language Resources and Evaluation (LREC 2004)*, pages 1083–1086.

Fangzhong Su and Katja Markert. 2008. From words to senses: A case study of subjectivity recognition. In *Proceedings of the 22nd International Conference on Computational Linguistics (Coling 2008)*, pages 825–832, Manchester, UK, August. Coling 2008 Organizing Committee.

Julie Elizabeth Weeds. 2003. *Measures and Applications of Lexical Distributional Similarity*. Ph.D. thesis, University of Sussex.

Simon Whitehead and Lawrence Cavedon. 2010. Generating shifting sentiment for a conversational agent. In *Proceedings of the NAACL-HLT 2010 Workshop on Computational Approaches to Analysis and Generation of Emotion in Text* (caa, 2010), pages 89–97.

Janyce Wiebe, Theresa Wilson, and Claire Cardie. 2005. Annotating expressions of opinions and emotions in language. *Language Resources and Evaluation*, 39(2–3):165–210.

Theresa Wilson, Janyce Wiebe, and Paul Hoffmann. 2005. Recognizing contextual polarity in phrase-level sentiment analysis. In *Proceedings of Human Language Technologies Conference/Conference on Empirical Methods in Natural Language Processing (HLT/EMNLP 2005)*, Vancouver, Canada.

Yiming Yang and Jan O. Pedersen. 1997. A comparative study on feature selection in text categorization. In *Proceedings of the Fourteenth International Conference on Machine Learning*, pages 412–420, San Francisco, USA. Morgan Kaufmann Publishers Inc.

Experimental Evaluation of a Lexicon- and Corpus-based Ensemble for Multi-way Sentiment Analysis*

Minh Duc Cao
School of Chemistry and Molecular Biosciences
The University of Queensland
St Lucia, QLD 4072, Australia
m.cao1@uq.edu.au

Ingrid Zukerman
Clayton School of Information Technology
Monash University
Clayton, VIC 3800, Australia
Ingrid.Zukerman@monash.edu

Abstract

We describe a probabilistic approach that combines information obtained from a lexicon with information obtained from a Naïve Bayes (NB) classifier for multi-way sentiment analysis. Our approach also employs grammatical structures to perform adjustments for negations, modifiers and sentence connectives. The performance of this method is compared with that of an NB classifier with feature selection, and MCST – a state-of-the-art system. The results of our evaluation show that the performance of our hybrid approach is at least as good as that of these systems. We also examine the influence of three factors on performance: (1) sentiment-ambiguous sentences, (2) probability of the most probable star rating, and (3) coverage of the lexicon and the NB classifier. Our results indicate that the consideration of these factors supports the identification of regions of improved reliability for sentiment analysis.

1 Introduction

A key problem in sentiment analysis is to determine the polarity of sentiment in text. Much of the work on this problem has considered binary sentiment polarity (positive or negative) at granularity levels ranging from sentences (Mao and Lebanon, 2006; McDonald et al., 2007) to documents (Wilson et al., 2005; Allison, 2008). Multi-way polarity classification, i.e., the problem of inferring the "star" rating associated with a review, has been attempted in several domains, e.g., restaurant reviews (Snyder and Barzilay, 2007) and movie reviews (Bickerstaffe and Zukerman, 2010; Pang and Lee, 2005). Star ratings are more informative than positive/negative ratings, and are commonly given in reviews of films, restaurants, books and consumer goods. However, because of this finer grain, multi-way sentiment classification is a more difficult task than binary classification. Hence, the results for multi-way classification are typically inferior to those obtained for the binary case.

Most of the research on sentiment analysis uses supervised classification methods such as Maximum Entropy (Berger et al., 1996), Support Vector Machines (SVMs) (Cortes and Vapnik, 1995) or Naïve Bayes (NB) (Domingos and Pazzani, 1997). The sentiment expressed in word patterns has been exploited by considering word n-grams (Hu et al., 2007), applying feature selection to handle the resultant proliferation of features (Mukras et al., 2007). In addition, when performing multi-way classification, approaches that consider class-label similarities (Bickerstaffe and Zukerman, 2010; Pang and Lee, 2005) generally outperform those that do not.

Lexicon-based methods for sentiment analysis have been investigated in (Beineke et al., 2004; Taboada et al., 2011; Andreevskaia and Bergler, 2008; Melville et al., 2009) in the context of binary, rather than multi-way, sentiment classifiers. These methods often require intensive labour (e.g., via the Mechanical Turk service) to build up the lexicon (Taboada et al., 2011) or use a small, generic lexicon enhanced by sources from the Internet (Beineke et al., 2004). Andreevskaia and Bergler (2008) and Melville et al. (2009) employ a weighted average to combine information from the lexicon with the classifi-

*The majority of this work was done while the first author was at Monash University.

cation produced by a supervised machine learning method. Their results demonstrate the effectiveness of these methods only on small datasets, where the contribution of the machine-learning component is limited.

This paper examines the performance of a hybrid lexicon/supervised-learning approach and two supervised machine learning methods in multi-way sentiment analysis. The hybrid approach combines information obtained from the lexicon with information obtained from an NB classifier with feature selection. Information is obtained from a lexicon by means of a novel function based on the Beta distribution. This function, which employs heuristics to account for negations, adverbial modifiers and sentence connectives, combines the sentiment of words into the sentiment of phrases, sentences, and eventually an entire review (Section 2). The supervised learning methods are: an NB classifier with feature selection, and MCST (Bickerstaffe and Zukerman, 2010) – a state-of-the-art classifier based on hierarchical SVMs which considers label similarity (MCST outperforms Pang and Lee's (2005) best-performing methods on the Movies dataset described in Section 5.1).

We also investigate the influence of three factors on sentiment-classification performance: (1) presence of sentiment-ambiguous sentences, which we identify by means of a heuristic (Section 4); (2) probability of the most probable star rating; and (3) coverage of the lexicon and the NB classifier, i.e., fraction of words in a review being "understood".

Our results show that (1) the hybrid approach generally performs at least as well as NB with feature selection and MCST; (2) NB with feature selection generally outperforms MCST, highlighting the importance of choosing stringent baselines in algorithm evaluation; (3) the performance of sentiment analysis algorithms deteriorates as the number of sentiment-ambiguous sentences in a review increases, and improves as the probability of the most probable star rating of a review increases (beyond 50%), and as the coverage of the lexicon and the NB classifier increases (between 50% and 80%).

In the next section, we present our lexicon-based approach. Section 3 describes the combination of the lexicon with an NB classifier, followed by our heuristic for identifying sentiment-ambiguous sentences. Section 5 presents the results of our evaluation, and Section 6 offers concluding remarks.

2 Harnessing the Lexicon

In this section, we present our framework for representing information from a lexicon, and combining this information into phrases, sentences and entire reviews, and our heuristics for modifying the sentiment of a word or phrase based on grammatical information. We report on the results obtained with the lexicon collected by Wilson et al. (2005), which contains 8221 sentiment-carrying words (most are open-class words, but there are a few modals, conjunctions and prepositions); each word is identified as positive, negative or neutral, and either strong or weak.[1]

The numeric rating of a review is inferred from the sentiment of the words in it, while taking into account the uncertainty arising from (1) the ambiguous sentiment of individual words, and (2) our ignorance due to the lack of understanding of the sentiment of some words. Instead of committing to a particular star rating for a review, we assign a probability to each star rating and return the most probable star rating. This probability is modelled by a *unimodal* distribution, as the rating of a review is likely to be centered around the most probable star rating. For example, if a review is most likely to be in the 4-star class, the probability of this review having 3 stars should be higher than the probability of 2 stars.

We chose the Beta distribution to represent sentiment information because (1) its parameters α and β, which encode the *positiveness* and *negativeness* of the distribution respectively, are well-suited to represent the sentiment of every linguistic entity (i.e., word, phrase, sentence or review); and (2) it has appealing computational properties which facilitate the combination of the Beta distributions of those entities. The combination of the distributions of the words in a sentence yield a Beta distribution for the sentence, and the combination of the distributions for the sentences in a review yield a Beta distribution for the review.

To fully exploit the grammatical structure of a sentence, we first parse the sentence using the Stanford parser (Klein and Manning, 2003). We

[1]We also considered SentiWordNet (Baccianella et al., 2010), but it yielded inferior results.

then map the sentiment values of a word from the lexicon to the α and β parameters of the Beta distribution for the word, while maintaining the constraint $\alpha + \beta = 1$ (this constraint is relaxed for phrases, sentences and the entire review). Specifically, $\alpha = 1$ for a strong positive word, and $\beta = 1$ for a strong negative word; a weak positive word is assigned $\alpha = 0.75$, and a weak negative word $\beta = 0.75$; and $\alpha = \beta = 0.5$ for a neutral word.

We employ the function $\oplus$ to combine the distributions of individual words into distributions of successively higher-level segments in the parse tree, until we obtain the distribution of a whole sentence and then an entire review. For example, given review $R = \{(w_1w_2).(w_3(w_4w_5))\}$ comprising two main sentences w_1w_2 and $w_3(w_4w_5)$, its density function f is defined as $f(R) = (w_1 \oplus w_2) \oplus (w_3 \oplus (w_4 \oplus w_5))$. Unless otherwise specified, $\oplus$ multiplies the probabilities of consecutive segments. This is conveniently equivalent to adding the α and β values of the segments, i.e., $f(\alpha_1, \beta_1)f(\alpha_2, \beta_2) = f(\alpha_1 + \alpha_2, \beta_1 + \beta_2)$.

The probability that review R has a rating k is

$$\Pr(\mathit{rating}(R) = k) = \int_{b_{k-1}}^{b_k} f(y)dy \qquad (1)$$

where b_i is the upper boundary of rating i ($0 = b_0 < b_1 < \ldots < b_N = 1$), and N is the highest star rating. These boundaries were determined by a hill-climbing algorithm that maximizes classification accuracy on the training set.

Special operators, such as negations, adverbial modifiers and sentence connectives, alter the definition of the $\oplus$ function as follows (our identification of negations and modifiers resembles that in (Taboada et al., 2011), but our mappings are probabilistic).

Negations. Negations often shift the sentiment of a word or a phrase in the opposite direction (rather than inverting its polarity), e.g., "not outstanding" is better than "not good" (Taboada et al., 2011). This idea is implemented by adjusting the α and β parameters so that the new parameters α' and β' obey the constraint $\alpha' + \beta' = \alpha + \beta$, and the new mean of the distribution is

$$\frac{\alpha'}{\alpha' + \beta'} = \frac{\alpha}{\alpha + \beta} + \lambda$$

where $\lambda = -0.5$ for positive words/phrases and $+0.5$ for negative ones. For instance, based on the lexicon, $\alpha_{\text{good}} = 0.75$ ($\beta_{\text{good}} = 0.25$), which yields $\alpha'_{\text{not good}} = 0.25$ ($\beta'_{\text{not good}} = 0.75$). This procedure is also applied to antonyms of words in the lexicon, which are identified by removing a negation prefix from an input word (e.g., *un-*, *in-*, *il-*, *im-*, *de-*, *ab-*, *non-*, *dis-*), and matching with the lexicon, e.g., "*un*able" shifts the sentiment of "able". The combination of a negation and a phrase, e.g., "I *don't* think (the staff is friendly and efficient enough)", has the same effect.

Table 1: Sample modifications of the word *polite* ($\alpha = 0.75$ and $\beta = 0.25$)

Adverb	γ	α'	β'
hardly	-0.9	0.525	0.475
relatively	-0.1	0.725	0.275
more	0.4	0.850	0.150
really	0.7	0.925	0.075
absurdly	0.8	0.950	0.050
completely	1.0	1.000	0

Adverbial modifiers. Adverbs normally change the intensity of adjectives or verbs (e.g., "very" is an intensifier, while "hardly" is a diminisher). Like Taboada et al. (2011), we increase or decrease the sentiment level of a word based on the meaning of its modifier. This is done by adjusting the α' and β' of weak adjectives and verbs as follows (currently, we leave strong words unchanged as it is unusual to apply adverbial modifiers to such words, e.g., "somewhat excellent"): $\alpha' = \alpha \pm \gamma\beta$ and $\beta' = \beta \mp \gamma\beta$, where the sign is determined by the polarity of the word, and γ is determined by the adverb. For example, $\gamma = -0.2$ for "fairly" and $\gamma = 0.5$ for "very". Thus, "fairly polite" moves "polite" from $\alpha = 0.75$ ($\beta = 0.25$) to $\alpha = 0.7$ ($\beta = 0.3$). Table 1 shows the intensity level γ of several adverbs, and their effect on the polarity of the adjective "polite".

Dealing with uncertainty. When reading a text, the number of words a reader understands affects his/her confidence in his/her comprehension. The fewer words are understood, the higher the reader's uncertainty. We estimate w_i, the level of comprehension of sentence s_i, by means of the fraction of open-class and lexicon words in the sentence that appear in the lexicon (recall that the lexicon contains some closed-class words). When combining the sentiment derived from two sentences s_1 and s_2, we want the sentence that is less understood to carry a lower weight than the sentence that is better understood. To implement this idea, we adjust the probability of the star rating of a sentence by a function of the certainty of understanding it. We employ an exponential function as follows, where the exponents are the above weights w_i.

$$\Pr(y|s_1, s_2) \propto \Pr(y|s_1)^{w_1} \Pr(y|s_2)^{w_2} \quad (2)$$

Since $0 \leq w_i \leq 1$, a low certainty for w_i yields a value close to 1, which has relatively little effect on the outcome, while a high certainty has a large effect on the outcome.

Sentence connectives. When we have little confidence in our understanding of a sentence, sentence connectives, such as adversatives (e.g., "but", "however") or intensifiers (e.g., "furthermore"), may prove helpful. Assume that sentence s_1 has an adversative relation with sentence s_2, and w.l.o.g., assume that s_1 is better understood than s_2 (i.e., $w_1 > w_2$, where w_i is the level of comprehension of sentence s_i). We model the idea that in this case, the sentiment of s_2 is likely to contradict that of s_1 by shifting the sentiment of s_2 closer to that of $\bar{s_1}$ (the negation of s_1) in proportion to the difference between the weights of these sentences.

$$\Pr'(y|s_2) = \frac{\Pr(y|s_2)w_2 + \Pr(y|\bar{s_1})(w_1 - w_2)}{w_1} \quad (3)$$

In addition, owing to the interaction between s_2 and s_1, w_2 increases to $w'_2 = \frac{1}{2}(w_1 + w_2)$ to indicate that s_2 is now better understood. For example, consider a situation where the probability that sentence s_1 conveys a 4-star rating is 0.2 with $w_1 = 0.8$ (four fifths of the words in s_1 were understood), and the probability that s_2 conveys a 4-star rating is 0.4 with $w_2 = 0.2$. Further, assume that there is an adversative relation between s_1 and s_2, e.g., "s_1. However, s_2". After applying Equation 3 to adjust the probability of the less understood sentence, s_2, we obtain $\Pr'(y = 4\,\text{stars}|s2) = (0.4 \times 0.2 + 0.6\,(0.8 - 0.2))/0.8 = 0.55$, and $w'_2 = 0.5$ (the 0.6 is obtained by negating s_1). Thus, the probability that s_2 conveys a 4-star rating has increased, as has the certainty of this assessment.

Parameterization and heuristics. The values of the different parameters $(\alpha, \beta, \gamma, \delta, \lambda)$ were manually determined. We tried several combinations, but the effect was negligible, arguably due to the low coverage of the lexicon (Section 5). Further, we employ different types of heuristics, e.g., the modification of the probabilities of individual sentences is additive, while sentence combination is multiplicative (as per the Beta distribution). The application of machine learning techniques or a hill-climbing procedure to determine parameter values that yield improved performance, as well as the consideration of different heuristics for negations, adverbial modifiers, sentence connectives and dealing with uncertainty, may be a profitable avenue of investigation after lexicon coverage is increased.

3 Combining the Lexicon with a Naïve Bayes Classifier

Beineke et al. (2004) combined a lexicon with an NB classifier by sourcing from a large corpus words that co-occur with known sentimental "anchor" words, and employing these words to train the classifier. In contrast, like Andreevskaia and Bergler (2008) and Melville et al. (2009), we combine information from a lexicon with the classification produced by a supervised machine learning method. However, in their systems, the weights assigned to each contributing method are based on this method's performance on the training set, while our weights represent a method's coverage of the current text. In addition, we employ much larger datasets in our experiments than those used in (Andreevskaia and Bergler, 2008) and (Melville et al., 2009), and unlike them, we take into account negations, adverbial modifiers and sentence connectives to modify the sentiment of lexicon words.

Our system incorporates corpus-based information by training an NB classifier with unigrams and bigrams as features, and applying information gain (Yang and Pedersen, 1997) to select the top K $(= 4000)$ features.[2] This version of NB is denoted **NB4000**. The probability obtained from the classifier for a review is combined with that obtained from the lexicon by means of a weighted average.[3]

[2] According to our experiments, NB classifiers trained using unigrams and bigrams, combined with feature selection, are among the best sentiment classifiers.

[3] We also applied this combination procedure at the sentence level, but with inferior results.

$$\text{Pr}_{COMB}(D|s) = \frac{\text{Pr}_{NB}(D|s)w_{NB} + \text{Pr}_{LEX}(D|s)w_{LEX}}{w_{NB} + w_{LEX}} \quad (4)$$

where D is a document; w_{LEX} is the fraction of open-class and lexicon words in the review that appear in the lexicon; and w_{NB} represents the fraction of *all* the words in the review that appear in the NB features (this is because unigrams and bigrams selected as NB features contain both open- and closed-class words).

4 Identifying Bimodal Sentences

Sentiment analysis is a difficult problem, as opinions are often expressed in subtle ways, such as irony and sarcasm (Pang and Lee, 2008), which may confuse human readers, creating uncertainty over their understanding. In Section 2, we discussed the incorporation of uncertainty into the lexicon-based framework. Here we offer a method for identifying reviews that contain sentiment-ambiguous sentences, which also affect the ability to understand a review.

As mentioned above, the probability distribution of the sentiment in a review is likely to be unimodal. The Beta distribution obtained from the lexicon guarantees this property, but the multinomial distribution used to train the NB classifier does not. Further, the combination of the distributions obtained from the lexicon and the NB classifier can lead to a bimodal distribution due to inconsistencies between the two input distributions. We posit that such bimodal sentences are unreliable, and propose the following heuristic to identify bimodal sentences.[4]

> The sentiment distribution in a sentence is bimodal if (1) the two most probable classes are not adjacent (e.g., 2-star and 4-star rating), and (2) the probability of the second most probable class is more than half of that of the most probable class.

Examples of sentences identified by this heuristic are "It is pretty *boring*, but you do not worry because the picture will be *beautiful*, and you have these *gorgeous* stars too" (NB⇒1, Lexicon⇒3, actual = 1) and " 'The Wonderful, Horrible Life of Leni Riefenstahl' is a *excellent* film, *but it needed* Riefenstahl to edit it more" (NB⇒2&4,Lexicon⇒3, actual=4). The impact of bimodal sentences on performance is examined in Section 5.2.

5 Evaluation

5.1 Datasets

Our datasets were sourced from reviews in various domains: movies, kitchen appliances, music, and post office. These datasets differ in review length, word usage and writing style.

- **Movies**[5]: This is the *Sentiment Scale* dataset collected and pre-processed by Pang and Lee (2005), which contains movie reviews collected from the Internet. They separated the dataset into four sub-corpora, each written by a different author, to avoid the need to calibrate the ratings given by different authors. The authors, denoted A, B, C and D, wrote 1770, 902, 1307 and 1027 reviews respectively. Each author's reviews were grouped into three and four classes, denoted **Author***X***3** and **Author***X***4** respectively, where $X \in \{A, B, C, D\}$.

- **Kitchen**[6]: This dataset was sourced from a large collection of kitchen appliance reviews collected by Blitzer et al. (2007) from Amazon product reviews. We selected 1000 reviews from each of the four classes considered by Blitzer *et al.*, totalling 4000 reviews. The resultant dataset is denoted **Kitchen4**.

- **Music**[7]: We selected 4039 text samples of music reviews from the Amazon product review dataset compiled by Jindal and Liu (2008). To obtain a dataset with some degree of item consistency and reviewer reliability, we selected reviews for items that have at least 10 reviews written by users who have authored at least 10 reviews. The original reviews are associated with a 5-point rating scale, but we grouped the reviews with low ratings (≤ 3 stars) into one class due to their low numbers. The resultant dataset, denoted

[4] A statistical method for identifying bi-modality is described in (Jackson et al., 1989).

[5] http://www.cs.cornell.edu/home/llee/data/

[6] http://www.cs.jhu.edu/~mdredze/datasets/sentiment/

[7] http://www.cs.uic.edu/~liub/FBS/sentiment-analysis.html

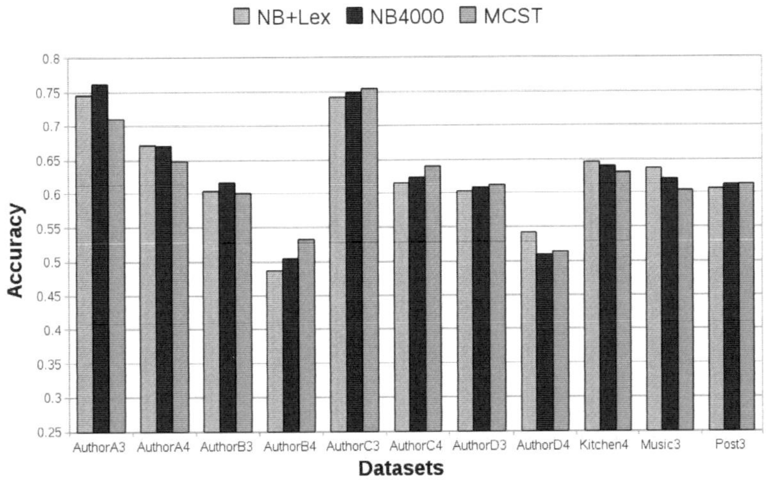

Figure 1: Average classification accuracy for NB+Lex, compared with NB4000 and MCST; all datasets.

Music3, contains three classes: 860 low reviews (≤ 3 stars), 1409 medium (4 stars) and 1770 high (5 stars).

- **PostOffice**: contains 3966 reviews of post-office outlets written by "mystery shoppers" hired by a contractor. The reviews are very short, typically comprising one to three sentences, and focus on specific aspects of the service, e.g., attitude of the staff and cleanliness of the stores. The reviews were originally associated with a seven-point rating scale. However, as for the Music dataset, owing to the low numbers of reviews with low ratings (≤ 5 stars), we grouped the reviews into three balanced classes denoted **Post3**: 1277 low reviews (≤ 5 stars), 1267 medium (6 stars), and 1422 high (7 stars).

5.2 Results

Figure 1 shows the average accuracy obtained by the hybrid approach (NB+Lex using NB4000),[8] compared with the accuracy obtained by the best-performing version of MCST (Bickerstaffe and Zukerman, 2010) (which was evaluated on the Movies dataset, using the algorithms presented in (Pang and Lee, 2005) as baselines), and by NB4000 (NB plus feature selection with 4000 features selected using information gain). All trials employed 10-fold cross-validation. For the NB+Lex method, we investigated different combinations of settings (with and without negations, modifiers, sentence connectives, and inter-sentence weighting). However, these variations had a marginal effect on performance, arguably owing to the low coverage of the lexicon. Here we report on the results obtained with all the options turned on. Statistical significance was computed using a two-tailed paired t-test for each fold with $p = 0.05$ (we mention only statistically significant differences in our discussion).

- NB+Lex outperforms MCST on three datasets (AuthorA3, AuthorA4 and Music3), while the inverse happens only for AuthorB4. NB+Lex also outperforms NB4000 on AuthorD4 and Music3. No other differences are statistically significant.
- Interestingly, NB4000 outperforms MCST for AuthorA3 and Music3, with no other statistically significant differences, which highlights the importance of judicious baseline selection.

Despite showing some promise, it is somewhat disappointing that the combination approach does not yield significantly better results than NB4000 for all the datasets. The small contribution of the lexicon to the performance of NB+Lex may be partially attributed to its low coverage of the vocabulary of the datasets compared with the coverage of NB4000 alone. Specifically, only a small

[8] We omit the results obtained with the lexicon alone, as its coverage is too low.

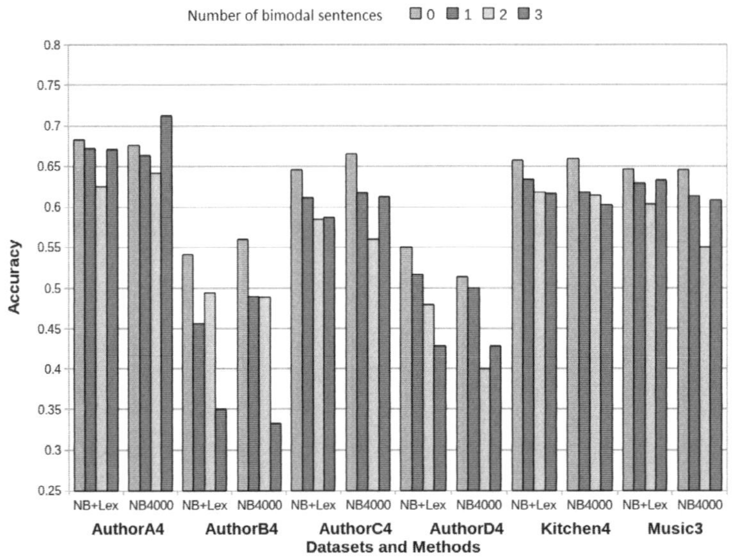

Figure 2: Effect of bimodal sentences on performance (average accuracy): NB+Lex and NB4000; datasets AuthorA4-D4, Kitchen4, Music3.

fraction of the words in our datasets is covered by the lexicon (between 5.5% for AuthorC and 7% for PostOffice), compared with the NB4000 coverage (between 31% for AuthorA3 and 67% for PostOffice). Further, as indicated above, the formulas for estimating the influence of negations, adverbial modifiers and sentence connectives are rather *ad hoc*, and the parameters were manually set. Different heuristics and statistical methods to set their parameters warrant future investigation.

It is interesting to note that the overlap between the words in the corpora covered by the lexicon and the words covered by the 4000 features used by NB is rather small. Specifically, in all datasets except PostOffice, which has an unusually small vocabulary (less than 3000 words), between half and two thirds of the lexicon-covered words are *not* covered by the set of 4000 features. This discrepancy in coverage means that the unigrams in the lexicon have a lower information gain, and hence are less discriminative, than many of the 4000 features selected for the NB classifier, which include a large number of bigrams.

We also analyzed the effect of the presence of sentiment-ambiguous (bimodal) sentences on the predictability of a review, using the method described in Section 4 to identify bimodal sentences. Figure 2 displays the accuracy obtained by NB+Lex and NB4000 on the datasets Authors4A-D, Kitchen4 and Music3 as a function of the number of bimodal sentences in a review (the Authors3A-D datasets were omitted, as they are "easier" than Authors4A-D, and Post3 was omitted because of the low number of sentences per review). We display only results for reviews with 0 to 3 bimodal sentences, as there were very few reviews with more bimodal sentences. As expected, performance was substantially better for reviews with no bimodal sentences (with the exception of NB4000 on AuthorsA4 with 3 bimodal sentences per review). These results suggest that the identification of bimodal sentences is worth pursuing, possibly in combination with additional lexicon coverage, to discriminate between reviews whose sentiment can be reliably detected and reviews where this is not the case. Further, it would be interesting to ascertain the views of human annotators with respect to the sentences we identify as bimodal.

In the context of identifying difficult reviews, we also investigated the relationship between prediction confidence (the probability of the most probable star rating in a review) and performance (Figure 3(a)), and between the coverage provided by both the lexicon and the NB classifier and performance (Figure 3(b)[9]). As seen in Figure 3(a), for all datasets, except AuthorB4, accuracy improves as prediction confidence increases. This

[9]We do not display results for less than 50 documents with a particular coverage.

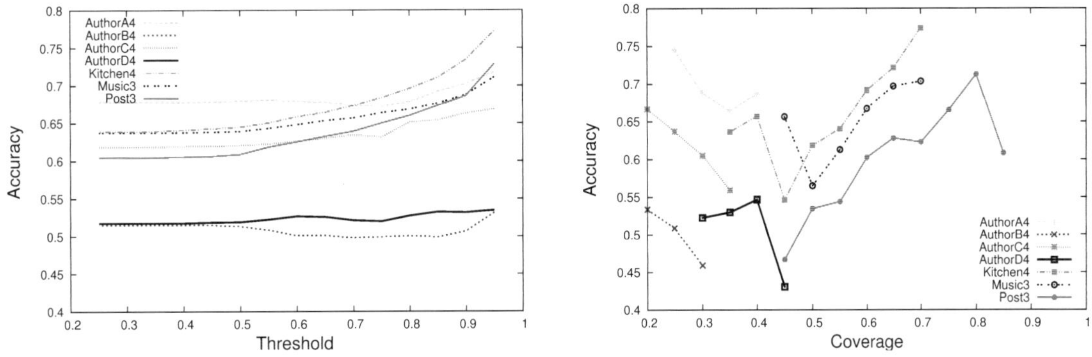

(a) Probability of the most probable star rating.

(b) Lexicon and NB coverage.

Figure 3: Relationship between probability of the most probable star rating and accuracy, and between lexicon/NB coverage and accuracy; datasets AuthorsA4-D4, Kitchen4, Music3 and Post3.

improvement is steadier and sharper for Kitchen4, Music3 and Post3, which as seen in Figure 3(b), have a higher lexicon and NB coverage than the Authors datasets. As one would expect, performance improves for the first three datasets as coverage increases from 50% to 80%. However, outside this range, the results are counter-intuitive: overall, accuracy decreases between 20% and 50% coverage, and also drops for Post3 at 85% coverage (a level of coverage that is not obtained for any other dataset); and a high level of accuracy is obtained for very low levels of coverage ($\leq$ 25%) for AuthorA4 and AuthorC4. These observations indicate that other factors, such as style and vocabulary, should be considered in conjunction with coverage, and that the use of coverage in Equations 2 and 4 may require fine-tuning to take into account the level of coverage.

6 Conclusion

We have examined the performance of three methods based on supervised machine learning applied to multi-way sentiment analysis: (1) sentiment lexicon combined with NB with feature selection, (2) NB with feature selection, and (3) MCST (which considers label similarity). The lexicon is harnessed by applying a probabilistic procedure that combines words, phrases and sentences, and performs adjustments for negations, modifiers and sentence connectives. This information is combined with corpus-based information by taking into account the uncertainty arising from the extent to which the text is "understood".

Our methods were evaluated on seven datasets of different sizes, review lengths and writing styles. The results of our evaluation show that the combination of lexicon- and corpus-based information performs at least as well as state-of-the-art systems. The fact that this improvement is achieved with a small contribution from the lexicon indicates that there may be promise in increasing lexicon coverage and improving the domain specificity of lexicons. At the same time, the observation that NB+Lex (with a small lexicon), NB4000 and MCST exhibit similar performance for several datasets leads us to posit that pure n-gram based statistical systems have plateaued, thus reinforcing the point that additional factors must be brought to bear to achieve significant performance improvements.

The negative result that an NB classifier with feature selection achieves state-of-the-art performance indicates that careful baseline selection is warranted when evaluating new algorithms.

Finally, we studied the effect of three factors on the reliability of a sentiment-analysis algorithm: (1) number of bimodal sentences in a review; (2) probability of the most probable star rating; and (3) coverage provided by the lexicon and the NB classifier. Our results show that these factors may be used to predict regions of reliable sentiment-analysis performance, but further investigation is required regarding the interaction between coverage and the stylistic features of a review.

References

B. Allison. 2008. Sentiment detection using lexically-based classifiers. In *Proceedings of the 11th International Conference on Text, Speech and Dialogue*, pages 21–28, Brno, Czech Republic.

A. Andreevskaia and S. Bergler. 2008. When specialists and generalists work together: Overcoming domain dependence in sentiment tagging. In *ACL'08 – Proceedings of the 46th Annual Meeting of the Association for Computational Linguistics*, pages 290–298, Columbus, Ohio.

S. Baccianella, A. Esuli, and F. Sebastiani. 2010. SentiWordNet 3.0: An enhanced lexical resource for sentiment analysis and opinion mining. In N. Calzolari, K. Choukri, B. Maegaard, J. Mariani, J. Odijk, S. Piperidis, M. Rosner, and D. Tapias, editors, *LREC'10 – Proceedings of the 7th Conference on International Language Resources and Evaluation*, Valletta, Malta.

P. Beineke, T. Hastie, and S. Vaithyanathan. 2004. The sentimental factor: Improving review classification via human-provided information. In *ACL'04 – Proceedings of the 42nd Annual Meeting of the Association for Computational Linguistics*, pages 263–270, Barcelona, Spain.

A.L. Berger, Stephen A. Della Pietra, and Vincent J. Della Pietra. 1996. A maximum entropy approach to natural language processing. *Computational Linguistics*, 22(1):39–71.

A. Bickerstaffe and I. Zukerman. 2010. A hierarchical classifier applied to multi-way sentiment detection. In *COLING'2010 – Proceedings of the 23rd International Conference on Computational Linguistics*, pages 62–70, Beijing, China.

J. Blitzer, M. Dredze, and F. Pereira. 2007. Biographies, Bollywood, boom-boxes and blenders: Domain adaptation for sentiment classification. In *ACL'07 – Proceedings of the 45th Annual Meeting of the Association for Computational Linguistics*, pages 440–447, Prague, Czech Republic.

C. Cortes and V. Vapnik. 1995. Support Vector Networks. *Machine Learning*, 20(3):273–297.

P. Domingos and M. Pazzani. 1997. On the optimality of the simple Bayesian classifier under zero-one loss. *Machine Learning*, 29:103–130.

Y. Hu, R. Lu, X. Li, Y. Chen, and J. Duan. 2007. A language modeling approach to sentiment analysis. In *ICCS07 – Proceedings of the 7th International Conference on Computational Science, Part II*, pages 1186–1193, Beijing, China.

P.R. Jackson, G.T. Tucker, and H.F. Woods. 1989. Testing for bimodality in frequency distributions of data suggesting polymorphisms of drug metabolism-hypothesis testing. *British Journal of Clinical Pharmacology*, 28:655–662.

N. Jindal and B. Liu. 2008. Opinion spam and analysis. In *WSDM-2008 – Proceedings of the 1st International Conference on Web Search and Web Data Mining*, pages 219–230, Palo Alto, California.

D. Klein and C.D. Manning. 2003. Accurate unlexicalized parsing. In *ACL'03 – Proceedings of the 41st Annual Meeting of the Association for Computational Linguistics*, pages 423–430, Sapporo, Japan.

Y. Mao and G. Lebanon. 2006. Isotonic conditional random fields and local sentiment flow. In *NIPS 2006 – Proceedings of the 20th Annual Conference on Neural Information Processing Systems*, pages 961–968, British Columbia, Canada.

R. McDonald, K. Hannan, T. Neylon, M. Wells, and J. Reynar. 2007. Structured models for fine-to-coarse sentiment analysis. In *ACL'07 – Proceedings of the 45th Annual Meeting of the Association for Computational Linguistics*, pages 432–439, Prague, Czech Republic.

P. Melville, W. Gryc, and R.D. Lawrence. 2009. Sentiment analysis of blogs by combining lexical knowledge with text classification. In *KDD'09 – Proceedings of the 15th ACM SIGKDD International Conference on Knowledge Discovery and Data Mining*, pages 1275–1284, Paris, France.

R. Mukras, N. Wiratunga, R. Lothian, S. Chakraborti, and D. Harper. 2007. Information gain feature selection for ordinal text classification using probability re-distribution. In *Proceedings of the IJCAI-07 TextLink Workshop*, Hyderabad, India.

B. Pang and L. Lee. 2005. Seeing stars: Exploiting class relationships for sentiment categorization with respect to rating scales. In *ACL'05 – Proceedings of the 43rd Annual Meeting of the Association for Computational Linguistics*, pages 115–124, Ann Arbor, Michigan.

B. Pang and L. Lee. 2008. Opinion mining and sentiment analysis. *Foundations and Trends in Information Retrieval*, Vol. 2(1-2):pp. 1–135.

B. Snyder and R. Barzilay. 2007. Multiple aspect ranking using the Good Grief algorithm. In *NAACL-HLT 2007 – Proceedings of Human Language Technologies: The Annual Conference of the North American Chapter of the Association for Computational Linguistics*, pages 300–307, Rochester, New York.

M. Taboada, J. Brooke, M. Tofiloskiy, K. Vollz, and M. Stede. 2011. Lexicon-based methods for sentiment analysis. *Computational Linguistics*, 37(2):267–307.

T. Wilson, J. Wiebe, and P. Hoffmann. 2005. Recognizing contextual polarity in phrase-level sentiment analysis. In *EMNLP'2005 – Proceedings of the Conference on Empirical Methods in Natural Language Processing*, pages 347–354, Vancouver, Canada.

Y. Yang and J.O. Pedersen. 1997. A comparative study on feature selection in text categorization. In *ICML'97 – Proceedings of the 14th International Conference on Machine Learning*, pages 412–420, Nashville, Tennessee.

Segmentation and Translation of Japanese Multi-word Loanwords

James Breen
The University of Melbourne
jimbreen@gmail.com

Timothy Baldwin
The University of Melbourne
tb@ldwin.net

Francis Bond
Nanyang Technological University, Singapore
bond@ieee.org

Abstract

The Japanese language has absorbed large numbers of loanwords from many languages, in particular English. As well as using single loanwords, compound nouns, multiword expressions (MWEs), etc. constructed from loanwords can be found in use in very large quantities. In this paper we describe a system which has been developed to segment Japanese loanword MWEs and construct likely English translations. The system, which leverages the availability of large bilingual dictionaries of loanwords and English *n*-gram corpora, achieves high levels of accuracy in discriminating between single loanwords and MWEs, and in segmenting MWEs. It also generates useful translations of MWEs, and has the potential to being a major aid to lexicographers in this area.

1 Introduction

The work described in this paper is part of a broader project to identify unrecorded lexemes, including neologisms, in Japanese corpora. Since such lexemes include the range of lexical units capable of inclusion in Japanese monolingual and bilingual dictionaries, it is important to be able to identify and extract a range of such units, including compound nouns, collocations and other multiword expressions (MWEs: Sag et al. (2002; Baldwin and Kim (2009)).

Unlike some languages, where there is official opposition to the incorporation of foreign words, Japanese has assimilated a large number of such words, to the extent that they constitute a sizeable proportion of the lexicon. For example, over 10% of the entries and sub-entries in the major Kenkyūsha New Japanese-English Dictionary (5th ed.) (Toshiro et al., 2003) are wholly or partly made up of loanwords. In addition there are several published dictionaries consisting solely of such loanwords. Estimates of the number of loanwords and particularly MWEs incorporating loanwords in Japanese range into the hundreds of thousands. While a considerable number of loanwords have been taken from Portuguese, Dutch, French, etc., the overwhelming majority are from English.

Loanwords are taken into Japanese by adapting the source language pronunciation to conform to the relatively restricted set of syllabic phonemes used in Japanese. Thus "blog" becomes *burogu*, and "elastic" becomes *erasutikku*. When written, the syllables of the loanword are transcribed in the *katakana* syllabic script (ブログ, エラスティック), which in modern Japanese is primarily used for this purpose. This use of a specific script means possible loanwords are generally readily identifiable in text and can be extracted without complex morphological analysis.

The focus of this study is on multiword loanwords. This is because there are now large collections of basic Japanese loanwords along with their translations, and it appears that many new loanwords are formed by adopting or assembling MWEs using known loanwords. As evidence of this, we can cite the numbers of *katakana* sequences in the the Google Japanese *n*-gram corpus (Kudo and Kazawa, 2007). Of the 2.6 million 1-grams in that corpus, approximately 1.6 million are in *katakana* or other characters used in loanwords.[1] Inspection of those 1-grams indicates that once the words that are in available dictionaries are removed, the majority of the more common members are MWEs which had not been segmented during the generation of the corpus. Moreover the *n*-gram corpus also contains 2.6 million 2-grams and 900,000 3-grams written in *katakana*. Even after allowing for the multiple-counting between the 1, 2 and 3-grams, and the imperfections in the segmentation of the katakana sequences, it is clear that the vast numbers of multiword loanwords in use are a fruitful area for investigation with a view to extraction and translation.

In the work presented in this paper we describe a system which has been developed to segment Japanese loanword MWEs and construct likely English translations, with the ultimate aim of being part of a toolkit to aid the lexicographer. The system builds on the availability of large collections of translated loanwords and a large English *n*-gram corpus, and in testing is performing with high levels of precision and recall.

2 Prior Work

There has not been a large amount of work published on the automatic and semi-automatic extraction and translation of Japanese loanwords. Much that has been reported has been in areas such as back-transliteration (Matsuo et al., 1996; Knight and Graehl, 1998; Bilac and Tanaka, 2004), or on extraction from parallel bilingual corpora (Brill et al., 2001). More recently work has been carried out exploring combinations of dictionaries and corpora (Nakazawa et al., 2005), although this lead does not seem to have been followed further.

Both Bilac and Tanaka (2004) and Nakazawa et al. (2005) address the issue of segmentation of MWEs. This is discussed in 3.1 below.

[1] In addition to *katakana*, loanwords use the ー (*chōoN*) character for indicating lengthened vowels, and on rare occasions the ヽ and ヾ syllable repetition characters.

3 Role and Nature of Katakana Words in Japanese

As mentioned above, loan words in Japanese are currently written in the *katakana* script. This is an orthographical convention that has been applied relatively strictly since the late 1940s, when major script reforms were carried out. Prior to then loanwords were also written using the *hiragana* syllabary and on occasions *kanji* (Chinese characters).

The *katakana* script is not used exclusively for loanwords. Other usage includes:

a. transcription of foreign person and place names and other named entities. Many Japanese companies use names which are transcribed in *katakana*. Chinese (and Korean) place names and person names, although they are usually available in *kanji* are often written in *katakana* transliterations;
b. the scientific names of plants, animals, etc.
c. onomatopoeic words and expressions, although these are often also written in *hiragana;*
d. occasionally for emphasis and in some contexts for slang words, in a similar fashion to the use of italics in English.

The proportion of *katakana* words that were not loanwords was measured by Brill et al. (2001) at about 13%. (The impact and handling of these is discussed briefly at the end of Section 4.)

When considering the extraction of Japanese loan words from text, there are a number of issues which need to be addressed.

3.1 Segmentation

As mentioned above, many loanwords appear in the form of MWEs, and their correct analysis and handling often requires separation into their composite words. In Japanese there is a convention that loanword MWEs have a "middle-dot" punctuation character (・) inserted between the components, however while this convention is usually followed in dictionaries, it is rarely applied elsewhere. Web search engines typically ignore this character when indexing, and a search for a very common MWE: トマトソース

tomatosōsu "tomato sauce", reveals that it almost always appears as an undifferentiated string. Moreover, the situation is confused by the common use of the ・ character to separate items in lists, in a manner similar to a semi-colon in English. In practical terms, systems dealing with loanwords MWEs must be prepared to do their own segmentation.

One approach to segmentation is to utilize a Japanese morphological analysis system. These have traditionally been weak in the area of segmentation of loanwords, and tend to default to treating long *katakana* strings as 1-grams. In testing a list of loanwords and MWEs using the ChaSen system (Matsumoto et al., 2003), Bilac and Tanaka (2004) report a precision and recall of approximately 0.65 on the segmentation, with a tendency to under-segment being the main problem. Nakazawa et al. (2005) report a similar tendency with the JUMAN morphological analyzer (Kurohashi and Nagao, 1998). The problem was most likely due to the relatively poor representation of loanwords in the morpheme lexicons used by these systems. For example the IPADIC lexicon (Asahara and Matsumoto, 2003) used at that time only had about 20,000 words in *katakana*, and many of those were proper nouns.

In this study, we use the MeCab morphological analyzer (Kudo et al., 2004) with the recently-developed *UniDic* lexicon (Den et al., 2007), as discussed below.

As they were largely dealing with non-lexicalized words, Bilac and Tanaka (2004) used a dynamic programming model trained on a relatively small (13,000) list of *katakana* words, and reported a high precision in their segmentation. Nakazawa et al. (2005) used a larger lexicon in combination with the JUMAN analyzer and reported a similar high precision.

3.2 Non-English Words

A number of loanwords are taken from languages other than English. The JMdict dictionary (Breen, 2004) has approximately 44,000 loanwords, of which 4% are marked as coming from other languages. Inspection of a sample of the 22,000 entries in the Gakken *A Dictionary of Katakana Words* (Kabasawa and Satō, 2003) indicates a similar proportion. (In both dictionaries loanwords from languages other than English are marked with their source language.) This relatively small number is known to cause some problems with generating translations through transliterations based on English, but the overall impact is not very significant.

3.3 Pseudo-English Constructions

A number of *katakana* MWEs are constructions of two or more English words forming a term which does not occur in English. An example is バージョンアップ *bājon'appu* "version up", meaning upgrading software, etc. These constructions are known in Japanese as 和製英語 *wasei eigo* "Japanese-made English". Inspection of the JMdict and Gakken dictionaries indicate they make up approximately 2% of *katakana* terms, and while a nuisance are not considered to be a significant problem.

3.4 Orthographical Variants

Written Japanese has a relatively high incidence of multiple surface forms of words, and this particularly applies to loan words. Many result from different interpretations of the pronunciation of the source language term, e.g. the word for "diamond" is both ダイヤモンド *daiyamondo* and ダイアモンド *daiamondo*, with the two occurring in approximately equal proportions. (The JMdict dictionary records 10 variants for the word "vibraphone", and 9 each for "whiskey" and "vodka".) In some cases two different words have been formed from the one source word, e.g. the English word "truck" was borrowed twice to form トラック *torakku* meaning "truck, lorry" and トロッコ *torokku* meaning "trolley, rail car". Having reasonably complete coverage of alternative surface forms is important in the present project.

4 Approach to Segmentation and MWE Translation

As our goal is the extraction and translation of loanword MWEs, we need to address the twin tasks of segmentation of the MWEs into their constituent source-language components, and generation of appropriate translations for the MWEs as a whole. While the back-transliteration approaches in previous studies have been quite successful, and have an important role in handling single-word loanwords, we decided to experiment with an alternative approach which builds on the large lexicon and *n*-gram corpus resources which are now available. This approach, which we have labelled "CLST" (Corpus-based Loanword Segmentation and Translation) builds upon a direction suggested in Nakazawa et al. (2005) in that it uses a large English *n*-gram corpus both to validate alternative segmentations and select candidate translations.

The three key resources used in CLST are:

a. a dictionary of *katakana* words which has been assembled from:
   i. the entries with *katakana* headwords or readings in the JMdict dictionary;
   ii. the entries with *katakana* headwords in the Kenkyūsha New Japanese-English Dictionary;
   iii. the *katakana* entries in the Eijiro dictionary database;[2]
   iv. the *katakana* entries in a number of technical glossaries covering biomedical topics, engineering, finance, law, etc.
   v. the named-entities in *katakana* from the JMnedict named-entity database.[3]

   This dictionary, which contains both base words and MWEs, includes short English translations which, where appropriate, have been split into identifiable senses. It contains a total of 270,000 entries.

b. a collection of 160,000 *katakana* words drawn from the headwords of the dictionary above. It has been formed by splitting the known MWEs into their components where this can be carried out reliably;

c. the Google English *n*-gram corpus[4]. This contains 1-grams to 5-grams collected from the Web in 2006, along with frequency counts. In the present project we use a subset of the corpus consisting only of case-folded alphabetic tokens.

ソーシャル・ブックマーク・サービス
ソーシャル・ブックマーク・サー・ビス
ソーシャル・ブック・マーク・サービス
ソーシャル・ブック・マーク・サー・ビス
ソー・シャル・ブックマーク・サービス
ソー・シャル・ブックマーク・サー・ビス
ソー・シャル・ブック・マーク・サービス
ソー・シャル・ブック・マーク・サー・ビス

Table 1: Segmentation Example

The process of segmenting an MWE and deriving a translation is as follows:

a. using the *katakana* words in (b) above, generate all possible segmentations of the MWE. A recursive algorithm is used for this. Table 1 shows the segments derived for the MWE ソーシャルブックマークサービス *sōsharubukkumākusābisu* "social bookmark service".

b. for each possible segmentation of an MWE, assemble one or more possible glosses as follows:
   i. take each element in the segmented MWE, extract the first gloss in the dictionary and assemble a composite potential translation by simply concatenating the glosses. Where there are multiple senses, extract the first gloss from each and assemble all possible combinations. (The first gloss is being used as lexicographers typically place the most relevant and succinct translation first, and this has been observed to be often the most useful when building composite glosses.) As examples, for ソーシャル・ブックマーク・サービス the element サービス has two senses "service" and "goods or services without charge", so the possible glosses were "social bookmark service" and "social bookmark goods or services without charge". For ソーシャル・ブック・マーク・サービス the element マーク has senses of "mark", "paying attention",

[2]`http://www.eijiro.jp/e/index.htm`

[3]`http://www.csse.monash.edu.au/~jwb/enamdict_doc.html`

[4]`http://www.ldc.upenn.edu/Catalog/CatalogEntry.jsp?catalogId=LDC2006T13`

"markup" and "Mach", so the potential glosses were "social book mark service", "social book markup service", "social book Mach service", etc. A total of 48 potential translations were assembled for this MWE.

   ii. where the senses are tagged as being affixes, also create combinations where the gloss is attached to the preceding or following gloss as appropriate.

   iii. if the entire MWE is in the dictionary, extract its gloss as well.

It may seem unusual that a single sense is being sought for an MWE with polysemous elements. This comes about because in Japanese polysemous loanwords are almost always due to them being derived from multiple source words. For example ランプ *ranpu* has three senses reflecting that it results from the borrowing of three distinct English words: "lamp", "ramp" and "rump". On the other hand, MWEs containing ランプ, such as ハロゲンランプ *harogenranpu* "halogen lamp" or オンランプ *onranpu* "on-ramp" almost invariably are associated with one sense or another.

c. attempt to match the potential translations with the English *n*-grams, and where a match does exist, extract the frequency data. For the example above, only "social bookmark service", which resulted from the ソーシャル・ブックマーク・サービス segmentation, was matched successfully;

d. where match(es) result, choose the one with the highest frequency as both the most likely segmentation of the MWE and the candidate translation.

The approach described above assumes that the term being analyzed is a MWE, when in fact it may well be a single word. In the case of as-yet unrecorded words we would expect that either no segmentation is accepted or that any possible segmentations have relatively low frequencies associated with the potential translations, and hence can be flagged for closer inspection. As some of the testing described below involves deciding whether a term is or is not a MWE, we have enabled the system to handle single terms as well by checking the unsegmented term against the dictionary and extracting *n*-gram frequency counts for the glosses. This enables the detection and rejection of possible spurious segmentations. As an example of this, the word ボールト *bōruto* "vault" occurs in one of the test files described in the following section. A possible segmentation (ボー・ルト) was generated with potential translations of "bow root" and "baud root". The first of these occurs in the English 2-grams with a frequency of 63, however "vault" itself has a very high frequency in the 1-grams so the segmentation would be rejected.

As pointed out above, a number of *katakana* words are not loanwords. For the most part these would not be handled by the CLST segmentation/translation process as they would not be reduced to a set of known segments, and would be typically reported as failures. The transliteration approaches in earlier studies also have problems with these words. Some of the non-loanwords, such as scientific names of plants, animals, etc. or words written in *katakana* for emphasis, can be detected and filtered prior to attempted processing simply by comparing the *katakana* form with the equivalent *hiragana* form found in dictionaries. Some of the occurrences of Chinese and Japanese names in text can be detected at extraction time, as such names are often written in forms such as "...金鍾泌(キムジョンピル)..."[5].

5 Evaluation

Evaluation of the CLST system was carried out in two stages: testing the segmentation using data used in previous studies to ensure it was discriminating between single loanwords and MWEs, and testing against a collection of MWEs to evaluate the quality of the translations proposed.

5.1 Segmentation

The initial tests of CLST were of the segmentation function and the identification of single words/MWEs. We were fortunate to be

[5]Kim Jong-Pil, a former South Korean politician.

Method	Set	Recall	Precision	F
CLST	EDR	98.67	100.00	99.33
MeCab	EDR	92.67	97.20	94.88
CLST	NTCIR-2	94.87	100.00	97.37
MeCab	NTCIR-2	95.52	92.75	89.37

Table 2: Results from Segmentation Tests

able to use the same data used by Bilac and Tanaka (2004), which consisted of 150 out-of-lexicon *katakana* terms from the EDR corpus (EDR, 1995) and 78 from the NTCIR-2 test collection (Kando et al., 2001). The terms were hand-marked as to whether they were single words or MWEs. Unfortunately we detected some problems with this marking, for example シェークスピア *shēkusupia* "Shakespeare" had been segmented (shake + spear) whereas ホールバーニング *hōrubāningu* "hole burning" had been left as a single word. We considered it inappropriate to use this data without amending these terms. As a consequence of this we are not able to make a direct comparison with the results reported in Bilac and Tanaka (2004). Using the corrected data we analyzed the two datasets and report the results in Table 2. We include the results from analyzing the data using *MeCab/UniDic* as well for comparison. The precision and recall achieved was higher than that reported in Bilac and Tanaka (2004). As in Bilac and Tanaka (2004), we calculate the scores as follows: N is the number of terms in the set, c is the number of terms correctly segmented or identified as 1-grams, e is the number of terms incorrectly segmented or identified, and $n = c + e$. Recall is calculated as $\frac{c}{N}$, precision as $\frac{c}{n}$, and the F-measure as $\frac{2 \times precision \times recall}{precision + recall}$.

As can be seen our CLST approach has achieved a high degree of accuracy in identifying 1-grams and segmenting the MWEs. Although it was not part of the test, it also proposed the correct translations for almost all the MWEs. The less-than-perfect recall is entirely due to the few cases where either no segmentation was proposed, or where the proposed segmentation could not be validated with the English n-grams.

The performance of *MeCab/UniDic* is interesting, as it also has achieved a high level of accuracy. This is despite the *UniDic* lexicon only having approximately 55,000 *katakana* words, and the fact that it is operating outside the textual context for which it has been trained. Its main shortcoming is that it tends to over-segment, which is a contrast to the performance of *ChaSen/IPADIC* reported in Bilac and Tanaka (2004) where under-segmentation was the problem.

5.2 Translation

The second set of tests of CLST was directed at developing translations for MWEs. The initial translation tests were carried out on two sets of data, each containing 100 MWEs. The sets of data were obtained as follows:

a. the 100 highest-frequency MWEs were selected from the Google Japanese 2-grams. The list of potential MWEs had to be manually edited as the 2-grams contain a large number of over-segmented words, e.g. アイコン *aikon* "icon" was split: アイコ+ン, and オークション *ōkushon* "auction" was split オーク+ション;
b. the *katakana* sequences were extracted from a large collection of articles from 1999 in the *Mainichi Shimbun* (a Japanese daily newspaper), and the 100 highest-frequency MWEs extracted.

After the data sets were processed by CLST the results were examined to determine if the segmentations had been carried out correctly, and to assess the quality of the proposed translations. The translations were graded into three groups: (1) acceptable as a dictionary gloss, (2) understandable, but in need of improvement, and (3) wrong or inadequate. An example of a translation graded as 2 is マイナスイオン *mainasuion* "minus ion", where "negative ion" would be better, and one graded as 3 is フリーマーケット *furīmāketto* "free market", where the correct translation is "flea market". For the most part the translations receiving a grading of 2 were the same as would have been produced by a back-transliteration system, and in many cases they were the *wasei eigo* constructions described above.

Some example segmentations, possible translations and gradings are in Table 3.

MWE	Segmentation	Possible Translation	Frequency	Grade
ログインヘルプ	ログイン・ヘルプ	login help	541097	1
ログインヘルプ	ログ・イン・ヘルプ	log in help	169972	-
キーワードランキング	キーワード・ランキング	keyword ranking	39818	1
キーワードランキング	キー・ワード・ランキング	key word ranking	74	-
キャリアアップ	キャリア・アップ	career up	13043	2
キャリアアップ	キャリア・アップ	carrier up	2552	-
キャリアアップ	キャリア・アップ	career close up	195	-
キャリアアップ	キャリア・アップ	career being over	188	-
キャリアアップ	キャリア・アップ	carrier increasing	54	-

Table 3: Sample Segmentations and Translations

Data Set	Failed Segmentations	Translation Grades 1	2	3	Precision	Recall	F
Google	9	66	24	1	98.90	90.00	94.24
Mainichi (Set 1)	3	77	19	1	98.97	96.00	97.46
Mainichi (Set 2)	1	83	16	0	100.00	99.00	99.50

Table 4: Results from Translation Tests

The assessments of the segmentation and the gradings of the translations are given in Table 4. The precision, recall and F measures have been calculated on the basis that a grade of 2 or better for a translation is a satisfactory outcome.

A brief analysis was conducted on samples of 25 MWEs from each test set to ascertain whether they were already in dictionaries, or the degree to which they were suitable for inclusion in a dictionary. The dictionaries used for this evaluation were the commercial Kenkyusha Online Dictionary Service[6] which has eighteen Japanese, Japanese-English and English-Japanese dictionaries in its search tool, and the free WWWJDIC online dictionary[7], which has the JMdict and JMnedict dictionaries, as well as numerous glossaries.

Of the 50 MWEs sampled:

a. 34 (68%) were in dictionaries;
b. 11 (22%) were considered suitable for inclusion in a dictionary. In some cases the generated translation was not considered appropriate without some modification, i.e. it had been categorized as "2";
c. 3 (6%) were proper names (e.g. hotels, software packages);
d. 2 (4%) were not considered suitable for inclusion in a dictionary as they were simple collocations such as メニューエリア *menyūeria* "menu area".

As the tests described above were carried out on sets of frequently-occurring MWEs, it was considered appropriate that some further testing be carried out on less common loanword MWEs. Therefore an additional set of 100 lower-frequency MWEs which did not occur in the dictionaries mentioned above were extracted from the *Mainichi Shimbun* articles and were processed by the CLST system. Of these 100 MWEs:

a. 1 was not successfully segmented;
b. 83 of the derived translations were classified as "1" and 16 as "2";
c. 8 were proper names.

The suitability of these MWEs for possible inclusion in a bilingual dictionary was also evaluated. In fact the overwhelming majority of the MWEs were relatively straightforward collocations, e.g. マラソンランナー *marasonrannā* "marathon runner" and ロックコンサート *rokkukonsāto* "rock concert", and were deemed to be not really appropriate as dictionary entries. 5 terms were assessed as being dictionary candidates.

[6] http://kod.kenkyusha.co.jp/service/

[7] http://www.edrdg.org/cgi-bin/wwwjdic/wwwjdic?1C

Several of these, e.g. ゴールドプラン *gōru-dopuran* "gold plan" and エースストライカー *ēsusutoraikā* "ace striker" were category 2 translations, and their possible inclusion in a dictionary would largely be because their meanings are not readily apparent from the component words, and an expanded gloss would be required.

Some points which emerge from the analysis of the results of the tests described above are:

a. to some extent, the Google *n*-gram test data had a bias towards the types of constructions favoured by Japanese web-page designers, e.g. ショッピングトップ *shoppingutoppu* "shopping top", which possibly inflated the proportion of translations being scored with a 2;

b. some of the problems leading to a failure to segment the MWEs were due to the way the English *n*-gram files were constructed. Words with apostrophes were split, so that "men's" was recorded as a bigram: "men+'s". This situation is not currently handled in CLST, which led to some of the segmentation failures, e.g. with メンズアイテム *menzuaitemu* "men's item";

6 Conclusion and Future Work

In this paper we have described the CLST (Corpus-based Loanword Segmentation and Translation) system which has been developed to segment Japanese loanword MWEs and construct likely English translations. The system, which leverages the availability of large bilingual dictionaries of loanwords and English *n*-gram corpora, is achieving high levels of accuracy in discriminating between single loanwords and MWEs, and in segmenting MWEs. It is also generating useful translations of MWEs, and has the potential to being a major aide both to lexicography in this area, and to translating.

The apparent success of an approach based on a combination of large corpora and relatively simple heuristics is consistent with the conclusions reached in a number of earlier investigations (Banko and Brill, 2001; Lapata and Keller, 2004).

Although the CLST system is performing at a high level, there are a number of areas where refinement and experimentation on possible enhancements can be carried out. They include:

a. instead of using the "first-gloss" heuristic, experiment with using all available glosses. This would be at the price of increased processing time, but may improve the performance of the segmentation and translation;

b. align the searching of the *n*-gram corpus to cater for the manner in which words with apostrophes, etc. are segmented. At present this is not handled correctly;

c. tune the presentation of the glosses in the dictionaries so that they will match better with the contents of the *n*-gram corpus. At present the dictionary used is simply a concatenation of several sources, and does not take into account such things as the *n*-gram corpus having hyphenated words segmented;

d. extend the system by incorporating a back-transliteration module such as that reported in Bilac and Tanaka (2004). This would cater for single loanwords and thus provide more complete coverage.

References

Masayuki Asahara and Yuji Matsumoto. 2003. *IPADIC version 2.7.0 User's Manual (in Japanese).* NAIST, Information Science Division.

Timothy Baldwin and Su Nam Kim. 2009. Multiword expressions. In Nitin Indurkhya and Fred J. Damerau, editors, *Handbook of Natural Language Processing.* CRC Press, Boca Raton, USA, 2nd edition.

Michele Banko and Eric Brill. 2001. Scaling to very very large corpora for natural language disambiguation. In *Proceedings of the 39th Annual Meeting of the ACL and 10th Conference of the EACL (ACL-EACL 2001)*, Toulouse, France.

Slaven Bilac and Hozumi Tanaka. 2004. A Hybrid Back-transliteration System for Japanese. In *Proceedings of the 20th international conference on Computational Linguistics*, COLING '04, Geneva, Switzerland.

James Breen. 2004. JMdict: a Japanese-Multilingual Dictionary. In *Proceedings of the COLING-2004 Workshop on Multilingual Resources*, pages 65–72, Geneva, Switzerland.

Eric Brill, Gary Kacmarcik, and Chris Brockett. 2001. Automatically Harvesting Katakana-

English Term Pairs from Search Engine Query Logs. In *Proceedings of the Sixth Natural Language Processing Pacific Rim Symposium, November 27-30, 2001, Hitotsubashi Memorial Hall, National Center of Sciences, Tokyo, Japan*, pages 393–399.

Yasuharu Den, Toshinobu Ogiso, Hideki Ogura, Atsushi Yamada, Nobuaki Minematsu, Kiyotaka Uchimoto, and Hanae Koiso. 2007. The development of an electronic dictionary for morphological analysis and its application to Japanese corpus linguistics (in Japanese). *Japanese Linguistics*, 22:101–123.

EDR, 1995. *EDR Electronic Dictionary Technical Guide.* Japan Electronic Dictionary Research Institute, Ltd. (in Japanese).

Yōichi Kabasawa and Morio Satō, editors. 2003. *A Dictionary of Katakana Words.* Gakken.

Noriko Kando, Kazuko Kuriyama, and Masaharu Yoshioka. 2001. Overview of Japanese and English Information Retrieval Tasks (JEIR) at the Second NTCIR Workshop. In *Proceedings of the Second NTCIR Workshop*, Jeju, Korea.

Kevin Knight and Jonathan Graehl. 1998. Machine Transliteration. *Comput. Linguist.*, 24(4):599–612, December.

Taku Kudo and Hideto Kazawa. 2007. Japanese Web N-gram Corpus version 1. `http://www.ldc.upenn.edu/Catalog/docs/LDC2009T08/`.

Taku Kudo, Kaoru Yamamoto, and Yuji Matsumoto. 2004. Applying conditional random fields to Japanese morphological analysis. In *Proceedings of the 2004 Conference on Empirical Methods in Natural Language Processing (EMNLP 2004)*, pages 230–237, Barcelona, Spain.

Sadao Kurohashi and Makoto Nagao. 1998. *Nihongo keitai-kaiseki sisutemu JUMAN* [Japanese morphological analysis system JUMAN] version 3.5. Technical report, Kyoto University. (in Japanese).

Mirella Lapata and Frank Keller. 2004. The web as a baseline: Evaluating the performance of unsupervised web-based models for a range of NLP tasks. In *Proceedings of the Human Langauge Techinology Conference and Conference on Empirical Methods in National Language Processing (HLT/NAACL-2004)*, pages 121–128, Boston, USA.

Yuji Matsumoto, Akira Kitauchi, Tatsuo Yamashita, Yoshitaka Hirano, Hiroshi Matsuda, Kazuma Takaoka, and Masayuki Asahara. 2003. *Japanese Morphological Analysis System ChaSen Version 2.3.3 Manual.* Technical report, NAIST.

Yoshihiro Matsuo, Mamiko Hatayama, and Satoru Ikehara. 1996. Translation of 'katakana' words using an English dictionary and grammar (in Japanese). In *Proceedings of the Information Processing Society of Japan*, volume 53, pages 65–66.

Toshiaki Nakazawa, Daisuke Kawahara, and Sadao Kurohashi. 2005. Automatic Acquisition of Basic Katakana Lexicon from a Given Corpus. In *Proceedings of the 2nd International Joint Conference on Natural Language Processing (IJCNLP-05)*, pages 682–693, Jeju, Korea.

Ivan A. Sag, Timothy Baldwin, Francis Bond, Ann Copestake, and Dan Flickinger. 2002. Multiword expressions: A pain in the neck for NLP. In *Proceedings of the 3rd International Conference on Intelligent Text Processing and Computational Linguistics (CICLing-2002)*, pages 1–15, Mexico City, Mexico.

Watanabe Toshiro, Edmund Skrzypczak, and Paul Snowdon (eds). 2003. *Kenkyûsha New Japanese-English Dictionary, 5th Edition.* Kenkyûsha.

Measurement of Progress in Machine Translation

Yvette Graham **Timothy Baldwin** **Aaron Harwood** **Alistair Moffat** **Justin Zobel**
Department of Computing and Information Systems
The University of Melbourne
{ygraham,tbaldwin,aharwood,amoffat,jzobel}@unimelb.edu.au

Abstract

Machine translation (MT) systems can only be improved if their performance can be reliably measured and compared. However, measurement of the quality of MT output is not straightforward, and, as we discuss in this paper, relies on correlation with inconsistent human judgments. Even when the question is captured via "is translation A better than translation B" pairwise comparisons, empirical evidence shows that inter-annotator consistency in such experiments is not particularly high; for intra-judge consistency – computed by showing the same judge the same pair of candidate translations twice – only low levels of agreement are achieved. In this paper we review current and past methodologies for human evaluation of translation quality, and explore the ramifications of current practices for automatic MT evaluation. Our goal is to document how the methodologies used for collecting human judgments of machine translation quality have evolved; as a result, we raise key questions in connection with the low levels of judgment agreement and the lack of mechanisms for longitudinal evaluation.

1 Introduction

Measurement is central to all scientific endeavor. In computing, we rely on impartial and scrutable evaluations of phenomena in order to determine the extent to which progress is being made in that discipline area. We then use those measurements to predict performance on unseen data. That is, we need accurate measurement to know that we have made progress, and we need those measurements to be predictive, so that we can have confidence that we will benefit from the improvements that have been attained. The particular focus of this paper is measurement of translation quality in the field of machine translation (MT).

In some areas of computing, measurement techniques are unambiguous, directly comparable between systems, and enduring over time. For example, a proposed new approach to text compression can be evaluated on a wide range of files, and the criteria to be measured in each case are straightforward: execution time for encoding and decoding; memory space used during encoding and decoding; and, of course, compressed file size. All of these facets are objective, in that, if the same file is compressed a second time on the same hardware, the same measurements (to within some predictable tolerance, in the case of execution speed) will result; and compressing the same file with the same technique on different hardware ten years later should still result in consistent measures of memory use and file size. To compare two approaches to text compression, therefore, the only real complexity is in assembling a collection of documents which is "representative" of utility in general or over some specific domain (for example, compression of microposts from a service such as Twitter). Beyond this, as long as the evaluation is carried out using a fixed computing environment (OS, hardware, and, ideally, programming environment), establishing the superiority of one method over another is clear-cut and predictivity is high.

In other areas of computing, the measurement

techniques used are, of necessity, more subjective, and predictivity is harder to achieve. Areas that often require subjective human judgments for evaluation are those where the work product is for human consumption, such as natural language processing (NLP) and information retrieval (IR). In IR, systems are measured with reference to subjective human relevance judgments over results for a sample set of topics; a recent longitudinal study has indicated that, despite a considerable volume of published work, there is serious question as to the extent to which actual long-term improvements in effectiveness have been attained (Armstrong et al., 2009). Moreover, while it is possible to achieve predictivity through the use of a fixed set of topics, a fixed document collection, and a static set of relevance judgments (often based on pooling (Voorhees and Harman, 2005)), the set of topics is often small and not necessarily representative of the universe of possible topics, which raises concerns about true predictivity.

The work of Armstrong et al. (2009) raises another important question, one that is relevant in all fields of computing: that any experimentation carried out today should, if at all possible, also lay the necessary groundwork to allow, ten years hence, a retrospective evaluation of "have we made quantifiable progress over the last decade?"

2 Automatic Measurement of MT

The automatic evaluation of MT system output has long been an objective of MT research, with several of the recommendations of the early ALPAC Report (ALPAC, 1966), for example, relating to evaluation:

> 1. Practical methods for evaluation of translations; ... 3. Evaluation of quality and cost of various sources of translations;

In practical terms, improvements are often established through the use of an automatic measure that computes a similarity score between the candidate translation and one or more human-generated reference translations. However it is well-known that automatic measures are not necessarily a good substitute for human judgments of translation quality, primarily because:

- There are different valid ways of translating the same source input, and therefore comparison with a single or even multiple references risks ranking highly those translations that happen to be more reference-like compared to those that made different choices; and
- There are different ways to compute the syntactic similarity between a system output translation and reference translations, and given two possible system translations for a source input, different measures can disagree on which output is more similar to the set of reference translation.

Moreover, with any mechanical method of measurement, there is a tendency for researchers to work to improve their MT system's ability to score highly rather than produce better translations.

To alleviate these concerns, direct human judgments of translation quality are also collected when possible. During the evaluation of MT shared tasks, for example, human judgments of MT outputs have been used to determine the ranking of participating systems. The same human judgments can also be used in the evaluation of automatic measures, by comparing the degree to which automatic scores (or ranks) of translations correlate with them. This aspect of MT measurement is discussed shortly.

One well-known example of an automatic metric is the BLEU (bilingual evaluation understudy) score (Papineni et al., 2002). Computation of a BLEU score for a system, based on a set of candidate translations it has generated, requires only that sets of corresponding reference translations be made available, one per candidate. The ease – and repeatability – of such testing has meant that BLEU is popular as a translation effectiveness measure. But that popularity does not bestow any particular superiority, and, BLEU suffers from drawbacks (Callison-Burch et al., 2006). (As an aside, we note that in all such repeatable scoring arrangements, every subsequent experiment must be designed so that there is clear separation between training and test data, to avoid any risk of hill-climbing and hence over-fitting.)

3 Human Assessment in MT

The standard process by which researchers have tested automatic MT evaluation measures is through analysis of correlation with human judgments of MT quality, as depicted in Figure 1.

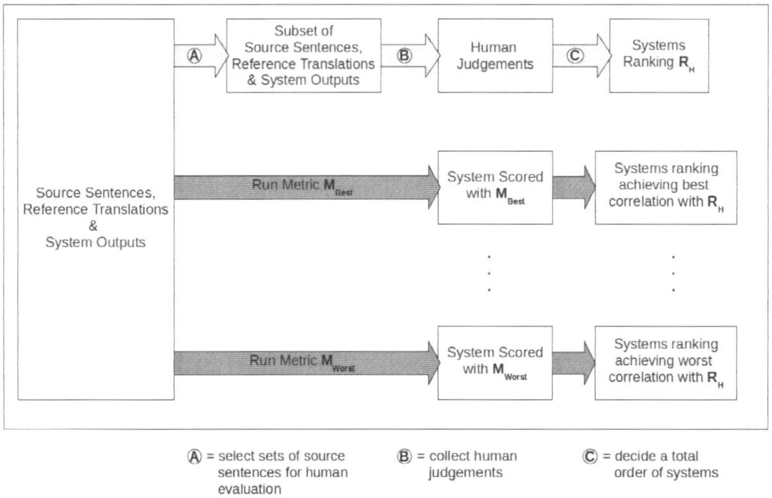

Figure 1: The process by which human assessment is used to confirm (or not) automatic MT evaluation measures.

In this process, a suite of different MT systems are each given the same corpus of sentences to translate, across a variety of languages, and required to output a 1-best translation for each input in the required target language. Since the total number of translations in the resulting set is too large for exhaustive human assessment, a sample of translations is selected, and this process is labeled A in Figure 1. To increase the likelihood of a fair evaluation, translations are selected at random, with some number of translations repeated, to facilitate later measurement of consistency levels.

Label B in Figure 1 indicates the assessment of the sample of translations by human judges, where judges are required to examine translated sentences, perhaps several at a time, and assess their quality. It is this issue in particular that we are most concerned with: to consider different possibilities for acquiring human judgments of translation quality in order to facilitate more consistent assessments.

Once sufficient human judgments have been collected, they are used to decide a best-to-worst ranking of the participating machine translation systems, shown as R_H in Figure 1. The process of computing that ranking is labeled C. The best approach to process C, that is, going from raw human judgments to a total-order rank, to some degree still remains an open research question (Bojar et al., 2011; Lopez, 2012; Callison-Burch et al., 2012), and is not considered further in this paper.

Once the suite of participating systems has been ordered, any existing or new automatic MT evaluation metric can be used to construct another ordered ranking of the same set. The ranking generated by the metric can then be compared with the ranking R_H generated by the human assessment, using statistics such as Spearman's coefficient, with a high correlation being interpreted as evidence that the metric is sound.

Since the validity of an automatic MT evaluation measure is assessed relative to human judgments, it is vital that the judgments acquired are reliable. In practice, however, human judgments, as evaluated by intra- and inter-annotator agreement, can be inconsistent with each other. For example, inter-annotator agreement for human assessment of translation quality, as measured using Cohen's Kappa coefficient (Cohen, 1960), in recent WMT shared tasks are reported to be at as low levels as $k = 0.44$ (2010), $k = 0.38$ (2011) and $k = 0.28$ (2012), with intra-annotator agreement levels not faring much better: $k = 0.60$ (2010), $k = 0.56$ (2011) and $k = 0.46$ (2012) (Callison-Burch et al., 2010; Callison-Burch et al., 2011; Callison-Burch et al., 2012). This lack of coherence amongst human assessments then forces the question: *are assessments of MT evalu-*

ation metrics robust, if they are validated via low-quality human judgments of translation quality?

While one valid response to this question is that the automatic evaluation measures are no worse than human assessment, a more robust approach is to find ways of increasing the reliability of the human judgments we use as the yard-stick for automatic metrics by endeavoring to find better ways of collecting and assessing translation quality. Considering just how important human assessment of translation quality is to empirical machine translation, although there is a significant amount of research into developing metrics that correlate with human judgments of translation quality, the underlying topic of finding ways of increasing the reliability of those judgments to date has received a limited amount of attention (Callison-Burch et al., 2007; Callison-Burch et al., 2008; Przybocki et al., 2009; Callison-Burch et al., 2009; Callison-Burch et al., 2010; Denkowski and Lavie, 2010).

4 Human Assessment of Quality

To really improve the consistency of the human judgments of translation quality, we may need to take a step back and ask ourselves *what are we really asking human judges to do when we require them to assess translation quality?* In the philosophy of science, the concept of *translation quality* would be considered a (hypothetical) *construct*. MacCorquodale and Meehl (1948) describe a construct as follows:

> ... constructs involve terms which are not wholly reducible to empirical terms; they refer to processes or entities that are not directly observed (although they need not be in principle unobservable); the mathematical expression of them cannot be formed simply by a suitable grouping of terms in a direct empirical equation; and the truth of the empirical laws involved is a necessary but not a sufficient condition for the truth of these conceptions.

Translation quality is an abstract notion that exists in theory and can be observed in practice but cannot be measured directly. Psychology often deals with the measurement of such abstract notions, and provides established methods of measurement and validation of those measurement techniques. Although "translation quality" is not a psychological construct as such, we believe these methods of measurement and validation could be used to develop more reliable and valid measures of translation quality.

Psychological constructs are measured indirectly, with the task of defining and measuring a construct known as *operationalizing* the construct. The task requires examination of the mutual or common-sense understanding of the construct to come up with a set of items that together can be used to indirectly measure it. In psychology, the term *construct validity* refers to the degree to which inferences can legitimately be made from the operationalizations in a study to the theoretical constructs on which those operationalizations were based.

Given some data, it is possible then to examine each pair of constructs within the semantic net, and evidence of convergence between theoretically similar constructs supports the inclusion of both constructs (Campbell and Fiske, 1959). To put it more simply, when two theoretically *similar* constructs that *should* (in theory) relate to one another do in fact *highly correlate* on the data, it is evidence to support their use. Similarly, when a *lack of correlation* is observed for a pair of constructs that theoretically *should not* relate to each, this also validates their use. This is just one example of a range of methods used in psychology to validate techniques used in the measurement of psychological constructs (see Trochim (1999) for a general introduction to construct validity).

5 Past and Current Methodologies

The ALPAC Report (ALPAC, 1966) was one of the earliest published attempts to perform cross-system MT evaluation, in determining whether progress had been made over the preceding decade. The (somewhat anecdotal) conclusion was that:

> (t)he reader will find it instructive to compare the samples above with the results obtained on simple, selected, text 10 years earlier ... in that the earlier samples are more readable than the later ones.

The DARPA Machine Translation Initiative of the 1990s incorporated MT evaluation as a central tenet, and periodically evaluated the three MT systems funded by the program (CANDIDE, PANGLOSS and LINGSTAT). It led to the proposal of *adequacy* and *fluency* as the primary means of human MT evaluation, in addition to human-assisted measurements. For instance, the DARPA initiative examined whether post-editing of MT system output was faster than simply translating the original from scratch (White et al., 1994). Adequacy is the degree to which the information in the source language string is preserved in the translation,[1] while fluency is the determination of whether the translation is a well-formed utterance in the target language and fluent in context.

Subsequently, many of the large corporate machine translation systems used regression testing to establish whether changes or new modules had a positive impact on machine translation quality. Annotators were asked to select which of two randomly-ordered translations (one from each system) they preferred (Bond et al., 1995; Schwartz et al., 2003), and this was often performed over a reference set of translation pairs (Ikehara et al., 1994). While this methodology is capable of capturing longitudinal progress for a given MT system, it is prohibitively expensive and doesn't scale well to multi-system comparison.

The annual workshop for statistical machine translation (WMT) has, over recent years, been the main forum for collection of human assessment of translation quality, despite this not being the main focus of the workshop (which is to provide a regular cross-system comparison over standardized datasets for a variety of language pairs by means of a shared translation task) (Koehn and Monz, 2006; Callison-Burch et al., 2007; Callison-Burch et al., 2008; Callison-Burch et al., 2009; Callison-Burch et al., 2010; Callison-Burch et al., 2011; Callison-Burch et al., 2012). Figure 2 shows the approaches used for human judgments of translation quality at the annual workshops.

To summarize, across the field of machine translation human judges have been asked to assess translation quality in a variety of ways:

- Single-item or two-items (for example, *fluency* and *adequacy* being a two-item assessment);
- Using different labels (for example, asking which translation is *better* or asking which is more *adequate*);
- Ordinal level scales (ranking a number of translations from best-to-worst) or interval-level scales (for example, interval-level fluency or adequacy judgments);
- Different lexical units (for example, whole sentences rather than sub-sentential constituents);
- Different numbers of points on interval-level scale;
- Displaying interval-level scale numbering to judges or not displaying it;
- Simultaneously judging fluency and adequacy items or separating the assessment of fluency and adequacy;
- Displaying a reference translation to the judge or not displaying it;
- Including the reference translation present among the set being judged or not including it;
- Displaying a preceding and following context of the judged translation or not displaying any surrounding context;
- Displaying session/overall participation meta-information to the judge (for example, the number of translations judged so far, the time taken so far, or the number of translations left to be judged) or not displaying session meta-information;
- Allowing judges to assess translations that may have originated with their own system versus holding out these translations;
- Including crowd-sourced judgments or not.

5.1 Pre 2007 Methodologies

A widely used methodology for human evaluation of MT output up to 2007 was to assess translations under the two items, fluency and adequacy, each on a five-point scale (Callison-Burch et al., 2007). Fluency and adequacy had originally been part of the US Government guidelines for assessment of manually produced translations and was adopted by DARPA for the evaluation of machine translation output, as the fact that these established criteria had originally been designed for the more general purpose of grading translators helped validate their use (White et al., 1994).

When WMT began in 2006 the fluency and adequacy measures were again adopted, as had also

[1] Or, in the case of White et al. (1994), the degree to which the information in a professional *translation* can be found in the translation, as judged by monolingual speakers of the target language.

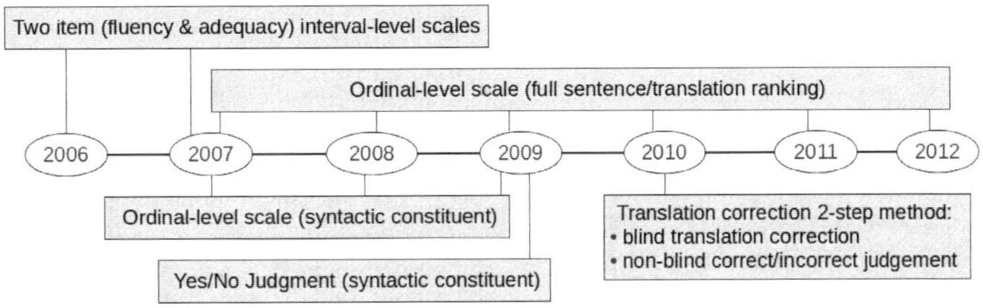

Figure 2: Methodologies of human assessment of translation quality at statistical machine translation workshops

been used in LDC (2005), to assess output of shared task participating systems in the form of a two item interval-level scale. Too few human assessments were recorded in the first year to be able to estimate the reliability of human judgments (Koehn and Monz, 2006). In 2007, the workshop sought to better assess the reliability of human judgments in order to increase the reliability of results reported for the shared translation task. Reliability of human judgments was estimated by measuring levels of agreement as well as adding two new supplementary methods of human assessment. In addition to asking judges to measure the fluency and adequacy of translations, they were now also requested in a separate evaluation set-up to rank translations of full sentences from best-to-worst (the method of assessment that has been sustained to the present), in addition to ranking translations of sub-sentential source syntactic constituents.[2] Both of the new methods used a single item ordinal-level scale, as opposed to the original two item interval-level fluency and adequacy scales.

Highest levels of agreement were reported for the sub-sentential source syntactic constituent ranking method ($k_{\text{inter}} = 0.54$, $k_{\text{intra}} = 0.74$), followed by the full sentence ranking method ($k_{\text{inter}} = 0.37$, $k_{\text{intra}} = 0.62$), with the lowest agreement levels observed for two-item fluency ($k_{\text{inter}} = 0.28$, $k_{\text{intra}} = 0.54$) and adequacy ($k_{\text{inter}} = 0.31$, $k_{\text{intra}} = 0.54$) scales. Additional methods of human assessment were trialled in subsequent experimental rounds; but the only method still currently used is ranking of translations of full sentences.

When the WMT 2007 report is revisited, it is difficult to interpret reported differences in levels of agreement between the original fluency/adequacy method of assessment and the sentence ranking method. Given the limited resources available and huge amount of effort involved in carrying out a large-scale human evaluation of this kind, it is not surprising that instead of systematically investigating the effects of individual changes in method, several changes were made at once to quickly find a more consistent method of human assessment. In addition, the method of assessment of translation quality is required to facilitate speedy judgments in order to collect sufficient judgments within a short time frame for the overall results to be reliable, an inevitable trade-off between bulk and quality must be taken into account. However, some questions remain unanswered: *to what degree was the increase in consistency caused by the change from a two item scale to a single item scale and to what degree was it caused by the change from an interval level scale to an ordinal level scale?* For example, it is wholly possible that the increase in observed consistency resulted from the combined effect of a reduction in consistency (perhaps caused by the change from a two item scale to a single item scale) with a simultaneous increase in consistency (due to the change from an interval-level scale to an ordinal-level scale). We are not suggesting this is in fact what happened, just that an overall observed increase in consistency resulting from multiple changes to method cannot be interpreted as each individual alteration causing an increase in consistency. Although a more consistent method of human assessment was indeed found, we cannot be at all certain of the reasons behind the improvement.

[2]Ties are allowed for both methods.

A high correlation between fluency and adequacy across all language pairs included in the evaluation is also reported, presented as follows (Callison-Burch et al., 2007):

> ..., in principle it seems that people have a hard time separating these two aspects (referring to fluency and adequacy) of translation. The high correlation between people's fluency and adequacy scores ... indicates that the distinction might be false.

The observed high correlation between fluency and adequacy is interpreted as a negative. However, in the field of psychology according to construct validity, an observed high correlation between two items that in theory should relate to each other is interpreted as evidence of the measure in fact being valid (see Section 4), and there is no doubt that in theory the concepts of fluency and adequacy do relate to each other. Moreover, in general in psychology, a measure that employs more items as opposed to fewer (given the validity of those items), is regarded as better.

In addition, human judges were asked to assess fluency and adequacy at the same time, and this could have inflated the observed correlation. A fairer examination of the degree to which fluency and adequacy of translations correlate, would have judges assess the two criteria of translations on separate occasions, so that each judgment could be made independently of the other. Another advantage of judging fluency and adequacy separately might be to avoid revealing the reference translation to judges before they make their fluency assessment. A fluency judgment of translations without a reference translation would increase the objectivity of the assessment and avoid the possibility of a bias in favor of systems that produce reference-like translations.

Confusion around how well fluency and adequacy can be used to measure translation quality, to some degree may stem from the implicit relationship between the two notions. For instance, does the adequacy of a translation imply its fluency, and, if so, why would we want to assess translations under both these criteria? However, the argument for assessing adequacy on its own and dropping fluency, only stands for translations that are fully fluent. The fluency of a translation judged to be fully adequate can quite rightly be assumed. However, when the adequacy of a translation is less than perfect, very little can be assumed from an adequacy judgment about the fluency of the translation. Moving from a two-item fluency/adequacy scale to a single-item scale loses some information that could be useful for analyzing the kinds of errors present in translations.

5.2 Post 2007 Methodologies

Since 2007, the use of a single item scale for human assessment of translation quality has been common, as opposed to the more traditional two item fluency/adequacy scale, sometimes citing the high correlation reported in WMT 2007 as motivation for its non-use other times not (Przybocki et al., 2009; Denkowski and Lavie, 2010). For example, Przybocki et al. (2009) use (as part of their larger human evaluation) a single item (7-point) scale for assessing the quality of translations (with the scale labeled *adequacy*) and report inter-annotator agreement of $k = 0.25$, lower than those reported for the two item fluency/adequacy scales in WMT 2007. Although caution needs to be taken when directly comparing such agreement measurements, this again raises questions about the validity of methodologies used for human assessment of translation quality.

When we look at the trend in consistency levels for human assessments acquired during the three most recent WMT shared tasks, where the only surviving method of human assessment of translation quality is full sentence ranking (or translation ranking as it is also known), we unfortunately see ever-decreasing consistency levels. Agreement levels reported in the most recent 2012 WMT using translation ranking are lower than those reported in 2007 for the two item fluency and adequacy interval-level scales. Although caution must again be taken when making direct comparisons, this may cause us to revisit our motivation for moving away from more traditional methods. In addition, due to the introduction of the new kind of shared task, quality estimation, the traditional ordinal-level scale has again resurfaced for human assessment of translation quality, although on this occasion in the guise of a 4-point scale (Callison-Burch et al., 2012). This causes us to pose the question *is the route we have chosen in the search of more reliable human assessment of translation quality really going to lead to an optimal method?* Machine translation may benefit from a systematic investigation into which methods of human assessment of translation quality are in fact most reliable and result in most consistent judgments.

Planning for the future: Two major components of evaluation are not catered for by current approaches. The first is the value of longitudinal evaluation, the ability to measure how much improvement is occurring over time. Mechanisms that could be used include: capture of the output of systems that is not evaluated at the time; strategic re-use of evaluation data in different events; probably others. In the TREC context, a long-held belief that systems were measurably improving is not supported by longitudinal study, demonstrating the value of such mechanisms. In other contexts, longitudinal mechanisms allow meta studies that yield insights that would not otherwise be available.

Context for judgments: The other omitted component is sufficient consideration of what might be called "role", the persona that the assessor is expected to adopt as they make their decisions. An MT system that is used to determine, for example, whether a statement in another language is factually correct may be very different from one that is used to translate news for a general audience. Without understanding of role, assessors can only be given very broad instructions, and may have varying interpretations of what is expected of them. The design of such instructions needs to be considered with extreme caution, however, as a seemingly unambiguous instruction inevitably has the potential to bias judgments in some unexpected way.

6 Open Questions

Our review of approaches to MT system evaluation illustrates that a range of questions need to be asked:

- What are the effects of context and specificity of task on human assessment of translation quality?
- Can we identify the key "components" annotators draw on in evaluating translation quality? Could insights allow us to develop more reliable evaluation methodology?
- Should we reconsider how conclusions are drawn from results by taking into account the degree to which automatic metrics correlate with human judgments as well as levels of consistency of those judgments? How do these factors effect the practical significance of a result?
- What can be done to enhance the reusability of previous experimental data? Can current regimes be adapted to testing of new systems that did not originally participate in particular experimental rounds?
- Is data being collected now that would allow retrospective evaluation in ten years, to know if the state of the art has changed? Similarly, is it possible to demonstrate with the evaluation data that MT systems today are better than they were ten years ago?

7 Summary

Regular competitive evaluation of systems in a common framework has become widespread in computing, in areas as diverse as message understanding and genome assembly. However, at core these evaluations are dependent on principled, robust measurement of systems and their ability to solve particular tasks. Our review has established that there are significant issues with current approaches to measurement in MT, and should provide the basis of development of new approaches that will allow researchers to be confident of the value of different MT technologies.

Acknowledgments

This work was funded by the Australian Research Council.

References

ALPAC. 1966. Languages and machines: Computers in translation and linguistics. A report by the Automatic Language Processing Advisory Committee, Division of Behavioral Sciences, National Academy of Sciences, National Research Council.

T. G. Armstrong, A. Moffat, W. Webber, and J. Zobel. 2009. Improvements that don't add up: Ad-hoc retrieval results since 1998. In *Proc. 18th ACM CIKM Int. Conf. on Information and Knowledge Management*, pages 601–610, Hong Kong, China, November.

O. Bojar, M. Ercegovčevic, M. Popel, and O. Zaidan. 2011. A grain of salt for the WMT manual evaluation. In *Proc. 6th Wkshp. Statistical Machine Translation*, pages 1–11, Edinburgh, Scotland. Assoc. Computational Linguistics.

F. Bond, K. Ogura, and S. Ikehara. 1995. Possessive pronouns as determiners in Japanese-to-English machine translation. In *Proc. 2nd Conf. Pacific Assoc. Computational Linguistics*, pages 32–38, Brisbane, Australia.

C. Callison-Burch, M. Osborne, and P. Koehn. 2006. Re-evaluating the role of BLEU in machine translation research. In *Proc. 11th Conf. European Chapter of the Assoc. Computational Linguistics*, pages 249–256, Trento, Italy, April. Assoc. for Computational Linguistics.

C. Callison-Burch, C. Fordyce, P. Koehn, C. Monz, and J. Schroeder. 2007. (Meta-) evaluation of machine translation. In *Proc. 2nd Wkshp. Statistical Machine Translation*, pages 136–158, Prague, Czech Republic. Assoc. Computational Linguistics.

C. Callison-Burch, C. Fordyce, P. Koehn, C. Monz, and J. Schroeder. 2008. Further meta-evaluation of machine translation. In *Proc. 3rd Wkshp. Statistical Machine Translation*, pages 70–106, Columbus, Ohio. Assoc. Computational Linguistics.

C. Callison-Burch, P. Koehn, C. Monz, and J. Schroeder. 2009. Findings of the 2009 Workshop on Statistical Machine Translation. In *Proc. 4th Wkshp. Statistical Machine Translation*, pages 1–28, Athens, Greece. Assoc. Computational Linguistics.

C. Callison-Burch, P. Koehn, C. Monz, K. Peterson, M. Przybocki, and O. Zaidan. 2010. Findings of the 2010 Joint Workshop on Statistical Machine Translation and Metrics for Machine Translation. In *Proc. 5th Wkshp. Statistical Machine Translation*, Uppsala, Sweden. Assoc. Computational Linguistics.

C. Callison-Burch, P. Koehn, C. Monz, and O. Zaidan. 2011. Findings of the 2011 Workshop on Statistical Machine Translation. In *Proc. 6th Wkshp. Statistical Machine Translation*, pages 22–64, Edinburgh, Scotland. Assoc. Computational Linguistics.

C. Callison-Burch, P. Koehn, C. Monz, M. Post, R. Soricut, and L. Specia. 2012. Findings of the 2012 Workshop on Statistical Machine Translation. In *Proc. 7th Wkshp. Statistical Machine Translation*, pages 10–51, Montreal, Canada, June. Assoc. Computational Linguistics.

D. T. Campbell and D. W. Fiske. 1959. Convergent and discriminant validation by the muultitrait-multimethod matrix. 56:81–105.

J. Cohen. 1960. A coefficient of agreement for nominal scales. *Educational and Psychological Measurement*, 20(1):37–46.

M. Denkowski and A. Lavie. 2010. Choosing the right evaluation for machine translation: an examination of annotator and automatic metric performance on human judgement tasks. In *Proc. 9th Conf. Assoc. Machine Translation in the Americas (AMTA)*.

S. Ikehara, S. Shirai, and K. Ogura. 1994. Criteria for evaluating the linguistic quality of Japanese to English machine translations. *J. Japanese Soc. Artificial Intelligence*, 9. (in Japanese).

P. Koehn and C. Monz. 2006. Manual and automatic evaluation of machine translation between european languages. In *Proc. Wkshp. Statistical Machine Translation*, pages 102–121.

LDC. 2005. Linguistic data annotation specification: Assessment of fluency and adequacy in translations. Technical report, Linguistic Data Consortium. Revision 1.5.

A. Lopez. 2012. Putting human machine translation systems in order. In *Proc. 7th Wkshp. Statistical Machine Translation*, pages 1–9, Montreal, Canada, June. Assoc. Computational Linguistics.

K. MacCorquodale and P.E. Meehl. 1948. On a distinction between hypothetical constructs and intervening variables. *Psychological Review*, 55(2):307–321.

K. Papineni, S. Roukos, T. Ward, and W.-J. Zhu. 2002. Bleu: A method for automatic evaluation of machine translation. In *Proc. 40th Ann. Meet. Assoc. Computational Linguistics*, pages 311–318, Philadelphia, PA, July. Assoc. Computational Linguistics.

M. Przybocki, K. Peterson, S. Bronsart, and G. Sanders. 2009. The NIST 2008 metrics for machine translation challenge – overview, methodology, metrics and results. *Machine Translation*, 23(2-3):71–103.

L. Schwartz, T. Aikawa, and C. Quirk. 2003. Disambiguation of English PP attachment using multilingual aligned data. In *Proc. 9th Machine Translation Summit (MT Summit IX)*, New Orleans, LA.

William M.K. Trochim. 1999. *The Research Methods Knowledge Base*. Cornell University Custom Publishing, Ithaca, New York.

E. M. Voorhees and D. K. Harman. 2005. *TREC: Experiment and evaluation in information retrieval*. MIT Press, Cambridge, MA.

J. S. White, T. O'Connell, and F. O'Mara. 1994. The ARPA MT evaluation methodologies: Evolution, lessons, and future approaches. In *Proc. 1st Conf. Assoc. for Machine Translation in the Americas (AMTA'94)*, pages 193–205.

Towards Two-step Multi-document Summarisation for Evidence Based Medicine: A Quantitative Analysis

Abeed Sarker , Diego Mollá-Aliod
Centre for Language Technology
Macquarie University
Sydney, NSW 2109
{abeed.sarker, diego.molla-aliod}@mq.edu.au

Cécile Paris
CSIRO – ICT Centre
Sydney, NSW 2122
cecile.paris@csiro.au

Abstract

We perform a quantitative analysis of data in a corpus that specialises on summarisation for Evidence Based Medicine (EBM). The intent of the analysis is to discover possible directions for performing automatic evidence-based summarisation. Our analysis attempts to ascertain the extent to which good, evidence-based, multi-document summaries can be obtained from individual single-document summaries of the source texts. We define a set of scores, which we call *coverage scores*, to estimate the degree of information overlap between the multi-document summaries and source texts of various granularities. Based on our analysis, using several variants of the *coverage scores*, and the results of a simple task oriented evaluation, we argue that approaches for the automatic generation of evidence-based, bottom-line, multi-document summaries may benefit by utilising a two-step approach: in the first step, content-rich, single-document, query-focused summaries are generated; followed by a step to synthesise the information from the individual summaries.

1 Introduction

Automatic summarisation is the process of presenting the important information contained in a source text in a compressed format. Such approaches have important applications in domains where lexical resources are abundant and users face the problem of information overload. One such domain is the medical domain, with the largest online database (PubMed[1]) containing over 21 million published medical articles. Thus, a standard clinical query on this database returns numerous results, which are extremely time-consuming to read and analyse manually. This is a major obstacle to the practice of Evidence Based Medicine (EBM), which requires practitioners to refer to relevant published medical research when attempting to answer clinical queries. Research has shown that practitioners require botom-line evidence-based answers at point of care, but often fail to obtain them because of time constraints (Ely et al., 1999).

[1]http://www.ncbi.nlm.nih.gov/pubmed

1.1 Motivation

Due to the problems associated with the practise of EBM, there is a strong motivation for automatic summarisation/question-answering (QA) systems that can aid practitioners. While automatic text summarisation research in other domains (e.g., news) has made significant advances, research in the medical domain is still at an early stage. This can be attributed to various factors: (i) the process of answer generation for EBM requires practitioners to combine their own expertise with medical evidence, and automatic systems are only capable of summarising content present in the source texts; (ii) the medical domain is very complex with a large number of domain specific terminologies and relationships between the terms that systems need to take into account when performing summarisation; and (iii) while there is an abundance of medical documents available electronically, specialised corpora for performing summarisation research in this domain are scarce.

1.2 Contribution

We study a corpus that specialises on the task of summarisation for EBM and quantitatively analyse the contents of human generated evidence-based summaries. We compare bottom-line evidence-based summaries to source texts and human-generated, query-focused, single-document summaries of the source texts. This enables us to determine if good single-document summaries contain sufficient content, from source texts, to be used for the generation of multi-document, bottom-line summaries. We also study single-document extractive summaries generated by various summarisation systems and compare their performance relative to source texts and human generated summaries. In terms of content, our experiments reveal that there is no statistically significant difference between the source texts and the human-generated, single-document summaries, relative to the bottom-line summaries. This suggests that that the generation of bottom-line summaries *may be* considered to be a two step summarisation process in which the first step is single-document summarisation, and the second step involves information synthesis from the summaries, as illustrated in Figure 1. In the figure, d represents a source document, s represents a summary of a source document, and b represents a bottom-line summary generated from multiple single-document summaries.

In addition to this analysis, we attempt to make *estimations* about the extent to which the core contents of the bottom-line summaries come from the source texts. Such an analysis is of paramount importance in this domain because, if only a small proportion of the summaries contain information from the source articles, we can assume that the summaries are almost entirely generated from specialised human knowledge, making it impossible to perform text-to-text summarisation automatically in this domain without intensive use of domain-specific knowledge. We conclude that there is sufficient overlap between the source texts and evidence-based summaries for the process to be automated. Our analysis is purely numerical and is based on various statistics computed from the available corpus.

The rest of the paper is organised as follows: Section 2 presents a brief overview of research work related to ours; Section 3 provides a description of the corpus we study; Section 4 details our analytical techniques; Section 5 presents the results we obtain, along with a discussion; and Section 6 concludes the paper and provides a brief discussion of our planned future work.

2 Related Work

2.1 Evidence Based Medicine

There is a good amount of published work on EBM practice, which is defined by Sackett et al. (1996) as *"the conscientious, explicit, and judicious use of current best evidence in making decisions about the care of individual patients"*. The goal of EBM is to improve the quality of patient

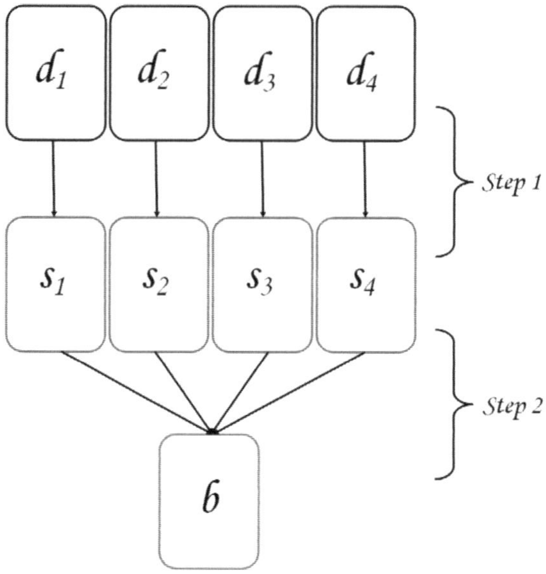

Figure 1: The two-step summarisation process.

care in the long run through the identification of practices that work, and the elimination of ineffective or harmful ones (Selvaraj et al., 2010). The necessity of searching for, appraising, and synthesising evidence makes EBM practice time-consuming. Research has shown that practitioners generally spend about 2 minutes to search for evidence (Ely et al., 2000). Consequently, practitioners often fail to provide evidence-based answers to clinical queries, particularly at point of care (Ely et al., 1999; Ely et al., 2002). The research findings strongly motivate the need for end-to-end medical text summarisation systems.

2.2 Summarisation for EBM

As already mentioned, the task of automatic text summarisation is particularly challenging for the medical domain because of the vast amount of domain-specific knowledge required (Lin and Demner-Fushman, 2007) and the highly complex domain-specific terminologies and semantic relationships (Athenikos and Han, 2009). Text processing systems in this domain generally use the Unified Medical Language System (UMLS)[2], which is a repository of biomedical vocabularies developed by the US National Library of Medicine. It covers over 1 million biomedical concepts and terms from various vocabularies, semantic categories for the concepts and both hier-

[2]http://www.nlm.nih.gov/research/umls/

archical and non-hierarchical relationships among the concepts (Aronson, 2001). In the UMLS vocabulary, each medical concept is represented using a *Concept Unique Identifier (CUI)*. Related concepts are grouped into generic categories called *semantic types*. Our analysis heavily relies on the CUIs and semantic types of medical terms.

There has been some progress in research for EBM text summarisation (i.e., query-focused summarisation of published medical texts) in recent years. Lin and Demner-Fushman (2007) showed the use of knowledge-based and statistical techniques in summary generation. Their summarisation system relies on the classification of text nuggets into various categories, including *Outcome*, and presents the sentences categorised as *outcomes* as the final summary. Niu et al. (2005, 2006) presented the EPoCare[3] system. The summarisation component of this system performs sentence-level polarity classification to determine if a sentence presents a positive, negative or neutral outcome. Polarised sentences are extracted to be part of the final summary. Shi et al. (2007) presented the BioSquash system that performs query-focused, extractive summarisation through the generation of text graphs and the identification of important groups of concepts from the graphs to be included in the final summaries. More recently, Cao et al. (2011) proposed the AskHermes[4] system that performs multi-document summarisation via key-word identification and clustering of information. The generated summaries are extracted, paragraph-like text segments. Sarker et al. (2012) showed the use of a specialised corpus to perform evidence-based summarisation. In their recent approach, the authors introduce target-sentence-specific, extractive, single-document summarisation, and use various statistics derived from the corpus to rank sentences for extraction. All these systems, however, have limitations. Inspired by this fact, our analyses attempt to test if automatic summairsation is in fact possible for EBM. We also attempt to identify possible summarisation approaches that are likely to be effective in this domain.

[3]http://www.cs.toronto.edu/km/epocare/index.html
[4]http://www.askhermes.org/

2.3 Evaluation and Analysis of Summarisation Systems

The most important research related to automatic evaluation of summarisation systems is perhaps that by Lin and Hovy (2003) . The authors propose a set of metrics called Recall-Oriented Understudy for Gisting Evaluation (ROUGE) that have become very much the standard for automatic summary evaluation. The intent of the ROUGE measures is to find the similarity between automatically generated summaries and reference summaries and it has been shown that ROUGE scores of summaries have a high correlation with human evaluations. We incorporate some ROUGE statistics in our analysis.

ROUGE has also been used for analysis tasks in automatic text summarisation, such as the analysis of extractive summarisation provided by Ceylan et al. (2011) . The authors use ROUGE to show that the combination of all possible extractive summaries follow a long-tailed gaussian distribution, causing most summarisation systems to achieve scores that are generally close to the mean and making it difficult for systems to achieve very high scores. This analysis of extractive summaries has opened a new direction for relative comparison of summarisation systems and the approach has been used in recent work (Sarker et al., 2012). Another recent analysis work on text summarisation, similar to the one we present here, is that by Louis and Nenkova (2011), who show that human-generated summaries generally contain a large proportion of generic content along with specific content. From the perspective of our research, this means that some of the disagreement between different summarisers, in terms of content, may be attributed to dissimilar generic (stylistic) content that are not contained in the source documents, rather than dissimilar query-specific content.

3 Data

3.1 Corpus

The corpus we study (Mollá-Aliod and Santiago-Martinez, 2011) was created from the Journal of Family Practice[5] (JFP). The 'Clinical Inquiries' section of the JFP contains clinical queries and evidence-based answers from real-life EBM practice, and the corpus was built from the information in this section. The corpus consists of a set

[5]www.jfponline.com

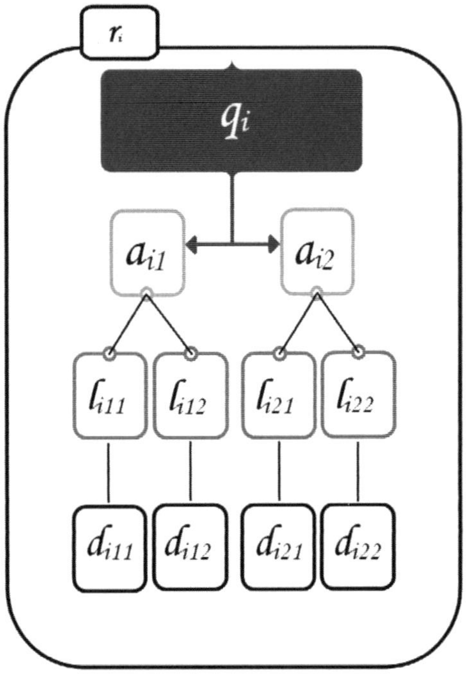

Figure 2: Structure of a sample record the corpus.

of records, $R = \{r_1 ... r_m\}$. Each record, r_i, contains one clinical query, q_i, so that we have a set of questions $Q = \{q_1 ... q_m\}$. Each r_i has associated with it a set of one or more bottom-line answers to the query, $A_i = \{a_{i1} ... a_{in}\}$. For each bottom-line answer of r_i, a_{ij}, there exists a set of human-authored detailed justifications (single-document summaries) $L_{ij} = \{l_{ij1} ... l_{ijo}\}$. Each detailed justification in turn l_{ijk} is associated with at least one source document d_{ijk}. Thus, the corpus has a set of source documents, which we denote as $D = \{d_{ij1} ... d_{ijo}\}$.

For the work described in this paper, we use the sets A, L and D from the corpus. Figure 2 visually illustrates a sample record from the corpus with two bottom-line summaries associated with the query. We analyse a total of 1,279 bottom-line summaries, associated with 456 queries, along with source texts and human summaries.

4 Methods

4.1 Coverage Analysis

Our first analytical experiments attempt to estimate the extent to which information in the set of bottom-line summaries, A, are contained in the source documents, D_a, associated with each summary (a). This gives us a measure of the extent to which extra information are added to the final summaries by the authors of the JFP articles from which the corpus has been built. For this, we define a set of scores, which we call *coverage scores*. The greater the score, the better is the bottom-line summary coverage. Consider a bottom-line summary a, which contains a set of m terms, and the associated source documents, D_a. The first variant of the coverage scores that we use is a term-based measure and is given by the following equation:

$$Coverage(a, D_a) = \frac{|a \cap D_a|}{m} \quad (1)$$

where $|a \cap D_a|$ represents the number of terms common to a summary and the associated source texts. We first preprocess the text by removing stop words and punctuations, lowercasing all terms and stemming the terms using the Porter stemmer (Porter, 1980). Term tokenisation is performed using the *word tokeniser* of the nltk[6] toolbox. Such a term-level coverage measurement, however, often fails to identify matches in the case of medical concepts that may be represented by multiple distinct terms. An example of this is the term *high blood pressure*. In our corpus, this term has various other representations including *hypertension* and *hbp*.

4.1.1 Incorporation of CUIs and Semantic Types

To address the problem of distinct lexical representations of the same concepts, we identify the semantic types and CUIs of all the terms in the corpus and incorporate this information in our coverage computation. Using CUIs in the computation reduces the dependence on direct string matching because distinct terms representing the same medical concept have the same CUI. For example, all the different variants of the term *high blood pressure* have the same CUI (C0020538). However, it is also possible for terms with different CUIs to have the same underlying meaning in our corpus. For example, the terms [African] women (CUI: C0043210) and African Americans (CUI:C008575) have different CUIs but have been used to represent the same population group. The two terms have the same UMLS semantic type: popg (population group) and this information may be used to match the two terms in our experiments.

[6]nltk.org

We use the MetaMap[7] tool to automatically identify the CUIs and semantic types for all the text in our corpus.

We introduce two more variants of the coverage scores. In our first variation, we use individual terms and CUIs; and in the second variation we use terms, CUIs and semantic types. We apply a sequence of functions that, given a and D_a, along with the CUIs and semantic types of the terms in a and D_a, compute $a \cap D_a$ utilising all the available information (i.e., terms, CUIs, semantic types). Term-based matching is first performed and the terms in a that are exactly matched by terms in D_a are collected. Next, for the unmatched terms in a, CUI matching is performed with the CUIs of D_a. This ensures that different lexical versions of the same concept are detected correctly. All the matched terms are added to the covered terms collection. In our first variant, this value is used for $|a \cap D_a|$ in equation 1. For the second variant, for terms that are still uncovered after CUI matching, semantic type matching is performed and the terms in a with matching semantic types are added to the covered terms collection before computing the coverage score.

A problem with the use of semantic types in coverage score computation is that they are too generic and often produce incorrect matches. For example, the terms *pneumonia* and *heart failure* are two completely distinct concepts but have the same semantic type (*dsyn*). The use of semantic types, therefore, leads to incorrect matches, resulting in high coverage scores. We still use semantic types along with terms and CUIs in our experiments because their coverage scores give an idea of the coverage upper limits.

4.1.2 Concept Coverage

In an attempt to reduce the number of non-medical terms in our coverage score computation, we introduce a fourth varaint to our coverage scores which we call *Concept Coverage* (CC). We noticed that often non-medical terms such as entities, numbers etc. are the primary causes of mismatch among different terms. This coverage score only takes into account the concepts (CUIs) in a and D_a. Referring to equation 1, m in this case represents the number of unique CUIs in a, while $|a \cap D_a|$ is computed as a combination of direct CUI matches and similarity measures among unmatched CUIs. That is, besides considering direct matches between CUIs, we also consider *similarities* among concepts when performing this calculation. This is important because often bottom-line summaries contain generic terms representing the more specific concepts in the source texts (e.g., the generic term *anti-depressant* in the bottom-line summary to represent *paroxetine*, *amitriptyline* and so on). The concept similarity between two concepts gives a measure of their *semantic relatedness* or how *close* two concepts are within a specific domain or ontology (Budanitsky and Hirst, 2006).

In our concept coverage computation, each CUI in a receives a score of 1.0 if it has an exact match with the CUIs in D_a. For each unmatched CUI in a, its concept similarity value with each unmatched concept in D_a is computed and the *maximum similarity* value is chosen as the score for that concept. To compute the similarity between two concepts, we use the similarity measure proposed by Jiang and Conrath (1997). The authors apply a corpus-based method that works in conjunction with lexical taxonomies to calculate semantic similarities between terms, and the approach has been shown to agree well with human judgements. We use the implementation provided by McInnes et al. (2009), and scale the scores so that they fall within the range [0.0,1.0), with 0.0 indicating no match and 0.99 representing near perfect match (theoretically). The direct match score or *maximum similarity* score of each CUI in a are added and divided by m to give the final concept coverage score.

4.1.3 Comparison of Coverage Scores

Our intent is to determine the extent to which the contents of the bottom-line summaries in the corpus are contained in source texts of different granularities. This gives us an estimate of the information loss that occurs when source text is compressed by various compression factors. More specifically, in our experiments, a (in equation 1) is always the bottom-line summary, while for D_a, we use:

i all the text from all the article abstracts associated with a (FullAbs),

ii all the text from all the human-generated, single-document summaries (from L) (HS),

iii all the text from all the *ideal* three-sentence

[7] http://metamap.nlm.nih.gov/

extractive summaries associated with a (IdealSum),

iv all the text from all the single document, three-sentence extractive summaries, produced by a state of the art summarisation system (Sarker et al., 2012), associated with a, and

v all the text from random three sentence extractive single document summaries associated with a (Random).

The IdealSum summaries are three-sentence, single-document, extractive summaries that have the highest ROUGE-L *f-scores* (Lin and Hovy, 2003; Lin, 2004) when compared with the human generated single document summaries (*l*)[8]. Using these five different sets enables us to estimate the degradation, if any, in coverage scores as the source text is compressed. Table 1 presents the coverage scores for these five data sets along with the concept coverage scores for (i) and (ii)[9].

For each data set, we also compute their ROUGE-L recall scores (after stemming and stop word removal) with the bottom-line summaries, and compare these scores. This enables us to compare the voerage of these data sets using another metric. Table 2 shows the recall scores along with the 95% confidence intervals.

4.2 Task Oriented Evaluation

To establish some estimates about the performances of these variants of the source texts, we performed simple task oriented evaluations. The evaluations required annotation of the data, which is extremely time-consuming. Therefore, we used a subset of the corpus for this task. We manually identified 33 questions from the corpus that focus on 'drug treatments for diseases/syndromes'. All the questions are of the generic form: *'What is the best drug treatment for disease X?'*. Given a question, the task for the system is to identify drug candidates for the disease from the source texts.

From the bottom-line summaries for each of the 33 questions, we manually collected the list of all mentioned drug interventions. Using these, we measured a system's performance by computing its recall for the drug interventions. Our intent, in fact, is not to evaluate the performances of different systems. Instead, it is to evaluate the performances of different source texts on the same task. To extract drug candidates from text, the system relies fully on the MetaMap system's annotation of the data set. All terms identified as *drugs* or *chemicals*[10] are extracted by the system and returned as a list. Recall and precision for each type of source text is computed from this list of drug names.

Using this technique we evaluate the performance of the five previously mentioned source texts. The recall for the FullAbs set acts as the upper limit and this evaluation enables us to determine how much information is lost when the source texts are summarised either manually or automatically. The performance of the Random data set indicates the lower limit. The results of this experiment are presented in the next section.

System	T	T & C	T, C & ST	CC
FullAbs	0.596	0.643	0.782	0.659
HS	0.595	0.630	0.737	0.644
IdealSum	0.468	0.511	0.654	..
Sarker et al.	0.502	0.546	0.683	..
Random	0.403	0.451	0.594	..

Table 1: Coverage scores for the five data sets with the bottom-line summaries. T = Terms, C = CUIs, ST = Semantic Types, and CC = Concept Coverage.

System	Recall	95% CI
FullAbs	0.418	0.40 - 0.44
HS	0.405	0.39 - 0.42
IdealSum	0.284	0.27 - 0.30
Sarker et al.	0.318	0.30 - 0.34
Random	0.229	0.21 - 0.24

Table 2: ROUGE-1 recall scoresand 95% confidence intervals for the five data sets with the bottom-line summaries.

5 Results and Discussion

Table 1 shows that, when terms and CUIs are used, the source texts cover approximately 65% of the summary texts, and incorporation of se-

[8]These summaries were produced by generating all three-sentence combinations for each source text, and then computing the ROUGE-L f-score for each combination.

[9]We only compute the concept coverage scores for these two sets because of the extremely long running time of our similarity measurement algorithm.

[10]The semantic types included in these two categories are: aapp, antb, hops, horm, nnon, orch, phsu, strd, vita, bacs, carb, eico, elii, enzy, imft, inch, lipd nsba, opco. A list of the current UMLS semantic types can be found at: www.nlm.nih.gov/research/umls/

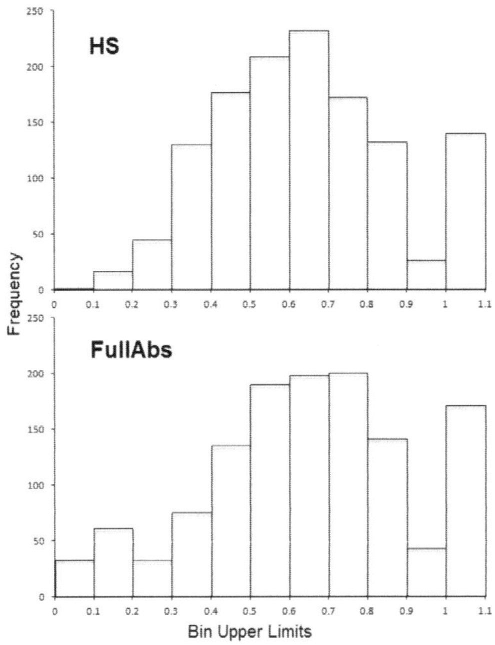

Figure 3: Distributions for concept coverage scores.

mantic types takes the coverage score to close to 80%. The concept coverage scores are similar to the term and CUI overlap scores. Analysis of the *uncovered* components reveal a number of reasons behind coverage mismatches. First of all, as already metioned earlier in this paper, authors often prefer using generalised medical terms in the bottom-line summaries while the source texts contain more specific terms (e.g., *antibiotics vs penicillin*). Incorporating semantic types ensures coverage in such cases, but also leads to false matches. Secondly, MetaMap has a relatively low word sense disambiguation accuracy (Plaza et al., 2011) and often fails to disambiguate terms correctly, causing variants of the same term to have different CUIs, and often different semantic types. Thirdly, a large portion of the uncovered components consists of text that improves the qualitative aspects of the summaries and do not represent important content. Considering the analysis presented by Louis and Nenkova (2011), it is no surprise that the texts of all granularities contain a significant amount of generic information, which may be added or lost during summarisation.

Interestingly, Table 1 reveals that the human generated single-document summaries have almost identical coverage scores to full source articles. Figure 3 shows the distributions of the con-

	T	T & C	CC
z	-1.5	-1.27	-1.33
p-value (2-tail)	0.13	0.20	0.16

Table 3: z and p-values for Wilcoxon rank sum tests.

cept coverage scores for the two sets, and it can be seen that the distributions are very similar. The coverage scores obtained by the two summarisation systems (IdealSum and Sarker et al.) also have high coverage scores compared to the Random summaries.

Table 2 shows that the ROUGE-L recall scores are also very similar for the HS and FullAbs data sets and lie within each other's 95% confidence intervals, indicating that there is no statistically significant difference between the contents of the HS and FullAbs sets.

To verify if the difference in the coverage scores between the HS and FullAbs sets are statistically significant, we perform statistical significance tests for the two pairs of coverage scores. Due to the paired nature of the data, we perform the Wilcoxon rank sum test with the null hypothesis that the coverage scores for the two sets are the same ($\mu_0 = 0$). Table 3 shows the z and p-values for the tests performed for the term, term and CUI and concept coverage scores for the HS and FullAbs sets. In all cases $p > 0.05$, meaning that we cannot reject the null hypothesis. Therefore, the difference in the two sets of coverage scores are not statistically significant. This adds further evidence to the hypothesis that single document summaries may contain sufficient content for bottom-line summary generation. This, in turn, strengthens our claim that the generation of bottom-line summaries by humans *may be* considered to be a two step process, in which the first step involves summarising individual documents, based on the information needs of queries, and the second step synthesises information from the individual summaries.

The compression factors (CF) in Table 4 show the relative compression rates required for the various source texts to generate the bottom-line summaries. It can be seen that generating bottom-line summaries from original source texts require approximately 5 times more compression compared to the generation from single document summaries, suggesting that the single document

System	Recall (%)	Precision (%)	CF
FullAbs	77	41	0.05
HS	75	68	0.26
IdealSum	66	48	0.20
Sarker et al.	68	45	0.15
Random	52	35	0.21

Table 4: Task oriented evaluation results and summary compression factors (CF) for the five sets of source texts.

summaries contain important information from the source texts in a much compressed manner. Thus, for a summarisation system that focuses on generating bottom-line summaries, it is perhaps better to use single document summaries as input rather than whole source texts, as the information in the source texts are generally very noisy. Considering the balance between coverage scores and compression factors of IdealSum and Sarker et al., such content-rich automatic summaries may prove to be better inputs for the generation of bottom-line summaries than original texts.

Table 4 also presents the drug name recall and precision values for the five source text sets from the task-oriented evaluation. The relative recall-based performances of the different source text sets closely resemble their coverage scores. The performance of the HS summaries is almost identical to the FullAbs system, and the systems IdealSum and Sarker et al. are close behind. Primary reasons for drops in recall are the use of generic terms in bottom-line summaries, as already discussed, and errors made by MetaMap. For the former problem, automatic summarisation systems such as IdealSum and Sarker et al. suffer the most, as the articles in the FullAbs set generally contain the generic terms (e.g., antibiotic) and also the specific terms (e.g., penicillin). However, the compressed versions of the source texts, in the IdealSum and Sarker et al. sets, only the specific terms tend to occur. Importantly, the low precision score for the FullAbs set illustrates the high amount of noise present. The precision scores for the HS set and the two summarisation systems are higher than the FullAbs set, indicating that selective compression of the source text may help to efficiently remove noise.

6 Conclusions and Future Work

We performed analyses on a corpus that is specialised for automatic evidence-based summarisation. Our intent was to analyse the extent to which: (i) information in the bottom-line summaries are directly contained in the source texts; and, (ii) good, evidence-based, multi-document summaries can be obtained from individual single-document summaries of the source texts. We applied various statistics from the corpus to ascertain the difference in content among source texts and summaries of the source texts.

Our analyses show that human summarisers rely significantly on information from published research when generating bottom-line evidence-based summaries. This is demonstrated by the coverage scores presented in the previous section and the manual analysis following it. This indicates that, content-wise, it is possible to generate summaries for EBM automatically in a text-to-text manner. Our experiments also show that human-generated single-document summaries contain approximately the same relevant information as the source texts but in a much more compressed format. This suggests that, for generating bottom-line summaries, it might be a good idea to apply a two-step summarisation. The first step involves single-document, query-focused summarisation. The second step, which is dependent on the output of the first step, performs further summarisation of the already compressed source texts to generate bottom-line answers. For such an approach, it is essential that the first step produces content-rich, high precision summaries. With the advent of new, efficient, single-document summarisation systems in this domain, a multi-step summarisation system has the potential of producing very good results.

Future work will focus on performing more comprehensive task-oriented experiments using these different datasets to evaluate their usefulness in the summarisation task. We will also attempt to develop a two-step summarisation system and compare its performance with other state of the art summarisation systems in this domain.

Acknowledgements

This research is jointly funded by Macquarie University and CSIRO. The authors would like to thank the anonymous reviewers for their valuable comments.

References

Alan R. Aronson. 2001. Effective mapping of biomedical text to the umls metathesaurus: The metamap program. In *Proceedings of the AMIA Annual Symposium*, pages 17–21.

Sofia J. Athenikos and Hyoil Han. 2009. Biomedical question answering: A survey. *Computer Methods and Programs in Biomedicine*, pages 1–24.

Alexander Budanitsky and Graeme Hirst. 2006. Evaluating WordNet-based Measures of Lexical Semantic Relatedness. *Computational Linguistics*, 32(1):13–47.

John W. Ely, Jerome A. Osheroff, Mark H. Ebell, George R. Bergus, Barcey T. Levy, Lee M. Chambliss, and Eric R. Evans. 1999. Analysis of questions asked by family doctors regarding patient care. *BMJ*, 319(7206):358–361.

John W. Ely, Jerome A. Osheroff, Paul Gorman, Mark H. Ebell, Lee M. Chambliss, Eric Pifer, and Zoe Stavri. 2000. A taxonomy of generic clinical questions: classification study. *BMJ*, 321:429–432.

John W. Ely, Jerome A. Osheroff, Mark H. Ebell, Lee M. Chambliss, DC Vinson, James J. Stevermer, and Eric A. Pifer. 2002. Obstacles to answering doctors' questions about patient care with evidence: Qualitative study. *BMJ*, 324(7339):710–716.

Jay J. Jiang and David W. Conrath. 1997. Semantic similarity based on corpus statistics and lexical taxonomy. In *Proceedings on International Conference on Research in Computational Linguistics*, pages pp. 19–33.

Jimmy J. Lin and Dina Demner-Fushman. 2007. Answering clinical questions with knowledge-based and statistical techniques. *Computational Linguistics*, 33(1):63–103.

Chin-Yew Lin and Eduard Hovy. 2003. Automatic Evaluation of Summaries Using N-gram Co-occurrence Statistics. In *Proceedings of HLT-NAACL 2003*, pages 71–78.

Chin-Yew Lin. 2004. Rouge: A package for automatic evaluation of summaries. In *Proceedings of NAACL-HLT 2004*, pages 74–81.

Annie Louis and Ani Nenkova. 2011. Text specificity and impact on quality of news summaries. In *Proceedings of the Workshop on Monolingual Text-To-Text Generation*, pages 34–42.

Bridget T. McInnes, Ted Pedersen, and Serguei V. S. Pakhomov. 2009. UMLS-Interface and UMLS-Similarity : Open Source Software for Measuring Paths and Semantic Similarity. In *Proceedings of the AMIA Annual Symposium 2009*, pages 431–435.

Diego Mollá-Aliod and Maria Elena Santiago-Martinez. 2011. Development of a Corpus for Evidence Based Medicine Summarisation. In *Proceedings of the Australasian Language Technology Association Workshop 2011*, pages 86–94.

Yun Niu, Xiaodan Zhu, Jianhua Li, and Graeme Hirst. 2005. Analysis of polarity information in medical text. In *Proceedings of the AMIA Annual Symposium*, pages 570–574.

Yun Niu, Xiaodan Zhu, and Graeme Hirst. 2006. Using outcome polarity in sentence extraction for medical question-answering. In *Proceedings of the AMIA Annual Symposium*, pages 599–603.

Laura Plaza, Antonio Jimeno-Yepes, Alberto Diaz, and Alan Aronson. 2011. Studying the correlation between different word sense disambiguation methods and summarization effectiveness in biomedical texts. *BMC Bioinformatics*, 12(1):355–368.

Martin F. Porter. 1980. An algorithm for suffix stripping. *Program*, 14(3):130–137.

David L Sackett, William M C Rosenberg, J A Muir Gray, R Brian Haynes, and W Scott Richardson. 1996. Evidence based medicine: what it is and what it isn't. *BMJ*, 312(7023):71–72.

Abeed Sarker, Diego Mollá, and Cecile Paris. 2012. Extractive Evidence Based Medicine Summarisation Based on Sentence-Specific Statistics. In *Proceedings of the 25th IEEE International Symposium on CBMS*, pages 1–4.

Sanchaya Selvaraj, Yeshwant Kumar, Elakiya, Prarthana Saraswathi, Balaji, Nagamani, and SuraPaneni Krishna Mohan. 2010. Evidence-based medicine - a new approach to teach medicine: a basic review for beginners. *Biology and Medicine*, 2(1):1–5.

Zhongmin Shi, Gabor Melli, Yang Wang, Yudong Liu, Baohua Gu, Mehdi M. Kashani, Anoop Sarkar, and Fred Popowich. 2007. Question answering summarization of multiple biomedical documents. In *Proceedings of the 20th Canadian Conference on Aritificial Intelligence (CanAI '07)*.

Yonggang Cao and Feifan Liu and Pippa Simpson and Lamont D. Antieau and Andrew Bennett and James J. Cimino and John W. Ely and Hong Yu. 2011. AskHermes: An Online Question Answering System for Complex Clinical Questions. *Journal of Biomedical Informatics*, 44(2):277 – 288.

In Your Eyes: Identifying Clichés in Song Lyrics

Alex G. Smith, Christopher X. S. Zee and Alexandra L. Uitdenbogerd
School of Computer Science and Information Technology, RMIT University
GPO Box 2476V, Melbourne 3001, Australia

alex.geoffrey.smith@gmail.com xiashing@gmail.com sandrau@rmit.edu.au

Abstract

We investigated methods for the discovery of clichés from song lyrics. Trigrams and rhyme features were extracted from a collection of lyrics and ranked using term-weighting techniques such as tf-idf. These attributes were also examined over both time and genre. We present an application to produce a cliché score for lyrics based on these findings and show that number one hits are substantially more clichéd than the average published song.

1 Credits

2 Introduction

Song lyrics can be inspiring, moving, energetic and heart wrenching pieces of modern poetry. Other times, we find lyrics to be boring and uninspired, or *clichéd*. Some lyricists may aim to write truly original lyrics, while others are after a number one on the charts. The authors of *The Manual* (Drummond and Cauty, 1988), who have several hits to their credit, state that to succeed in achieving a number one hit one needs to "stick to the clichés" because "they deal with the emotional topics we all feel".

Despite dictionary definitions, it isn't easy to pinpoint what is cliché and what isn't. Dillon (2006) explains that linguists tend to prefer the term *idiom* or *fixed expression*. He also points out the subjective nature of the decision as to whether a phrase is a cliché, illustrating this with some frequently used phrases that are not considered clichéd, and other phrases such as 'armed to the teeth' that are, despite their relative infrequent appearance within corpora.

There is also a temporal component to whether something is cliché, since an expression would not be considered cliché on its first use, but only after widespread adoption. For song lyrics, clichés can arise due to the perceived need to make rhymes. Some words have limited possibilities for rhyme, and so using exact rhyme makes cliché more likely. Early songwriters believed that a good song must have perfect rhyme in its lyrics. However, recent thought is that alternatives, such as assonance and additive or subtractive rhymes, are valid alternatives in order to avoid clichéd writing (Pattison, 1991).

In this paper we use an information retrieval approach to defining what is clichéd in song lyrics, by using human judgements. We use statistical measures to build ranked lists of clichéd trigrams and rhymes, then combine these results to produce an overall cliché score for a song's lyrics. A simple count of the occurrences of terms in song lyrics, ranked according to frequency is likely to produce generic common phrases rather than lyric-specific terms. Therefore we investigated means of detecting typical rhymes and phrases in lyrics using a term-weighting technique. We examined trends in these attributes over musical genre and time. Using our results, we developed a cliché score for song lyrics.

The remainder of this paper is structured as follows: first, we discuss related work, then describe the data collection and preparation process. Next, our rhyme and collocation techniques and results are shown. Finally, we present our application for cliché scoring.

3 Related Work

There are several areas of research that are relevant to our topic, such as other studies of lyrics, analysis of text, and work on rhyme. However, we have not found any work specifically on identifying clichés in either songs or other works.

Song lyrics have previously been studied for a variety of applications, including determining artist similarity (Logan et al., 2005), genre classification (Mayer et al., 2008) and topic detection (Kleedorfer et al., 2008). Whissell (1996) combined traditional stylometric measures with a technique for emotional description in order to successfully differentiate between lyrics written by Beatles Paul McCartney and John Lennon. In addition, several studies have recently appeared for retrieving songs based on misheard lyrics (Ring and Uitdenbogerd, 2009; Xu et al., 2009; Hirjee and Brown, 2010b).

Rhyme in poetry has been studied statistically for many years (for example a study of Shakespeare and Swinburne (Skinner, 1941)). More recently Hirjee and Brown (2009) (Hirjee, 2010) introduced a probabilistic scoring model to identify rhymes in song lyrics based on prior study of the complex rhyme strategies found in Hip-Hop. They define a normal or 'perfect' rhyme as 'two syllables that share the same nucleus (vowel) and coda (ending consonants). They found this method more accurate than rule-based methods and developed a *Rhyme Analyzer* application based upon their model (Hirjee and Brown, 2010a).

In our work, we considered the use of collocation extraction for finding words that frequently appear together in lyrics. Smadja (1993) described several techniques for collocation extraction and implemented these in the *Xtract* tool. The precision of this tool is tested on a corpus of stock market reports and found to be 80% accurate. Lin (1998) defined a method for retrieving two word collocations using a broad coverage parser and applied this to compute word similarties. Word n-grams have been used elsewhere as features for authorship attribution of text (Pillay and Solorio, 2011; Koppel et al., 2009), and source code (Burrows et al., 2009).

Genre	Proportion
Rock	24.70%
Hip-Hop	21.63%
Punk	13.09%
World	11.17%
Electronic	10.15%
Metal	7.00%
Pop	3.58%
Alternative	3.57%
Other	2.97%
Folk	2.12%

Table 1: Genre distribution of lyrics.

4 Experiments

Our aim was to detect and measure clichés in song lyrics. In normal text, clichés are likely to be stock phrases, such as "par for the course". Frequently used phrases can be found by looking at n-grams or collocated terms in text. The second source of cliché in song lyrics arises from rhyme pairs. Due to the typical subject matter of pop songs, and the tendency toward perfect rhyme use, particular rhyme pairs are likely to be common.

Our approach was to obtain a large collection of song lyrics, observe the effect of different formulations for ranking rhyme pairs and collocated terms, then create a cliché measure for songs based on the most promising ranking formulae. These were to be evaluated with human judgements.

4.1 Lyrics Collection

The collection was composed of a subset of lyrics gathered from online lyrics database LyricWiki[1] using a web crawler. Song title and artist meta-data were also retrieved. All lyrics were converted to lower case and punctuation removed. Digits between one and ten were replaced with their written equivalent. Duplicate lyrics were found to be a problem, for example the song 'A-OK' by 'Face to Face' was submitted three times under different names as 'A.O.K', 'A-Ok' and 'AOK'. Variations between lyrics included case, punc-

[1] http://lyrics.wikia.com

R	F(Lyrics)	F(Gutenberg)	tf-idf
1	be me	the a	baby me
2	go know	an man	real feel
3	away day	there very	be me
4	day way	than an	go know
5	way say	very their	tonight right
6	baby me	manner an	right night
7	you to	to you	apart heart
8	right night	pretty little	heart start
9	away say	cannot an	away day
10	real feel	then again	soul control
11	night light	any then	la da
12	away stay	their there	good hood
13	day say	anything any	night tight
14	town down	man than	away say
15	head dead	the of	away stay

Table 2: Top fifteen rhyme pairs ranked by frequency and tf-idf.

tuation and white space. Removing these distinctions allowed us to identify and discard many duplicates. This process resulted in a collection of 39,236 items by 1847 artists.

As our focus was on English lyrics, therefore the world music items were also discarded, removing the majority of foreign language lyrics. This reduced our collection to 34,855 items by 1590 artists.

4.2 Genre distribution

Using collected meta-data, we were able to query music statistics website last.fm[2] to determine the genre of each artist. We considered the top three genre tags for each and performed a broad general categorisation of each. This was done by checking if the artist was tagged as one of our pre-defined genres. If not, we checked the tags against a list of subgenres; for example 'thrash metal' was classified as 'metal' and 'house' fit into 'electronic' music. This resulted in the genre distribution shown in Table 1.

4.3 Lyric Attributes

In order to find typical rhymes and phrases, we applied the term-weighting scheme *tf-idf* (Salton and Buckley, 1988) to our collection. As a bag-of-words approach, tf-idf considers terms with no regard to the order in which they appear in a document. The objective of this scheme was to highlight those terms that occur more frequently in a given document, but less often in the remainder of the corpus.

The term frequency *tf* for a document is given by the number of times the term appears in the document. The number of documents in the corpus containing the term determines document frequency, *df*. With the corpus size denoted D, we calculate a term t's weight by $tf(t) \times \ln(D/df(t))$.

4.4 Rhyme Pairs

We modified Hirjee and Brown's 'Rhyme Analyzer' software in order to gather a set of all rhymes from our LyricWiki dataset. The pairs were then sorted by frequency, with reversed pairs, such as *to/do* and *do/to*, being combined. To lower the ranking of pairs that are likely to occur in ordinary text rather than in songs, we used tf-idf values calculated for rhyme pairs extracted from a corpus consisting of eighty-two Project Gutenberg[3] texts. The size of this corpus was approximately the same as the lyric collection. Note that most of the corpus was ordinary prose.

Table 2 shows that tf-idf has increased the rank of rhyme pairs such as 'right night' and introduced new ones like 'heart apart' and 'night light'. While not occurring as frequently in the lyrics collection, these pairs are given a greater weight due to their less frequent appearance in the Gutenberg texts. Note also, that the "rhyme pairs" found in the Gutenberg texts are not what one would normally think of as rhymes in poetry or songs, even though they have some similarity. This is due to the nature of the rhyme analyser in use, in that it identifies rhymes regardless of where in a line they occur, and also includes other commonly used rhyme-like devices, such as *partial rhymes* (for example, "pretty" and "little" (Pattison, 1991)). The benefit of using the Gutenberg text in this way is that spurious rhymes of high frequency in normal text can easily be filtered out. The technique may also make a rhyme analyser more robust, but that is not our purpose in this paper.

The results of grouping the lyrics by genre and performing tf-idf weighting are shown in Table 3.

[2] http://www.last.fm

[3] http://www.gutenberg.org

Rock	Hip-Hop	Electronic	Punk	Metal	Pop	Alternative	Folk
day away	way day	stay away	da na	night light	sha la	sha la	la da
way day	way say	day away	day away	la da	way say	insane brain	light night
say away	right night	control soul	say away	day away	feel real	alright tonight	day say
night light	good hood	say way	day way	real feel	say ok	little pretty	hand stand
way say	away day	getting better	way say	near fear	said head	write tonight	away day
stay away	dead head	way day	play day	say away	oh know	know oh	wave brave
night right	feel real	night right	day say	head dead	say day	way say	stride fried
way away	little bit	say away	way away	soul control	la da	la da	head dead
oh know	say play	heart start	head dead	high sky	right night	said head	sunday monday
da la	pretty little	light night	bed head	eyes lies	sha na	real feel	radio na

Table 3: Genre specific top ten rhyme pairs ranked by tf-idf.

4.5 Collocations

All possible trigrams were extracted from the LyricWiki collection and Gutenberg texts. Again, tf-idf was used to rank the trigrams, with a second list removing trigrams containing terms from the NLTK list of English stopwords (Bird et al., 2009) and repeated syllables such as 'la'. Table 4 provides a comparison of these techniques with raw frequency weighting. Similar attempts using techniques such as Pointwise Mutual Information, Student's t-test, the Chi-Squared Test and Likelihood Ratio (Manning and Schütze, 1999) did not yield promising ranked lists and are not included in this paper.

From Table 4, we can see that the difference between frequency and tf-idf in the top fifteen are both positional changes and the introduction of new terms. For example, 'i love you' is ranked fifth by frequency, but fifteenth using tf-idf. Also note how phrases such as 'its time to' and 'i just wanna' rank higher using tf-idf. This shows the influence of the Gutenberg texts - common English phrasing is penalised and lyric-centric terminology emphasised.

Interestingly, the filtered tf-idf scores 'll cool j' the highest. This is the name of a rapper, whose name appears in 136 songs within our collection. Hirjee's work involving hip-hop lyrics found that rappers have a tendency to 'name-drop in their lyrics, including their own names, nicknames, and record label and group names' (Hirjee, 2010). Examining these lyrics, we determined that many of these occurrences can be attributed to this practice, while others are annotations in the lyrics showing the parts performed by LL Cool J which we did not remove prior to experimentation.

Substituting document frequency for term frequency in the lyric collection, as in Table 6, decreases the weight of trigrams that occur repeatedly in fewer songs. As a result, this 'df-idf' should increase the quality of the ranked list. We see that the syllable repetition is largely absent from the top ranking terms and among other positional changes, the phrase 'rock n roll' drops from second place to thirteenth.

Decade	Collection
2000 - 2010	55.41%
1990 - 2000	33.49%
1980 - 1990	7.08%
1970 - 1980	2.88%
1960 - 1970	0.52%

Table 7: Time distribution of lyrics.

Several interesting trends are present in Table 5, which shows df-idf ranked trigrams by genre. Firstly, Hip-hop shows a tendency to use coarse language more frequently and genre-specific phrasing like 'in the club' and 'in the hood'. Repeated terms as in 'oh oh oh' and 'yeah yeah yeah' were more prevalent in pop and rock music. Such vocal hooks may be attempts to create catchy lyrics to sing along to. Love appears to be a common theme in pop music, with phrases like 'you and me', 'youre the one' and of course, 'i love you' ranking high. This terminology is shared by the the other genres to a lesser extent, except in the cases of hip-hop, punk and metal, where it seems largely absent. The term 'words music by' within the metal category is the result of author attribution annotations within the lyrics.

4.6 Time

There is a temporal component to clichés. There was probably a time when the lines "I'm begging you please, I'm down on my

Rank	Frequency	Frequency (filtered)	tf-idf	tf-idf (filtered)
1	la la la	ll cool j	la la la	ll cool j
2	i dont know	one two three	na na na	rock n roll
3	i want to	dont even know	yeah yeah yeah	cant get enough
4	na na na	rock n roll	i dont wanna	feel like im
5	i love you	cant get enough	oh oh oh	yeah oh yeah
6	i know you	theres nothing left	its time to	oh yeah oh
7	oh oh oh	feel like im	i wanna be	im gonna make
8	i got a	yeah oh yeah	i just wanna	theres nothing left
9	i dont want	cant live without	i just cant	dont wanna see
10	yeah yeah yeah	youll never know	give a f**k	cant live without
11	i dont wanna	two three four	dont give a	youll never know
12	up in the	oh yeah oh	du du du	let em know
13	i want you	im gonna make	i need to	im gonna get
14	i know that	never thought id	i need you	dont look back
15	you know i	dont wanna see	i love you	dont even know

Table 4: Top fifteen trigrams, ranked by term frequency and tf-idf.

Rock	Hip-Hop	Electronic	Punk	Metal	Pop	Alternative	Folk
its time to	_in the club_	its time to	its time to	its time to	i love you	and i know	and i know
i dont wanna	_give a f**k_	i dont wanna	i dont wanna	_time has come_	i dont wanna	i love you	_you are the_
i just cant	its time to	you and me	and i know	i can feel	and i know	its time to	i need to
i dont need	dont give a	i need you	_and i dont_	_in my mind_	you and me	_the way you_	close my eyes
i love you	_what the f**k_	cant you see	dont give a	its too late	oh oh oh	in your eyes	_i dont know_
yeah yeah yeah	_in the hood_	i need to	i wanna be	close my eyes	its time to	i try to	i love you
i need to	_i got a_	i love you	and i cant	_the time has_	i need you	_and you know_	_my heart is_
so hard to	_on the block_	what you want	i dont need	cant you see	yeah yeah yeah	i need you	_let it go_
i need you	_im in the_	_you feel the_	_i just dont_	_be the same_	in your eyes	_and i will_	i need you
in my eyes	i dont wanna	in your eyes	cant you see	_in the sky_	_to make you_	_you want me_	_i know youre_

Table 5: Top ten trigrams ranked by df-idf, grouped by genre. Terms that only occur in one genre's top 15 ranked list are *emphasised.*

1990-1995	1995-2000	2000-2005	2005-2010
da na	day away	away day	today away
way day	feel real	me be	town down
baby me	me be	know go	me be
go know	know go	wrong song	go know
be me	town down	day way	say away
soul control	day way	play day	right tonight
know show	oh know	right night	let better
tight night	stay away	say day	day away
down town	find mind	heart apart	alright light
day away	say away	say way	right night

Table 8: Top ten rhyme pairs ranked by tf-idf, five year period.

1990-1995	1995-2000	2000-2005	2005-2010
its time to	i got a	its time to	its time to
i got a	its time to	i got the	dont give a
i dont wanna	i dont wanna	dont give a	i got the
in the club	i need to	i got a	me and my
i need to	you need to	_i love you_	i got a
dont give a	_im in the_	and you know	i need to
and you know	and i know	_here we go_	check it out
and i know	in the back	check it out	in the back
in the back	i got the	in the back	i dont wanna
i got the	_i try to_	i dont wanna	you need to

Table 9: Top ten trigrams ranked by tf-idf, five year period. Terms that only occur in one genre's top 15 ranked list are *emphasised.*

knees", or the trigram "end of time" sounded fresh to the sophisticated audience. Fashions and habits in language also change over time. In this section we examine the rhyme pairs and trigrams across four time periods.

We queried the MusicBrainz[4] database using song title and artist in order to determine the first year of release for each song. This method was able to identify 22,419 songs, or 59% of our collection. Given the considerable size of MusicBrainz (10,761,729 tracks and 618,224 artists on 30th March 2011), this relatively low success rate can likely be attributed to incorrect or partial meta-data retrieved from LyricWiki rather than incompleteness of the database.

As shown in Table 7 our collection has a significant inclination towards music of the last twenty years, with over half in the last decade. It is suspected that this is again due to the nature of the source database — the users are likely to be younger and submitting lyrics they are more familiar with. Also, the distribution peak corresponds to the Web era, in which it has been easier to share lyrics electronically.

The lyrics were divided into 5 year periods

[4]http://musicbrainz.org

Rank	Frequency	Frequency (filtered)	df-idf	df-idf (filtered)
1	i dont know	dont even know	its time to	feel like im
2	i want to	one two three	i dont wanna	ll cool j
3	up in the	theres nothing left	give a f**k	dont wanna see
4	i know you	feel like im	dont give a	theres nothing left
5	i got a	ll cool j	i just cant	cant get enough
6	its time to	dont wanna see	yeah yeah yeah	dont even know
7	i know that	cant get enough	i need to	let em know
8	i love you	cant live without	what the f**k	im gonna make
9	and i dont	new york city	i wanna be	cant live without
10	you know i	let em know	in the club	im gonna get
11	you know what	im gonna make	im in the	dont look back
12	i dont want	two three four	check it out	new york city
13	i can see	never thought id	i just wanna	rock n roll
14	and if you	youll never know	i got a	never thought id
15	and i know	long time ago	i need you	im talkin bout

Table 6: Top fifteen trigrams, ranked by document frequency and df-idf.

from 1990 to 2010 and 2000 random songs selected from each. Rhyme pairs and trigrams were then found with the aforementioned methods, as shown in Tables 8 and 9.

4.7 Cliché Scores for Songs

We tested several cliché measures that combined the two components of our approach, being rhyme pairs and trigrams. We used precomputed tf-idf scores based on the Gutenberg collection for rhyme pairs and df-idf trigram weights. In this model, R and C are the sets of scored rhymes and trigrams respectively. The rhyme pairs and trigrams found in the given lyrics are represented by r and c. The length of the song lyrics in lines is denoted L, and $|R|$ denotes the number of rhyme pairs in the collection.

Our ground truth was based on human judgements. One coauthor prepared a list of ten songs, five of which were considered to be clichéd, and five less typical. The list was subjectively ranked by each coauthor from most to least clichéd. Spearman's rank-order correlation coefficient was used to compare each author's rankings of the songs. Two authors had a correlation of correlation of 0.79. The third author's rankings had correlations of -0.2 and -0.5 with each of the other authors, leading to a suspicion that the list was numbered in the opposite order. When reversed the correlations were very weak (0.09 and -0.1 respectively). We chose to work with an average of the two more highly correlated sets of judgements.

We report on results for the formulae shown below.

$$\frac{\sum R(r) + \sum C(c)}{L} \tag{1}$$

$$\frac{\frac{\sum (R(r))+1}{|R|+1} + \sum C(c)}{L} \tag{2}$$

$$(\frac{\sum (R(r)) + 1}{|R| + 1} + \sum C(c)) \times \ln(L + 1) \tag{3}$$

$$(\frac{\sum (R(r)) + 1}{|R| + 1} \times \sum C(c)) \times \ln(L + 1) \tag{4}$$

The lyrics were then ranked according to each equation.

An average rank list was prepared, and as the rankings of the third coauthor were an outlier, they were not included. Kendall's Tau and Spearman's rho were then used to compare this list to the equation rankings. These were chosen as they are useful for measuring correlation between two ordered datasets.

In order to test the accuracy of the application, we randomly selected ten songs from our collection and again subjectively ranked them from most to least cliché.

4.8 Results

Table 10 shows that the third equation produces the ranked list that best correlates with the coauthor-generated rankings. Table 11 shows the rankings obtained applying the

	Eq. 1		Eq. 2		Eq. 3		Eq. 4	
		p		p		p		p
τ	0.4222	0.0892	0.5555	0.0253	**0.7333**	0.0032	0.6888	0.0056
ρ	0.5640	0.0897	0.6969	0.0251	**0.8787**	0.0008	0.8666	0.0012

Table 10: Correlation measure results for training list using Kendall's tau (τ) and Spearman's rho (ρ).

	Ex. 1		Ex. 2		Ex. 3	
		p		p		p
τ	0.333	0.180	0.333	0.180	0.244	0.325
ρ	0.466	0.174	0.479	0.162	0.345	0.328

Table 12: Correlation measure results for random list, using Kendall's tau (τ) and Spearman's rho (ρ).

same formula to the test data. Table 12 shows the correlations obtained when compared to each author's ranked list. The results show a drop to about 50% of the values obtained using the training set.

4.9 Discussion

The third equation showed the greatest correlation with human ranking of songs by cliché. It suggests that log normalisation according to song length applied to the trigram score component in isolation, with the rhyme score normalised by the number of rhymes. Dividing the summed score by the length of the song (Equation 1) performed relatively poorly. It is possible that introducing a scaling factor into Equation 3 to modify the relative weights of the rhyme and trigram components may yield better results. Oddly, the somewhat less principled formulation, Equation 2, with its doubled normalisation of the rhyming component outperformed Equation 1. Perhaps this suggests that trigrams should dominate the formula.

The different expectations of what clichéd lyrics are resulted in three distinct lists. However, there are some common rankings, for example it was unanimous that *Walkin' on the Sidewalks* by Queens of the Stone Age was the least clichéd song. In this case, the application ranks did not correlate as well with the experimental lists as the training set. Our judgements about how clichéd a song is are generally based on what we have heard before. The application has a similar limitation in that it ranks according to the scores from our lyric collection. The discrepancy between the ranked lists may be due to this differerence in lyrical exposure, or more simply, a suboptimal scoring equation.

The list of songs was also more difficult to rank, as the songs in it probably didn't differ greatly in clichédness compared to the hand-selected set. For example, using Equation 3, the range of scores for the training set was 12.2 for *Carry*, and 5084 for *Just a Dream*, whereas, the test set had a range from 26.76 to 932.

Another difficulty when making the human judgements was the risk of judging on quality rather than lyric clichédness. While a poor quality lyric may be clichéd, the two attributes do not necessarily always go together.

Our results suggest that there are limitations in how closely human judges agree on how clichéd songs are relative to each other, which may mean that only a fairly coarse cliché measure is possible. Perhaps the use of expert judges, such as professional lyricists or songwriting educators, may result in greater convergence of opinion.

5 How Clichéd Are Number One Hits?

Building on this result, we compared the scores of popular music from 1990-2010 with our collection. A set of 286 number one hits as determined by the Billboard Hot 100[5] from this time period were retrieved and scored using the aforementioned method. We compared the distribution of scores with those from the LyricWiki collection over the same era. The score distribution is shown in Figure 1, and suggests that number one hits are more clichéd than other songs on average. There are several possible explanations for this result: it may be that number one

[5]http://www.billboard.com

Ex. 1	Ex. 2	Ex. 3	Score	Song Title - Artist
2	1	6	931.99	Fools Get Wise - B.B. King
8	8	1	876.10	Strange - R.E.M
1	7	7	837.14	Lonely Days - M.E.S.T.
3	2	4	625.93	Thief Of Always - Jaci Velasquez
9	4	9	372.41	Almost Independence Day - Van Morrison
7	6	3	343.87	Impossible - UB40
5	5	2	299.51	Try Me - Val Emmich
4	3	8	134.05	One Too Many - Baby Animals
6	9	5	131.38	Aries - Galahad
10	10	10	26.76	Walkin' On The Sidewalks - Queens of the Stone Age

Table 11: Expected and application rankings for ten randomly selected songs.

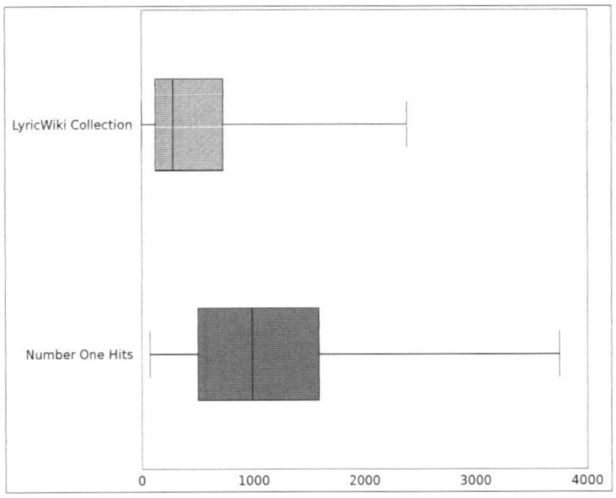

Figure 1: Boxplots showing the quartiles of lyric scores for the lyric collection from the 1990-2010 era, and the corresponding set of number one hits from the era.

hits are indeed more typical than other songs, or perhaps that a song that reaches number one influences other lyricists who then create works in a similar style. Earlier attempts to compare number one hits with the full collection of lyrics revealed an increase in cliché score over time for hit songs. We believe that this was not so much due to an increase in cliché in pop over time but that the language in the lyrics of popular music changes over time, as happens with all natural language.

6 Conclusion

We have explored the use of tf-idf weighting to find typical phrases and rhyme pairs in song lyrics. These attributes have been extracted with varying degrees of success, dependent on sample size. The use of a background model of text worked well in removing ordinary language from the results, and the technique may go towards improving rhyme detection software.

An application was developed that estimates how clichéd given song lyrics are. However, while results were reasonable for distinguishing very clichéd songs from songs that are fairly free from cliché, it was less successful with songs that are not at the extremes.

Our method of obtaining human judgements was not ideal, consisting of two rankings of ten songs by the research team involved in the project. For our future work we hope to obtain independent judgements, possibly of smaller snippets of songs to make the task easier. As it is unclear how consistent people are in judging the clichédness of songs, we expect to collect a larger set of judgements per lyric.

There were several instances where annotations in the lyrics influenced our results. Future work would benefit from a larger, more accurately transcribed collection. This could be achieved using Multiple Sequence Alignment as in Knees et al. (2005). Extending the model beyond trigrams may also yield interesting results.

A comparison of number one hits with a larger collection of lyrics from the same time period revealed that the typical number one hit is more clichéd, on average. While we have examined the relationship between our cliché score and song popularity, it is important to note that there is not necessarily a connection between these factors and writing quality, but this may also be an interesting area to explore.

References

Steven Bird, Edward Loper, and Ewan Klein. 2009. *Natural Language Processing with Python*. O'Reilly Media Inc.

S. Burrows, A. L. Uitdenbogerd, and A. Turpin. 2009. Application of information retrieval techniques for source code authorship attribution. In Ramamohanarao Kotagiri Xiaofang Zhou, Haruo Yokota and Xuemin Lin, editors, *International Conference on Database Systems for Advanced Applications*, volume 14, pages 699–713, Brisbane, Australia, April.

G. L. Dillon. 2006. Corpus, creativity, cliché: Where statistics meet aesthetics. *Journal of Literary Semantics*, 35(2):97–103.

B. Drummond and J. Cauty. 1988. *The Manual (How to Have a Number One the Easy Way)*. KLF Publications, UK.

H. Hirjee and D.G. Brown. 2009. Automatic detection of internal and imperfect rhymes in rap lyrics. In *Proceedings of the 10th International Society for Music Information Retrieval Conference.*

H. Hirjee and D.G. Brown. 2010a. Rhyme Analyzer: An Analysis Tool for Rap Lyrics. In *Proceedings of the 11th International Society for Music Information Retrieval Conference.*

H. Hirjee and D.G. Brown. 2010b. Solving misheard lyric search queries using a probabilistic model of speech sounds. In *Proc. 11th International Society ofor Music Information Retrieval Conference*, pages 147–152, Utrecht, Netherlands, August. ISMIR.

Hussein Hirjee. 2010. Rhyme, rhythm, and rhubarb: Using probabilistic methods to analyze hip hop, poetry, and misheard lyrics. Master's thesis, University of Waterloo.

Florian Kleedorfer, Peter Knees, and Tim Pohle. 2008. Oh Oh Oh Whoah! Towards Automatic Topic Detection In Song Lyrics. In *Proceedings of the 9th International Conference on Music Information Retrieval (ISMIR 2008)*, pages 287–292, September.

P. Knees, M. Schedl, and G. Widmer. 2005. Multiple lyrics alignment: Automatic retrieval of song lyrics. In *Proceedings of 6th international conference on music information retrieval (ismir05)*, pages 564–569.

M. Koppel, J. Schler, and S. Argamon. 2009. Computational methods in authorship attribution. *Journal of the American Society for information Science and Technology*, 60(1):9–26.

Dekang Lin. 1998. Extracting collocations from text corpora. In *First Workshop on Computational Terminology*, pages 57–63.

B. Logan, A. Kositsky, and P. Moreno. 2005. Semantic analysis of song lyrics. In *Multimedia and Expo, 2004. ICME'04. 2004 IEEE International Conference on*, volume 2, pages 827–830. IEEE.

Christopher D. Manning and Hinrich Schütze. 1999. *Foundations of statistical natural language processing*. MIT Press, Cambridge, MA, USA.

R. Mayer, R. Neumayer, and A. Rauber. 2008. Rhyme and style features for musical genre classification by song lyrics. In *ISMIR 2008: proceedings of the 9th International Conference of Music Information Retrieval*, page 337.

P. Pattison. 1991. *Songwriting : essential guide to rhyming : a step-by-step guide to better rhyming and lyrics*. Berklee Press, Boston.

S.R. Pillay and T. Solorio. 2011. Authorship attribution of web forum posts. In *eCrime Researchers Summit (eCrime), 2010*, pages 1–7. IEEE.

N. Ring and A. L. Uitdenbogerd. 2009. Finding 'Lucy in Disguise': the misheard lyric matching problem. In *The Fifth Asia Information Retrieval Symposium*, Sapporo, Japan, October.

Gerard Salton and Christopher Buckley. 1988. Term-weighting approaches in automatic text retrieval. *Inf. Process. Manage.*, 24:513–523, August.

B. F. Skinner. 1941. A quantitative estimate of certain types of sound-patterning in poetry. *American Journal of Psychology*, 54(1):64–79, January.

F. Smadja. 1993. Retrieving collocations from text: Xtract. *Computational linguistics*, 19(1):143–177.

C. Whissell. 1996. Traditional and emotional stylometric analysis of the songs of Beatles Paul McCartney and John Lennon. *Computers and the Humanities*, 30(3):257–265.

X. Xu, M. Naito, T. Kato, and K. Kawai. 2009. Robust and fast lyric search based on phonetic confusion matrix. In K. Hirata and G. Tzanetakis, editors, *Proc. 10th International Society ofor Music Information Retrieval Conference*, pages 417–422, Kobe, Japan, October. ISMIR.

Free-text input vs menu selection: exploring the difference with a tutorial dialogue system.

Jenny McDonald[1], **Alistair Knott**[2] **and Richard Zeng**[1]
[1]Higher Education Development Centre, University of Otago
[2]Department of Computer Science, University of Otago
jenny.mcdonald@otago.ac.nz

Abstract

We describe the in-class evaluation of two versions of a tutorial dialogue system with 338 volunteers from a first-year undergraduate health-sciences class. One version uses supervised machine-learning techniques to classify student free-text responses; the other requires students to select their preferred response from a series of options (menu-based). Our results indicate that both the free-text and menu-based tutors produced significant gains on immediate post-test scores compared to a control group. In addition, there was no significant difference in performance between students in the free-text and menu-based conditions. We note specific analysis work still to do as part of this research and speculate briefly on the potential for using tutorial dialogue systems in real class settings.

1 Introduction

In large undergraduate classes (1500-1800 students), it is time-consuming, costly and seldom practical to provide students with feedback on their conceptions other than by computer-based marking of formative assessments. Typical examples of this include Learning Management System (LMS) based multiple-choice quizzes or similar. Most computer-assisted assessment involves students being able to recognise a correct response rather than recall and independently generate an answer. In the context of the first-year undergraduate health sciences course that we studied, currently all computer-assisted assessment takes this form. In 2008, the coordinator of a first year undergraduate health sciences class asked us about ways in which technologies might assist students to practice writing short-answer questions. As a result of this request, we wanted to investigate whether students answering questions with free-text or multiple-choice(menu-based) selections in a tutorial dialogue setting would result in performance gains on student test scores and whether there would be any difference in performance between students who generated free-text answers and those who selected their preferred answer from a number of options. In the next section we begin with a brief literature review from the fields of both Education and Cognitive Science. Next, we briefly describe the design and features of our tutorial dialogue system. The experimental design, and results are described in subsequent sections and we conclude with a discussion of our key findings.

2 Background

This study is situated at the boundaries between at least three established fields of inquiry: educational assessment research; psychological research, in particular the study of memory, recognition and recall; and finally intelligent tutoring systems (ITS) and natural language processing (NLP) research.

Since the 1920s the positive benefits on student performance of answering practice, or formative assessment, questions have been demonstrated in classroom studies (Frederiksen, 1984). Similar positive effects have been demonstrated in psychology laboratory studies since the 1970s. (McDaniel et al., 2007) Large meta-analytic educational studies looking at the impact of practice tests on student outcomes indicate that on average, the provision of practice assessments during a course of study does confer a clear advantage, although the effect of increasing practice-test frequency is less clear. (Crooks, 1988). More recently, the role for computer-based assessment has been reviewed and Gipps (2005) writing in Studies in Higher Education has noted that,

> the provision of feedback to the learner, both motivational (evaluative) and substantive (descriptive), is crucially important to support learning. The developments in automated diagnostic feedback in short answer and multiple-choice tests are therefore potentially very valuable. If feedback from assessment could be automated, while maintaining quality in assessment, it could certainly be a powerful learning tool.

She goes on to say that use of computer-marking for anything other than MCQ-style questions, while showing some promise, is seldom used in practice in higher education institutions.

Recent research from the Cognitive Science and ITS domain, for example Chi (2009) and Van-Lehn (2011), suggests that tutor behaviour, human or machine, which encourages or promotes constructive or interactive behaviour by the student is likely to yield greater learning gains than passive or active behaviour. It also suggests that opportunities for extended interactive dialogue between teacher and student in a given domain are likely to produce the largest gains.

On the basis of this considerable body of research we felt that an opportunity to practice answering questions with formative feedback, in this case in a tutorial dialogue setting, should produce learning gains over and above those expected from working with existing study resources and formative tests. We were also interested to test whether there is a difference in performance between students who generate free-text responses and those who select an answer from a series of options in the course of a tutorial dialogue. There is some literature which specifically explores this, however the number of studies is limited and the results are inconclusive. Gay (1980) found that in retention tests students who practiced answering short-answer (SA) or free-text questions performed as well as or better than students who practiced MCQs but this effect was also dependent on the mode of retention testing. Specifically, retention test results where the test was conducted using SA were better for both MCQ-practice and SA-practice, whereas there was no difference between the two practice groups where the retention test mode was MCQ. In 1984, reviewing the education and psychology literature at the time, Frederiksen (1984) concluded that,

> testing increases retention of the material tested and that the effects are quite specific to what was tested. There is some evidence that short-answer or completion tests may be more conducive to long-term retention.

In a related area in his comprehensive review of classroom evaluation practice, Crooks (1988) suggested,

> there is no strong evidence...to support widespread adoption of any one [question] item format or style of task. Instead, the basis for selecting item formats should be their suitability for testing the skills and content that are to be evaluated.

Support for this view is found in a met-analysis of 67 empirical studies which investigated the contruct equivalence of MCQ and constructed-response (SA) questions (Rodriguez, 2003). Where the content or stem of the MCQ and short-answer questions were the same Rodriguez found a very high correlation between the different formats. In other words, where the questions relate to the same content they will measure the same trait in the student. However, even if the same traits are measured by performance on questions in different formats, this says nothing about whether using practice questions in different formats results in differential learning gains for the students on subsequent retention tests.

The closest studies to our current work examined the impact on student performance of constructing or generating free-text descriptions vs. selecting descriptions from a series of options in a Geometry Tutor (Aleven et al., 2004) and an Algebra Tutor (Corbett et al., 2006). The results from both these studies suggest that there is little difference between the two formats especially on immediate post-test but that the free-text option may yield some advantage for long-term retention and some benefit for performance in subsequent short-answer questions. These results are consistent with the much earlier educational review conducted by Frederiksen (1984).

In real-class settings, there is considerable time and effort involved in developing and implementing tutors which can provide immediate feedback on student short-answer responses and in particular, natural language dialogue systems (for example, Murray (1999)). This means that it is crucially important to understand what the potential benefits of these systems could be for both students and teachers.

The tutor we describe in the next section is substantially different from the Geometry and Algebra Tutors. Unlike these systems, it is not a formal step-based tutor; that is, it is not asking students to explain specific steps in a problem-solving process and providing feedback at each step. Our Dialogue Tutor simply engages students in a conversation, much like an online chat-session, where the Tutor poses questions which are directly related to students' current area of study about the human cardiovascular system and the student either types in their response or selects a response from a series of options. Nevertheless, in common with other ITS, our tutor does provide immediate formative feedback to the student and offers a series of options for proceeding depending on the student response.

3 Natural Language Tutor Design

3.1 Tutorial dialogue design

The structure of the tutorial dialogue is determined entirely by the dialogue script. We wanted to use a finite-state model for the dialogue since this permits an organic authoring process and imposes no theoretical limit to how deep or broad the dialogue becomes. The script structure is based on Core and Allen's (1997) dialogue coding scheme and has been described previously (McDonald et al., 2011).

The current study utilises a single-initiative directed dialogue; however the opportunity for limited mixed-initiative is incorporated into the system design through classifying question contributions at any stage of the dialogue and searching for possible answers within the dialogue script.

Design of the tutorial dialogue began with the development of an initial script covering the curriculum on cardiovascular homeostasis. This was developed in close consultation with course teaching staff and was written by a medical graduate using lecture notes, laboratory manuals and self-directed learning material from the course itself. The initial script was refined through a series of pilot interactions with student and staff volunteers and released to the first year undergraduate class on a voluntary basis at the beginning of their module on the human cardiovascular system. The default position in this early script was to provide the correct answer and move on unless confidence was high that an appropriate match had been made, using minimum-edit distance between student response and model answers. A handful of dialogues were interrupted because of system-related problems but the majority that terminated before completion did so because the students simply ended their session. Feedback from course tutors and comments from the students supported our intuition that poor system 'understanding' of student dialogue contributions was a key reason for the fall-off in use. Nevertheless, student perceptions of this early tutorial were broadly positive and it served its purpose in capturing a reasonable quantity of student responses (between 127-242 responses to 50 tutorial questions) for the next stage of tutorial dialogue development.

The next step in dialogue development involved building classifiers for each dialogue contribution from the student corpus and revising the script depending on the nature of student responses. We followed the XML schema of the NPSChat corpus provided with the NLTK (Bird, 2006) in marking-up the corpus. The classes used are specific to each dialogue contribution although three generic classes are used throughout the dialogue where context-specific classification fails: *question*, *dont-know* and *dont-understand*. A flow diagram of the classification process is illustrated in Figure 1: There is a classifier for each dialogue contribution (DC-Classifier). A-D represent possible classes for student input. If classifier confidence falls below a certain threshold for assigning input to one of the possible classes then the unclassified input is passed on to a series of generic binary classifiers: Question, Dont-know and Dont-understand which identify whether the input string is likely to be a question (Q) or some variation on 'I don't know' (DK) or 'I don't understand the question' (DU). If the input remains unclassified after each of these generic classifiers has been tried, the dialogue moves to the next default node in the script (Default).

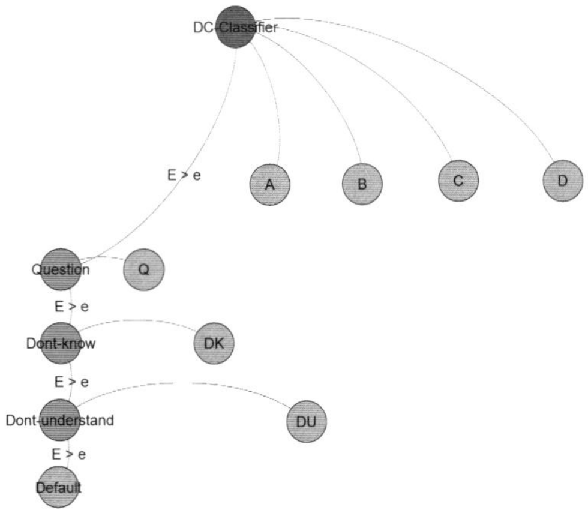

Figure 1: Classifier flow diagram.

For each dialogue context a training set was created from the corpus. Typically the first 100 student responses for each tutor question were classified by a human marker. This training set was divided into 5 folds and a Maximum Entropy classifier trained on 4/5 folds using simple *bag of words* as the featureset and then tested on the remaining fold. A 5-way cross-validation was carried out and accuracies for each of the 5 test sets calculated. The average accuracy across the 5 test sets and standard deviation was also recorded. This process was repeated using different combinations of featuresets (for example, bag of words, word length, first word, with/without stemming, with/without stopwords etc) until the highest accuracy and least variability in test set results was achieved. (The mean accuracy on test data across all 62 classifiers built for each dialogue context in the complete dialogue was 0.93. The minimum was 0.73, maximum was 1.00 and the first quartile was 0.89)

Tutor questions with multi-part answers, for example, *'Can you think of three main factors which affect cardiac contractility?'*, lent themselves to chaining together a series of binary classifiers, using the NLTK MultiBinary Classifier wrapper, rather than including all possible classes of response within a single classifier. This is the best approach given the relatively small amount of training data compared to the large number of possible classes of response. For example, in the question given above, three possible factors to list gives a total of eight possible classes of answer. For some combinations there are only very small, but nevertheless important training sets, and this leads to poor classfier performance overall. Training three binary classifiers which identify each of the factors sought as either present or not and then writing a function which returns a list of the factors found by all three binary classifiers for a given input effectively increases the amount of training data per factor. While this approach yielded some improvement, the *class imbalance problem* (Refer to, for example, Japkowicz(2000)) was still evident for some combinations.

The classifier is evaluated with previously unseen data and scored relative to a human marker. The entropy of the probability distribution (E) is calculated for each unseen response and this is used to determine appropriate thresholds for classification. For example, if E is close to zero the classifier confidence is generally very high. $E > 1$ indicates low confidence and less difference between the class rankings. An appropriate entropy threshold (e) for each classifier is determined by the script designer. This is really a subjective judgement and is made based on the classifier performance as well as the dialogue script context and the likely impact of a false negative or false positive classification. (The mean accuracy on unseen test data across all 62 classifiers with manually set entropy thresholds was 0.95. The minimum was 0.70, maximum was 1.00 and the first quartile was 0.93) There is the potential to automate this process however this will require a method to assess the cost of false positive and false negative classification for each dialogue context.

Finally the classifier is serialised, along with its associated feaureset parameters and e value and saved for use in the dialogue system itself.

3.2 Dialogue system architecture

The dialogue system is written in Python and utilises several NLTK libraries, Peter Norvig's 'toy' spell checker, and the Asyncore and Asynchat libraries to manage multiple simultaneous client connections. The server can readily communicate with any web-application front end using XML-formatted messages and we have built a java-based web application through which multiple clients can connect to the tutorial server. Figure 2. provides an overview of our system architecture.

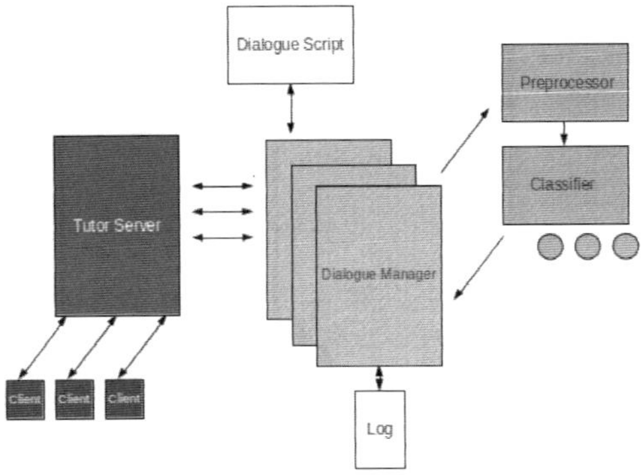

Figure 2: Architecture of Dialogue System.

Each client connection to the system creates an instance of the dialogue manager which sends tutor contributions to the client according to the preloaded script and receives student contributions which are then classified and determine the next tutor contribution. The dialogue manager design has been described previously (McDonald et al., 2011).

3.3 Free-text and menu based versions

A small addition to the dialogue script and the addition of a switch to the dialogue manager code allowed us to create two systems for the price of one. The free-text entry system uses the classifiers to categorise student responses and the menu-based system simply presents students with possible options added to the script from which they can select. The addition of <menu> tags to each dialogue context in the script is shown in the following example:

```
<contribution-node id="check-hr"
parent-node="start"
default="true">

<backward class="yes">
<acknowledge/>
</backward>

<forward>

<assert>We're going to talk about
what blood pressure is....
</assert>

<info-request value="How would you
check what someone&apos;s HR is?"
define="You could take their
pulse."/>

<menu>
<item value="correct">Count the
pulse.</item>
<item value="simpler">With a
blood pressure cuff and
stethoscope.</item>
<item value="simpler">Use an
ECG.</item>
<item value="incomplete">Pulse.
</item>
<item value="dont-know">I don't
know.</item>
</menu>

</forward>
</contribution-node>
```

Note that the menu options, like the classifier training data, are derived directly from student responses to the question. There are three things to note from this. Firstly, the menu-based options tend to have a slightly different flavour to conventional multiple-choice questions (MCQs) designed by teachers. For example, the incomplete response, *'Pulse'* would probably not be included in a conventional MCQ. It is here because this was a common response from students responding with free-text and resulted in a scripted reminder to students that short-answers do require complete descriptions or explanations. Secondly, *'I don't know'* is unlikely to be found in a teacher designed MCQ; however in this context it is useful and leads to scripted remedial action as it would if the student had typed in text with a similar meaning. Finally, two different options result in the same script action, labelled *'simpler'*, being taken. This reflects the free-text student data for this question. Both are acknowledged as possible ways to check someone's heart-rate, in either case, the student is prompted to think of a simpler method.

4 Experimental Design

Students from the 1st year Health Sciences course (N=1500) were asked to volunteer for the experiment. The first year Health Sciences course is a prerequisite for all professional health science programmes, such as Medicine, Dentistry, Pharmacy, ... Entry into these programmes is highly competitive and is dependent, amongst other things, on students achieving excellent grades in their 1st year courses. The only incentive offered to students was that taking part in the study would give them an opportunity to practice and develop their understanding of the cardiovascular section of the course by answering a series of questions related to the lectures they had received during the preceeding two weeks. Students were told that different styles of questions, short-answer and MCQ, might be used in different combinations and that not all students would receive the same style of questions. They were also told to allow 20-40 minutes to complete the questions. They could answer the questions by logging in to an online system at anytime during a three-week period which ran concurrently with their normal laboratory and self-paced study sessions on the cardiovascular system.

All student responses in the experiment were anonymised and appropriate ethics approval was obtained.

Students who logged into the system were randomly assigned to one of three conditions: A free-text condition where they completed a pre-test, then the free-text version of the tutorial dialogue, and concluded with an immediate post-test; a menu-based condition where they completed a pre-test, then the multi-choice version of the tutorial dialogue, followed by an immediate post-test, and a control condition where they simply completed pre- and post-tests.

The pre- and post-tests in each case consisted of equal numbers of MCQ and short-answers (3+3 for the pre-test and 7+7 for the post-test). The pre-test directly reflected material taught in the lectures students had just received and the post-test reflected material explicitly covered in the tutorial dialogues.

All student interactions with the system in each experimental condition were recorded and logged to a database. At the end of the experimental period only completed sessions (i.e. pre-test, post-test and tutorial condition completed) were included for analysis. The principal investigator marked all pre- and post-test short-answer questions and MCQs were scored automatically. One member of the teaching staff for the course also marked a sample of short-answer questions to check for inter-rater reliability.

Given the findings from the literature reported in Section 2, the hypotheses we wanted to test were: A. Any intervention results in better post-test performance than none; B. Free-text input results in better post-test performance overall than MCQ, because there is something special about students recalling and constructing their own response; C. Free-text tutorials lead to increased performance on short-answer questions; and D. MCQ tutorials lead to increased performance on MCQ questions.

Delayed post-tests are still to be completed and will involve correlation with short-answer and MCQ student results on the cardiovascular section of the final examination.

We describe our early results and analysis of the immediate post-test data in the next section.

5 Results

720 students logged into the experimental system during the 3 week period in which it was available. Of these, 578 students completed the session through to the end of the post-test and these were relatively evenly distributed across the three conditions suggesting that there are no sampling bias effects across conditions. We report here the results from the first 338 of the 578 completed tutorials/tests. Short-answer sections of both pre- and post-tests were checked for inter-rater reliability. A Cohen's kappa of 0.93 ($p=0$) confirmed very high agreement between 2 markers on pre- and post-test questions for a sample of 30 students.

Table 1 summarises the descriptive statistics for the three experimental conditions. Across all three conditions students performed well in the pre-test with a mean normalised score of 0.83. In the post-test, which was inherently harder, student scores dropped across all three conditions but the mean scores were higher in both the tutorial conditions compared to the control (0.75 and 0.77 c.f. 0.69).

	Control n=119		Free-text n=101		Menu-based n=118	
	mean	*sd*	*mean*	*sd*	*mean*	*sd*
Pre-test	0.83	0.15	0.83	0.14	0.84	0.14
Post-test	0.69	0.19	0.75	0.16	0.77	0.17

Table 1: Descriptive Statistics

The dependent variable to test our first hypothesis was taken as the difference between pre- and post-test performance for each student with the pre-test result serving as a common baseline in each case. The differences between pre- and post-test scores were normally distributed which allowed us to use parametric tests to see if there were differences between the means in each condition. A between subjects Anova gave an F value of 4.95 and a post-hoc Tukey multiple comparison of means at 95% confidence level showed a significant difference when compared with the control for both the free-text tutorial condition (p=0.03) and the menu-based tutorial condition (p=0.01) .

However, there was no support for our second hypothesis that free-text input results in better post-test performance overall than menu-based input; comparison between the mean scores for free-text condition and menu-based condition was not significant (p=0.94). Given this result it was also clear that there was no demonstrated benefit for free-text tutorials improving scores on free-text questions in the post-test nor multiple-choice questions improving post-test performance on the MCQs.

We discuss the implications of these early results in the final section and also outline our plan for further detailed analysis of the data obtained.

6 Discussion

Several features stand out from the results. The most striking initial feature is the much higher tutorial completion rate (80%) for this system compared with the original tutorial system (23%) which was fielded in order to collect student responses ((McDonald et al., 2011)) as discussed in Section 3. Formal evaluation of the free-text version classifier performance is currently underway and will be reported separately but the overall higher completion rate and only slightly lower numbers completing the dialogue tutorial (29% of the 578 completions) compared with the multi-choice tutorial (34% of the 578 completions) is suggestive of a considerable improvement.

On average, students performed better in the pre-test than they did in the post-test. This was expected: the pre-test was designed to measure the degree to which students had comprehended key points from the lectures they had just attended, while the post-test was designed to be more challenging. It is worth noting that in real in-class settings it is not uncommon for students to perform well in initial tests and subsequently perform less well as they work to make sense and meaning of the subject under study (see for example, Cree and Macaulay (2000)). However in this specific context, given that the pre-test was designed to measure the degree to which students had comprehended key points from the lectures they had just attended it is not too surprising that they did uniformly well in the pre-test. The post-test was designed to be more challenging and required an ability to demonstrate understanding as well as the ability to manipulate key cardiovascular variables and understand whether and how these relate to each other. These skills and abilities are developed through experience in the laboratory teaching sessions and with self-directed study materials; they are also directly covered in each of the tutorial conditions. Certainly the results confirmed that students in each condition started at a similar level and support our hypothesis that post-test performance is significantly improved through exposure to either tutorial condition when compared to the control condition.

In a practical sense it is important to see not only whether there are actual differences in performance but also whether these differences are large enough to be worth the additional effort for both teaching staff and students. Effect sizes are commonly reported in the educational literature and we believe it is worth doing so here. The standardised effect size is relatively small in each tutorial condition (0.17-0.22). Hattie (2008) and many others make the point that in general an effect size larger than 0.40 is suggestive of an intervention worth pursuing but that this also depends on local context. In the context of this study, for the 'price' of a single relatively brief intervention, an average effect size increase of between 6 to 8 percentage points on the immediate post-test suggests that engagement with either tutorial, particularly in a high stakes course, where every percentage point counts, does produce a gain worth having. With such a brief one-off intervention it would be surprising indeed to have found much larger effect sizes.

Examination of the variability of pre- and post-test results in each of the three conditions shows a highly consistent distribution of marks in all three conditions on the pre-test but a wider variation in results in the post-test control group (sd=0.19) than in either of the tutorial groups (sd=0.16 in menu-based condition and sd=0.17 in free-text condition). Again, given that the post-test was specifically testing material taught in the tutorial this is perhaps not suprising. You would hope that in any teaching situation student marks would start to converge in a positive direction! Nevertheless, once the complete set of student results is marked we will investigate this further. Of particular interest is to see whether poorer performing students benefit more from the tutorial than others.

Finally, the lack of difference between the two tutorial conditions, free-text and menu-based, was consistent with indications from existing literature. However, we found no advantage for free-text entry over menu-based choice overall, nor indeed did either condition confer any advantage in performance when post-testing was in the same mode. However, given previous research results we are keen to explore this further. In particular we want to examine specific questions from the post-test and see whether there is a difference between conditions on questions which required simple recall and those which required further analysis or description by the student. We also intend to look at several other factors: whether the average length of written responses to the tutorial in the free-text condition has any bearing on performance in either condition, time on task relative to performance and the stage at which the student logged in to the experimental system. (For example, did the group which took the tutorial later, once they had more laboratory work and self-study time under their belts, perform better in either condition than those who took the tutorial earlier?)

Additional work still to do includes correlating these experimental results with student performance on relevant questions in the final course examination (short-answer and MCQ); this will effectively provide delayed post-test data. Also, we will be gathering student feedback on their experience and perceptions of the tutorial systems via a course evaluation questionnaire.

Developing a deeper understanding of the potential role of natural language tutorial dialogue systems in improving student performance has been the focus of this paper. Nevertheless a striking side-effect from undertaking this research has been realising the role dialogue systems like this may be able to play in providing feedback to teachers on the conceptions held by students in large classes about the material they are being taught. The range and depth of large numbers of student free-text responses provide important clues about student conceptions. The ability to describe these conceptions is invaluable for teaching (Marton and Saljo, 1976). The facility to do this in an automated or semi-automated way for large classes, presumably, is even more so. Teaching staff who have had some involvement in the project have commented on the usefulness of being able to see student responses to questions grouped into categories: this grouping provides a powerful way for teachers to gauge the range of responses which they receive to their questions.

References

Vincent Aleven, Amy Ogan, Octav Popescu, Cristen Torrey, and Kenneth Koedinger. 2004. Evaluating the effectiveness of a tutorial dialogue system for self-explanation. In *In*, pages 443–454. Springer.

Steven Bird. 2006. NLTK: the natural language toolkit. In *Proceedings of the COLING/ACL on Interactive presentation sessions*, COLING-ACL '06, pages 69–72, Stroudsburg, PA, USA. Association for Computational Linguistics.

Michelene T. H. Chi. 2009. Active-constructive-interactive: A conceptual framework for differentiating learning activities. *Topics in Cognitive Science*, 1(1):73–105.

Albert Corbett, Angela Wagner, Sharon Lesgold, Harry Ulrich, and Scott Stevens. 2006. The impact on learning of generating vs. selecting descriptions in analyzing algebra example solutions. In *Proceedings of the 7th international conference on Learning sciences*, ICLS '06, pages 99–105. International Society of the Learning Sciences.

Mark G. Core and James F. Allen. 1997. Coding dialogs with the damsl annotation scheme. In *Working Notes of the AAAI Fall Symposium on Communicative Action in Humans and Machines*, pages 28–35, Cambridge, MA, November.

Viviene Cree and Cathlin Macaulay. 2000. *Transfer of Learning in Professional and Vocational Education*. Routledge, London: Psychology Press.

Terence J. Crooks. 1988. The impact of classroom evaluation practices on students. *Review of Educational Research*, 58(4):pp. 438–481.

Norman Frederiksen. 1984. The real test bias: Influences of testing on teaching and learning. *American Psychologist*, 39(3):193–202.

Lorraine R. Gay. 1980. The comparative effects of multiple-choice versus short-answer tests on retention. *Journal of Educational Measurement*, 17(1):45–50.

Caroline V. Gipps *. 2005. What is the role for ict-based assessment in universities? *Studies in Higher Education*, 30(2):171–180.

J. Hattie. 2008. *Visible Learning: A synthesis of over 800 meta-analyses relating to achievement*. Taylor & Francis.

N. Japkowicz. 2000. The class imbalance problem: Significance and strategies. In *Proceedings of the 2000 International Conference on Artificial Intelligence (ICAI2000)*, volume 1, pages 111–117.

F. Marton and R. Saljo. 1976. On qualitative differences in learning: Ioutcome and process*. *British Journal of Educational Psychology*, 46(1):4–11.

Mark A. McDaniel, Janis L. Anderson, Mary H. Derbish, and Nova Morrisette. 2007. Testing the testing effect in the classroom. *European Journal of Cognitive Psychology*, 19(4-5):494–513.

J. McDonald, A. Knott, R. Zeng, and A. Cohen. 2011. Learning from student responses: A domain-independent natural language tutor. In *Proceedings of the Australasian Language Technology Association Workshop 2011*, volume 148, page 156.

Tom Murray. 1999. Authoring intelligent tutoring systems: An analysis of state of the art. *International Journal of Artificial Intelligence in Education*, 10:98–129.

Michael C. Rodriguez. 2003. Construct equivalence of multiple-choice and constructed-response items: A random effects synthesis of correlations. *Journal of Educational Measurement*, 40(2):163–184.

Kurt VanLehn. 2011. The relative effectiveness of human tutoring, intelligent tutoring systems, and other tutoring systems. *Educational Psychologist*, 46(4):197–221.

Short papers

langid.py for better language modelling

Paul Cook♡ **and Marco Lui**♡♣
♡ Department of Computing and Information Systems
The University of Melbourne
Victoria 3010, Australia
♣ NICTA Victoria Research Laboratory
{paulcook,mhlui}@unimelb.edu.au

Abstract

Large corpora are crucial resources for building many statistical language technology systems, and the Web is a readily-available source of vast amounts of linguistic data from which to construct such corpora. Nevertheless, little research has considered how to best build corpora from the Web. In this study we consider the importance of language identification in Web corpus construction. Beginning with a Web crawl consisting of documents identified as English using a standard language identification tool, we build corpora of varying sizes both with, and without, further filtering of non-English documents with a state-of-the-art language identifier. We show that the perplexity of a standard English corpus is lower under a language model trained from a Web corpus built with this extra language identification step, demonstrating the importance of state-of-the-art language identification in Web corpus construction.

1 The need for large corpora

Corpora are essential resources for building language technology (LT) systems for a variety of applications. For example, frequency estimates for n-grams — which can be used to build a language model, a key component of many contemporary LT systems — are typically derived from corpora. Furthermore, bigger corpora are typically better. Banko and Brill (2001) show that for a classification task central to many LT problems, performance increases as a variety of models are trained on increasingly large corpora.

The Web is a source of vast amounts of linguistic data, and the need for large corpora has motivated a wide range of research into techniques for building corpora of various types from the Web (e.g., Baroni and Bernardini, 2004; Ferraresi et al., 2008; Kilgarriff et al., 2010; Murphy and Stemle, 2011). In stark contrast to manual corpus construction, such automatic methods enable large corpora to be built quickly and inexpensively. Moreover, large Web crawls have recently been produced which are readily-available to the LT community (e.g., ClueWeb09[1] and CommonCrawl[2]) and can easily be exploited to build corpora much larger than those currently available (and indeed Pomikálek et al. (2012) have already done so); based on the findings of Banko and Brill, such corpora could be exploited to improve LT systems.

Despite the importance of large Web corpora, the issue of how to best derive a corpus from a Web crawl remains an open question. Once a large collection of documents is obtained (from, e.g., either a Web crawl or the results of issuing queries to a commercial search engine) they must be post-processed to remove non-linguistic document portions, for example, boilerplate text such as menus; filter unwanted content such as documents in languages other than that intended for the corpus, and spam; and finally remove deduplicate or near-duplicate documents or document portions to produce a corpus. Furthermore, this document post-processing can potentially have a tremendous impact on corpus quality (Kilgarriff, 2007). For example, if texts in languages other than the target language(s) are not reliably identified and removed, n-gram frequency estimates for the target language will be less accurate than they would otherwise be, potentially having a negative

[1] http://lemurproject.org/clueweb09/
[2] http://commoncrawl.org/

impact on LT systems trained on such a corpus. Similar problems are encountered with the presence of boilerplate text, and duplicate or near-duplicate documents or text segments.

Although document post-processing is clearly important to corpus construction, little work has studied it directly, with the notable exception of CleanEval (Baroni et al., 2008), a shared task on cleaning webpages by removing boilerplate and markup. Liu and Curran (2006) and Versley and Panchenko (2012) compare Web corpora with standard corpora in task-based evaluations, but do not specifically consider the impact of document post-processing. Web corpus construction projects have tended to rely on readily-available tools, or simple heuristics, to accomplish this post-processing. This is not a criticism of these projects — their goals were to build useful language resources, not specifically to study the impact of document post-processing on corpora. Nevertheless, because of the immediate opportunities for improving LT by building larger Web corpora, and the importance of post-processing on the quality of the resulting corpora, there appear to be potential opportunities to improve LT by improving Web corpus construction methods.

In this paper we consider the importance of language identification — which has already been shown to benefit other LT tasks (e.g., Alex et al., 2007) — in Web corpus construction. We build corpora of varying sizes from a readily-available Web crawl (the English portion of ClueWeb09) using a standard corpus construction methodology. This dataset contains only documents classified as English according to a commonly-used language identification tool (TEXTCAT).[3] We then produce versions of these corpora from which non-English documents according to a state-of-the-art language identification tool (`langid.py`, Lui and Baldwin, 2012) are filtered. In this preliminary work, we measure the impact of language identification in a task-based evaluation. Specifically, we train language models on the Web corpora, and demonstrate that, for corpora built from equal amounts of crawl data, the perplexity of a standard (manually-constructed) corpus is lower under a language model trained on a corpus filtered using `langid.py`, than a model trained on a corpus without this filtering.

[3] `http://odur.let.rug.nl/vannoord/TextCat/`

2 Materials and methods

This section describes the language identification tools, corpus construction methods, and language modelling approach used in this study.

2.1 Language identification

The initial language identification for ClueWeb09 was performed using TEXTCAT, an implementation of the language identification method of Cavnar and Trenkle (1994),[4] which is based on the relative frequencies of byte n-grams. The reported language identification precision is over 99.7% across all 10 languages in ClueWeb09. However, the method of Cavnar and Trenkle has been shown to perform poorly when applied to test data outside the domain of the training data (Lui and Baldwin, 2011), as was the case for ClueWeb09 where the training data was drawn from newswire and European parliament corpora.

`langid.py` is an implementation of the method described in Lui and Baldwin (2011), which improves on the method of Cavnar and Trenkle (1994) in a number of ways; both classifiers are based on relative frequencies of byte n-grams, but `langid.py` uses a Naive Bayes classifier and cross-domain feature selection, allowing it to ignore non-linguistic content such as HTML, without the need to explicitly model such content. Lui and Baldwin (2012) show that `langid.py` significantly and systematically outperforms TEXTCAT on a number of domains, and we therefore use it in this study.

2.2 Corpora

We build corpora from subsets of the English portion of ClueWeb09, a Web crawl consisting of roughly 500 million webpages crawled from January–February 2009 that has been used in a number of shared tasks (e.g., Clarke et al., 2011). We build corpora of two types: corpora based on subsets of all documents in this crawl (which include only documents classified as English by TEXTCAT, but a small proportion of non-English documents according to `langid.py`) and corpora based on subsets of only those documents identified as English using `langid.py`.

Similar to Ferraresi et al. (2008), we select

[4] `http://boston.lti.cs.cmu.edu/clueweb09/wiki/tiki-index.php?page=Language+Identification+for+ClueWeb09`

documents of MIME type text/html with size between 5K and 200K bytes. Also following Ferraresi et al. we extract the textual portions of the selected HTML documents using the body text extraction algorithm (BTE, Finn et al., 2001) which heuristically removes removes boilerplate based on the frequency of HTML tags.[5] We use Pomikálek's (2011) implementation of BTE. We remove duplicate and near-duplicate paragraphs using onion (Pomikálek, 2011) — the same tool used by Pomikálek et al. (2012) — with its default settings. In this configuration onion makes a single pass through a corpus, and eliminates any paragraph which shares more than 50% of its 7-grams with the portion of the corpus analysed so far. Finally we tokenise and sentence split our corpora using tools provided by the Stanford Natural Language Processing Group.[6]

ClueWeb09 is broken into a number of files, each containing approximately 100M of compressed crawl data; we apply the above method to build corpora from the first 1, 5, 10, 50, and 100 files in English ClueWeb09.[7] The sizes, in tokens, of the resulting corpora are shown in Table 1.

2.3 Language modelling

We construct language models using SRILM (Stolcke, 2002), a commonly-used, off-the-shelf toolkit for building and applying statistical language models. For each corpus built from ClueWeb09, we build an open-vocabulary language model using the default settings of SRILM, which correspond to an order 3 language model with Good-Turing smoothing. All language models were built using the `make-big-lm` script provided with SRILM.

We evaluate our language models by measuring the perplexity of the written portion of the British National Corpus (BNC, Burnard, 2000), a corpus of roughly 87 million words of British English from the late twentieth century, spanning a variety of genres and topics. Perplexity is a standard evaluation metric for language models, with lower perplexity indicating the model better fits the test data. Perplexities were calculated using the `ngram` program from SRILM, and are normalized counting all input tokens, including end-of-sentence tags.

# files	− `langid.py`		+ `langid.py`	
	# tokens	PPL	# tokens	PPL
1	16M	457.1	15M	457.5
5	81M	384.2	77M	381.0
10	156M	361.8	148M	359.4
50	795M	297.1	760M	294.9
100	1.6B	277.1	1.5B	275.4

Table 1: Number of tokens in each corpus built from increasing numbers of ClueWeb09 files, with and without document filtering using `langid.py`. The perplexity (PPL) of the BNC under a language model trained on the corresponding corpus is also shown.

3 Experimental setup and results

We train language models on each corpus derived from ClueWeb09, and then measure the perplexity of the written portion of the BNC (as described in Section 2.3). Results are shown in Table 1.

We begin by noting that for all corpus sizes considered with the exception of the smallest, the perplexity of the BNC is lower under a language model from the corpus filtered using `langid.py` than under a language model trained on a corpus built from the same original data but without this extra language identification step. This suggests that state-of-the-art language identification can indeed enable the construction of better corpora — at least for training language models for the BNC.

To assess whether the observed differences are significant, for each corpus size (i.e., number of ClueWeb09 files) we measure the perplexity of each BNC document under the language model from the corpus with, and without, filtering with `langid.py`. For a given corpus size this then gives us independent paired measurements, which we compare using a Wilcoxon rank sum test. For each corpus size the difference with and without `langid.py` filtering is highly significant ($p < 10^{-23}$ in each case).

Further analysing the case of the smallest cor-

[5] We do not consider JusText (Pomikálek, 2011), a recent alternative to BTE, because it incorporates rudimentary language identification in the form of stopword frequency; our specific goal is to study the effects of state-of-the-art language identification in corpus construction. We leave studying the interaction between various steps of corpus construction — including text extraction and language identification — for future work. Furthermore, BTE has been widely used in previous corpus construction projects (e.g., Baroni and Bernardini, 2004; Sharoff, 2006; Ferraresi et al., 2008).

[6] `http://nlp.stanford.edu/software/tokenizer.shtml`

[7] We use the files in en0000, the first section of ClueWeb09.

pus size considered, the perplexity is quite high in both cases, suggesting that the language model is under-fitting due to insufficient training data. It seems that in such cases — which correspond to corpora far smaller than one would typically build from a Web crawl — there is little to be gained from improved language identification (at least for the task of building trigram language models considered here).

With the exception of the smallest corpus, as corpus size increases, the absolute reduction in perplexity with and without `langid.py` decreases. In future work we plan to build much larger corpora to further examine this trend.

In addition to the BNC, we considered a number of other corpora for evaluation, including the Brown Corpus (Francis and Kucera, 1964) and a sample of texts provided with NLTK (Bird et al., 2009) from Project Gutenberg,[8] and found the results to be consistent with those on the BNC.

4 Discussion

In addition to demonstrating the importance of language identification in Web corpus construction, the results in Table 1 confirm Banko and Brill's (2001) findings about corpus size; in particular, for corpora built using the same method (i.e., with or without `langid.py`) bigger is better. However, for each corpus size (i.e., each number of files from ClueWeb09) the corpus filtered with `langid.py` is roughly 5% smaller — and yet produces a better language model — than the corresponding corpus not filtered in this way. Furthermore, because of their smaller size, the corpora filtered with `langid.py` have lower storage and processing costs.

Based on these findings, it appears we can improve corpora in two ways: by getting more data, and by better processing the data we have. Although it is certainly possible to build a larger Web crawl than ClueWeb09, doing so comes at a substantial cost in terms of bandwidth, processing, and storage (although Suchomel and Pomikálek (2012) have recently considered how to more-efficiently crawl the Web for linguistic data). Resources which are readily-available at relatively-low cost (such as ClueWeb09) are likely to serve as the basis for many corpus construction efforts, and it is therefore important to determine how to best exploit such a fixed resource in building corpora.

The largest language-filtered corpus built in this study consists of roughly 1.5B tokens. Although we eventually intend to build much larger corpora, this corpus size is on par with that of the ukWaC (Ferraresi et al., 2008) — a corpus that has been widely used in computational linguistics and as the basis for lexicographical analysis (e.g., Atkins, 2010). Our findings are therefore helpful in that they demonstrate the possibility for improving Web corpora of a size already shown to be of practical use. Nevertheless, in future work we intend to explore the impact of language identification on much larger corpora by building corpora from roughly an order of magnitude more data.

In an effort to better understand the differences between the language identifiers, we examined 100 documents from English ClueWeb09 classified as non-English by `langid.py`. We found that 33 were entirely non-English, 30 contained some text in English as well as another language, 27 were in fact English, and 10 contained no linguistic content. The prevalence of multilingual documents suggests that language identification at the sub-document (e.g., paragraph) level, or language identification methods capable of detecting mixtures of languages could lead to further improvements.

5 Conclusions

In this paper we have considered the impact of language identification on corpus construction, and shown that state-of-the art language identification leads to better language models. The ultimate goal of this research is to determine how to best derive a linguistic corpus from a Web crawl. In future work, we intend to consider other aspects of the corpus construction process, including webpage cleaning (e.g., removing boilerplate text) and deduplication. In this preliminary study we only considered language modelling for evaluation; in the future, we plan to carry out a more-comprehensive evaluation, including classification and rankings tasks (e.g., Banko and Brill, 2001; Liu and Curran, 2006; Versley and Panchenko, 2012) in addition to language modelling. To encourage further research on this problem, code to replicate the corpora created for, and experiments carried out in, this paper will be made publicly available upon publication.

[8] `http://www.gutenberg.org/`

Acknowledgments

NICTA is funded by the Australian Government as represented by the Department of Broadband, Communications and the Digital Economy and the Australian Research Council through the ICT Centre of Excellence program.

References

Beatrice Alex, Amit Dubey, and Frank Keller. 2007. Using foreign inclusion detection to improve parsing performance. In *Proceedings of the 2007 Joint Conference on Empirical Methods in Natural Language Processing and Computational Natural Language Learning (EMNLP-CoNLL 2007)*, pages 151–160. Prague, Czech Republic.

B. T. Sue Atkins. 2010. The DANTE Database: Its contribution to English lexical research, and in particular to complementing the FrameNet data. In Gilles-Maurice De Schryver, editor, *A Way with Words: Recent Advances in Lexical Theory and Analysis. A Festschrift for Patrick Hanks*. Menha Publishers, Kampala, Uganda.

Michele Banko and Eric Brill. 2001. Scaling to very very large corpora for natural language disambiguation. In *Proceedings of 39th Annual Meeting of the Association for Computational Linguistics (ACL 2001)*, pages 26–33. Toulouse, France.

Marco Baroni and Silvia Bernardini. 2004. BootCaT: Bootstrapping corpora and terms from the Web. In *Proceedings of the Fourth International Conference on Language Resources and Evaluation (LREC 2004)*. Lisbon, Portugal.

Marco Baroni, Francis Chantree, Adam Kilgarriff, and Serge Sharoff. 2008. Cleaneval: A competition for cleaning Web pages. In *Proceedings of the Sixth International Conference on Language Resources and Evaluation (LREC 2008)*, pages 638–643. Marrakech, Morocco.

Steven Bird, Edward Loper, and Ewan Klein. 2009. *Natural Language Processing with Python*. O'Reilly Media Inc., Sebastopol, CA.

Lou Burnard. 2000. *The British National Corpus Users Reference Guide*. Oxford University Computing Services.

William B. Cavnar and John M. Trenkle. 1994. N-gram-based text categorization. In *Proceedings of the 3rd Annual Symposium on Document Analysis and Information Retrieval (SDAIR-94)*, pages 161–175. Las Vegas, USA.

Charles L. A. Clarke, Nick Craswell, Ian Soboroff, and Ellen M. Voorhees. 2011. Overview of the TREC 2011 Web Track. In *Proceedings of the Twentieth Text REtrieval Conference (TREC 2011), NIST Special Publication: SP 500-295*.

Adriano Ferraresi, Eros Zanchetta, Marco Baroni, and Silvia Bernardini. 2008. Introducing and evaluating ukWaC, a very large web-derived corpus of English. In *Proceedings of the 4th Web as Corpus Workshop: Can we beat Google*, pages 47–54. Marrakech, Morocco.

Aidan Finn, Nicholas Kushmerick, and Barry Smyth. 2001. Fact or fiction: Content classification for digital libraries. In *Proceedings of the Second DELOS Network of Excellence Workshop on Personalisation and Recommender Systems in Digital Libraries*. Dublin, Ireland.

W. Nelson Francis and Henry Kucera. 1964. *Manual of Information to accompany A Standard Corpus of Present-Day Edited American English, for use with Digital Computers*. Brown University.

Adam Kilgarriff. 2007. Googleology is bad science. *Computational Linguistics*, 33(1):147–151.

Adam Kilgarriff, Siva Reddy, Jan Pomikálek, and Avinesh PVS. 2010. A corpus factory for many languages. In *Proceedings of the Seventh International Conference on Language Resources and Evaluation (LREC 2010)*, pages 904–910. Valletta, Malta.

Vinci Liu and James Curran. 2006. Web text corpus for natural language processing. In *Proceedings of the 11th Meeting of the European Chapter of the Association for Computational Linguistics (EACL 2006)*, pages 233–240. Trento, Italy.

Marco Lui and Timothy Baldwin. 2011. Cross-domain feature selection for language identification. In *Proceedings of the 5th International Joint Conference on Natural Language Processing (IJCNLP 2011)*, pages 553–561. Chiang Mai, Thailand.

Marco Lui and Timothy Baldwin. 2012. langid.py: An off-the-shelf language identification tool. In *Proceedings of the 50th Annual Meeting of the Association for Computational Linguistics (ACL 2012) Demo Session*, pages 25–30. Jeju, Republic of Korea.

Brian Murphy and Egon Stemle. 2011. PaddyWaC: A minimally-supervised Web-corpus of Hiberno-English. In *Proceedings of the First Workshop on Algorithms and Resources for Modelling of Dialects and Language Varieties*, pages 22–29. Edinburgh, Scotland.

Jan Pomikálek. 2011. *Removing Boilerplate and Duplicate Content from Web Corpora*. Ph.D. thesis, Masaryk University.

Jan Pomikálek, Miloš Jakubíček, and Pavel Rychlý. 2012. Building a 70 billion word corpus of English from ClueWeb. In *Proceedings of the Eighth International Conference on Language Resources and Evaluation (LREC 2012)*, pages 502–506. Istanbul, Turkey.

Serge Sharoff. 2006. Creating general-purpose corpora using automated search engine queries. In Marco Baroni and Silvia Bernardini, editors, *Wacky! Working papers on the Web as Corpus*, pages 63–98. GEDIT, Bologna, Italy.

Andreas Stolcke. 2002. SRILM - an extensible language modeling toolkit. In *Proceedings of the International Conference on Spoken Language Processing*, volume 2, pages 901–904. Denver, USA.

Vit Suchomel and Jan Pomikálek. 2012. Efficient Web crawling for large text corpora. In *Proceedings of the seventh Web as Corpus Workshop (WAC7)*, pages 39–43. Lyon, France.

Yannick Versley and Yana Panchenko. 2012. Not just bigger: Towards better-quality Web corpora. In *Proceedings of the seventh Web as Corpus Workshop (WAC7)*, pages 44–52.

LaBB-CAT: an Annotation Store

Robert Fromont
NZILBB, University of Canterbury
Private Bag 4800
Christchurch, New Zealand
robert.fromont@canterbury.ac.nz

Jennifer Hay
NZILBB, University of Canterbury
Private Bag 4800
Christchurch, New Zealand
jen.hay@canterbury.ac.nz

Abstract

"ONZE Miner", an open-source tool for storing and automatically annotating Transcriber transcripts, has been redeveloped to use "annotation graphs" as its data model. The annotation graph framework provides the new software, "LaBB-CAT", greater flexibility for automatic and manual annotation of corpus data at various independent levels of granularity, and allows more sophisticated annotation structures, opening up new possibilities for corpus mining and conversion between tool formats.

1 Introduction

"ONZE Miner" (Fromont & Hay 2008) was a browser-based, searchable database tool for time-aligned transcripts of speech produced using Transcriber, a transcription and annotation tool developed by Barras et al. (2000). It has been used for a variety of research projects in various universities and labs, primarily for sociophonetic research.

ONZE Miner's original data structure was designed to closely mirror that of Transcriber, so transcripts are divided into topic-tagged *sections*, which contain speaker *turns*, divided up into utterance *lines* containing text and other 'event' annotations such as noises, comments, etc. In order to allow automatic annotation of lexical data from CELEX (Baayen *et al.*, 1995), and to facilitate storage for forced-alignments produced by the Hidden Markov Model Toolkit, HTK (Young et al. 2006), *lines* were tokenized into *words* that were stored as separately annotatable units, which could be further divided into *segments* for storage of phones produced by HTK.

For researchers with large collections of recordings and Transcriber transcripts, ONZE Miner was very useful for mining corpus data, but it had certain limitations related to its data structures, which are explained below.

1.1 Other Formats

Many corpora exist, or are being produced, using tools other than Transcriber. For example the Buckeye corpus (Pitt et al. 2007) includes aligned transcription files in the Xwaves (Hawkins 2008) format, and transcriptions for various other corpora are available as Praat (Boersma & Weenink 2005) textgrids.

For ONZE Miner, support for these was only available via conversion from these formats to Transcriber files before importing the data. The problem was that, in many cases, the data was not structured in a way that was compatible with the Transcriber model. For example, some formats include much finer-grained synchronisation than is typically available with Transcriber.

Simultaneous speech also presented problems for data conversion. In Transcriber, overlapping speech is modelled using a 'simultaneous speech' turn – i.e. a single turn that has multiple speakers attached to it, and multiple corresponding transcriptions. For example, if a second speaker started their turn before a first speaker finished theirs, this would be modelled as three turns:

1. a turn containing words spoken while only the first speaker is speaking,
2. a 'simultaneous speech' turn containing words spoken by both speakers, during the time that they are both speaking, and
3. a turn containing words spoken by the only second speaker, once the first speaker is no longer talking.

However, when researchers transcribe using other tools, they often treat cases like this as being two turns that overlap:

1. a turn containing words spoken by the first speaker, from the time they start talking to the time they stop, and
2. a turn containing words spoken by the second speaker, from the time they start talking to the time they stop, this turn having a start time earlier than the end time of the previous turn.

For ONZE Miner, the only option when importing non-Transcriber data was to convert this second model to the first model (i.e. break the two turns into three), which would have involved an inevitable loss of accuracy when trying to create the middle 'simultaneous speech' turn.

1.2 Different Annotation Granularities

Transcriber has facility for topic-tagging sections of transcripts, and for marking named entities, but beyond this, little facility for independent annotation of multiple words.

This meant that ONZE Miner couldn't be used to store annotations for multiple, independent, and possibly overlapping sets of such annotations. As a result, it was impossible to simultaneously have, for example, topic tags and speaker attitude tags dividing up the transcript in different ways, and also impossible to make more finely-grained multi-word annotations, e.g. phrasal verbs, genitive phrase constructions, syntactic parses, etc.

1.3 Development of a New Data Structure

As a result of these limitations, we decided to develop a new system, using ONZE Miner as a basis, keeping all of ONZE Miner's features and interfaces, but introducing new capabilities. The new system, LaBB-CAT (**La**nguage, **B**rain and **B**ehaviour – **C**orpus **A**nalysis **T**ool), adopts a different underlying data model, "annotation graphs", which is described in section 2. How annotation graphs solve the above problems, and introduces new possibilities, is discussed in section 3.

2 Annotation Graphs and LaBB-CAT

Bird and Liberman (1999 a&b) proposed a framework for modelling linguistic annotations, which seemed to provide potential solutions for the limitations faced by ONZE Miner. A new annotation storage tool was developed, called LaBB-CAT, which would maintain ONZE Miner's general way of working with recordings, transcripts, annotation, and search via web browser, but use a new data model based on annotation graphs.

2.1 Annotation Graphs

Bird and Liberman proposed a model for linguistic data which they claimed could encompass a wide variety of types of linguistic annotation. The commonality that Bird & Liberman saw between all approaches to linguistic annotation is that annotations are always:

1. some kind of contentful label, and
2. each label is usually 'anchored' to some portion of a 'source' (e.g. the recording).

They model this using digraphs, which consist of nodes that are joined by directional arcs. In their model:

1. labels are arcs, and
2. anchors are nodes.

In order to be specifically useful for linguistic annotation, there are some extra features to the model:

Arcs can have:

- a 'label' which represents the 'content' of the annotation (e.g. the orthography, the part of speech, the phonemic transcription, etc.)
- a 'type' which categorises the label (e.g. as being an 'orthography', or a 'part of speech', or a 'phonemic transcription', etc.)
- an optional 'class' which provides a mechanism for linking distal annotations by membership to an equivalence class.

In addition, nodes can have an 'offset' which represents the temporal position of the anchor (e.g. number of seconds since the beginning of the recording), but the offset is optional, so that annotations having no precise position in time can be represented.

By virtue of being a digraph, every arc has a start and end node, meaning that every annotation has a start point and an end point. However, these may have the same offset, to represent annotations of instants rather than intervals in time.

Annotations may share anchors, thereby reflecting a logical relationship between two annotations and conversely, two annotations may use two different anchors that have the same offset, thereby reflecting the lack of logical relationship between the annotations despite coincidence in time.

2.2 LaBB-CAT Implementation

The relational database schema we designed for LaBB-CAT is not dissimilar to that proposed for annotation graphs by Ma et al. (2002), but with some changes to enhance performance and meet specific needs for the time-aligned transcription data and annotations already stored using ONZE Miner.

In particular, both anchors (nodes) and annotations (arcs) carry a 'status' field that allows automatic annotations and alignments to be distinguished from manual ones. This is used, for example, to prevent HTK forced-alignment from overwriting alignments that have already been hand-corrected.

In addition, annotation records are kept in separate layer tables instead of a single table, and have a number of extra fields that allow, for example, a word's turn annotation to be immediately identified, without having to traverse the graph structure to find it (thus avoiding a constraint that the graph be connected between words and turns to make such a traversal possible).

These departures boost the performance of LaBB-CAT, both for searching and automatic annotation. However, they impose on the data an 'ontology' that isn't formally present in Bird & Liberman's original proposal. Essentially LaBB-CAT assumes that there are speaker turns, words, and sub-word segments.

In Bird & Liberman's definition anchor offsets are optional. In contrast, LaBB-CAT anchors are always given an offset. Where an accurate offset is not known, the offsets are computed by linear interpolation. These anchors are marked as having 'default' offsets using their status field, so they can be easily identified if required for data export, but having an approximate offset has two advantages:

- The anchors can always be sorted in relation to surrounding anchors, to help internal operations like displaying the transcript to the user.
- It provides research assistants a starting point to work with if they need to do manual alignment from scratch.

3 Advantages of Annotation Graphs

Having implemented essentially an annotation graph store, LaBB-CAT overcomes the limitations of ONZE Miner described is section 1, and supports a number of new possibilities for annotation creation and refinement.

3.1 Importing Data

Bird & Liberman's aim was to facilitate linguistic data exchange, and they demonstrated how annotation graphs could be used to model data from a number of linguistic tools.

LaBB-CAT modules can be implemented that convert data from the original format directly into LaBB-CAT's annotation graph structure, thereby escaping from any requirement that data be first convertible to a Transcriber file. We have already implemented converters for Transcriber files, Praat textgrids, Xwaves files as used by the Buckeye corpus, and ELAN (Sloetjes & Wittenburg, 2008) annotation files.

Simultaneous speech presented a particular problem for ONZE Miner's Transcriber-centric model. However with annotation graphs, either of the approaches to simultaneous-speech described in section 1.1 can be accommodated.

3.2 Exporting Data

Annotation graphs also allow for conversion of annotation data to a wider variety of formats.

As has already been expressed in the results from 2007 Multimodal Annotation Tools Workshops (Schmidt et al. 2008), and by the TILR2 Working Group 1 (Chochran et al. 2007), this is sometimes necessarily a lossy process, as different tools have different priorities, ontologies, and ways of structuring data (e.g. handling of simultaneous speech, as described in section 1.1). Thus not all of the information that was present in one file format when imported into LaBB-CAT will necessarily still be present when it's exported to a different format.

3.3 Round tripping

A further possibility that is suggested by import/export of data in various formats is that of re-importing data that has been exported and then refined. We have already implemented such round-trip data conversion, using algorithms that allow an annotation graph (or partial graph) to be merged into another:

1. A full Transcriber transcript is uploaded into LaBB-CAT, where an annotation graph is constructed.
2. Then a single utterance from the graph may be exported to Praat as a textgrid.
3. Edits are made in Praat to add, edit, and

re-align annotations.

4. The resulting textgrid can then be re-imported into LaBB-CAT, where it is converted into a graph fragment, which is compared to the full annotation graph stored in the database. The change deltas are then identified, validated, and saved to the database.

This is the kind of scenario presented by the TILR Working Group 1 as being a solution to the inevitable loss of information during conversion mentioned in section 3.2. They call this a "process-based" architecture for providing interoperability between different software tools.

With increased convertibility of LaBB-CAT annotation graphs from/to other formats, it's hoped that similar export/import interfaces can be developed involving other tools, using the annotation graph model as the pivot for annotation refinement. Information loss due to format conversion needn't always be a problem, as the central annotation store retains what gets lost in translation during export, and can thus use it to reconcile changes introduced during re-import, without loss of information.

3.4 Annotation Granularity and Structure

As annotation graphs don't include the compulsory definition of a single set of 'sections' with topic tags, any number of new layers can be created in LaBB-CAT and populated with independent sets of tags for annotating stretches of speech. These might contain annotations over long sections of transcript, or annotate only a few words at a time, or parts of words, e.g. stress-marked syllable annotations computed by combining HTK-produced phones within words and syllabification data from CELEX.

3.5 Syntactic Parses

In ONZE Miner, tree structures could not be modelled, so it was not possible to use readily available parsers like the Stanford Parser (Klein & Manning 2003) to provide syntactic parse annotations over utterances.

For annotation graphs, Bird and Liberman presented a possible technique for modelling trees using annotation graphs[1], where phrases can have their own bounding annotations, together marking the syntactic constituents of utterances.

We have taken this approach in LaBB-CAT, where a layer can be defined as containing trees. A newly created 'Stanford Parser' module can be configured to populate the layer with syntactic parses computed over words from another layer. These are represented in the annotation graph as arcs linking nodes, like all other annotations. We have also implemented an editor that allows these constructions to be viewed and edited using a tree layout more familiar to linguists.

4 Future Work

We have not yet implemented converters for some other commonly-used tools like Transana (Mavrikisa & Gernaniou 2011), Emu (Bombien et al. 2006), etc. While there will undoubtedly be some nuances to each of these cases, Bird & Liberman have shown that there should be no obstacle in principle to their representation as annotation graphs. Current and future work thus involves identifying tools and formats, both for import and export of data, making LaBB-CAT not only useful to a wider variety of researchers, but also making the data stored by it more shareable.

In addition there are many more possibilities for automatic annotation; lexical databases other than CELEX, other computations that may be useful, e.g. training classifiers for automated topic tagging, etc.

5 Conclusion

While ONZE Miner enabled several options for automatic and manual annotation of linguistic data, the adoption of an annotation graph framework for LaBB-CAT opens up new possible levels of granularity and sophistication for annotation and search.

The challenges that remain to be addressed reflect this new set of possibilities and the increasing diversity of domains in which LaBB-CAT can be of use as an annotation data store.

Acknowledgments

We would like to thank the anonymous reviewers for their helpful comments.

References

Baayen, H.; R. Piepenbrock; H. van Rijn, 1995. The CELEX Lexical Database (Release 2, CD-ROM), LDC Catalogue No.: LDC96L14, Linguistic Data Consortium, University of Pennsylvania, Philadelphia.

Barras, C.; E. Geoffrois; Z. Wu; M. Liberman, 2000. Transcriber: development and use of a tool for assisting speech corpora production, Speech

[1] For example Bird & Liberman 1999b §3.2 Figure 10

Communication 33 (special issue on Speech Annotation and Corpus Tools) Numbers 1–2.

Bird, Steven; Mark Liberman, 1999a. A Formal Framework for Linguistic Annotation, Technical Report MS-CIS-99-01, Department of Computer and Information Science, University of Pennsylvania, (arXiv:cs/9903003v1 [cs.CL]).

Bird, Steven; Mark Liberman, 1999b. Annotation graphs as a framework for multidimensional linguistic data analysis, in proceedings from the Association for Computational Linguistics workshops "Towards Standards and Tools for Discourse Tagging" workshop, pp. 1-10, (arXiv:cs/9907003v1 [cs.CL]).

Boersma, P.; D. Weenink, 2005. Praat: Doing Phonetics by Computer (Version 4.3.14) [http://www.praat.org/]

Bombien, L.; S. Cassidy; J. Harrington; T. John; S. Palethorpe, 2006. Recent Developments in the Emu Speech Database System, in Proceedings of the Australian Speech Science and Technology Conference, Auckland, December 2006.

Cochran, Michael; Jeff Good; Dan Loehr; S. A. Miller; Shane Stephens; Briony Williams; Imelda Udoh, 2007. Report from TILR Working Group 1: Tools interoperability and input/output formats, Working Group report from the "Toward the Interoperability of Language Resources" workshop, 2007 LSA Summer Institute. [http://linguistlist.org/tilr/]

Fromont, Robert; Jennifer Hay, 2008. ONZE Miner: the development of a browser-based research tool, Corpora, vol. 3, no. 2, pp. 173–193.

Hawkins, Sarah, 2008. Introduction to Xwaves+. [http://www.ling.cam.ac.uk/li9/waves_08.pdf]

Klein, Dan; Christopher D. Manning, 2003. Accurate Unlexicalized Parsing, in proceedings of the 41st Meeting of the Association for Computational Linguistics, pp. 423-430.

Ma, Xiaoyi; Haejoong Lee; Steven Bird; Kazuaki Maeda, 2002. Models and Tools for Collaborative Annotation, in proceedings of the Third International Conference on Language Resources and Evaluation (LREC 2002), European Language Resources Association, Paris.

Mavrikisa, Manolis; Eirini Geranioub, 2011. Using Qualitative Data Analysis Software to analyse students' computer-mediated interactions: the case of MiGen and Transana, International Journal of Social Research Methodology, Volume 14, Issue 3, pp. 245-252.

Pitt, M.A.; L. Dilley; K. Johnson; S. Kiesling; W. Raymond; E. Hume; E. Fosler-Lussier, 2007. Buckeye Corpus of Conversational Speech (2nd release), Department of Psychology, Ohio State University (Distributor).

[http://www.buckeyecorpus.osu.edu]

Schmidt, T.; S. Duncan; O. Ehmer; J. Hoyt; M. Kipp; D. Loehr; M. Magnusson; T. Rose; H. Sloetjes, 2008. An exchange format for multimodal annotations, in proceedings of the 6th International Conference on Language Resources and Evaluation (LREC 2008).

Sloetjes, H.; P. Wittenburg, 2008. Annotation by category - ELAN and ISO DCR, in proceedings of the 6th International Conference on Language Resources and Evaluation (LREC 2008).

Young, Steve; Gunnar Evermann; Mark Gales; Thomas Hain; Dan Kershaw; Xunying (Andrew) Liu; Gareth Moore; Julian Odell; Dave Ollason; Dan Povey; Valtcho Valtchev; Phil Woodland, 2006. The HTK Book (for HTK Version 3.4), Cambridge University Engineering Department.

Classification of Study Region in Environmental Science Abstracts

Jared Willett,[♠] **Timothy Baldwin,**[♠♡] **David Martinez**[♡] and **Angus Webb**[◇]
♠ Department of Computing and Information Systems
♡ NICTA Victoria Research Laboratory
◇ Department of Resource Management and Geography
The University of Melbourne, VIC 3010, Australia
jwillett@student.unimelb.edu.au, tb@ldwin.net,
davidm@csse.unimelb.edu.au, angus.webb@unimelb.edu.au

Abstract

One of the potentially most relevant pieces of metadata for filtering studies in environmental science is the geographic region in which the study took place (the "study region"). In this paper, we apply support vector machines to the automatic classification of study region in a dataset of titles and abstracts from environmental science literature, using features including frequency distributions of resolved toponyms and a bag of word unigrams. We found that we can determine the study region with high accuracy, with the strongest classifier achieving an accuracy of 0.892 combining toponym resolution from DBpedia and GeoNames with the bag-of-toponyms features.

1 Introduction

One of the potentially most relevant pieces of metadata for filtering studies in environmental science is the region in which the study took place, as users making queries are often looking for studies performed in a specific area. However, bibliographic databases do not systematically include information on study location. The Eco Evidence database, a compendium of literature citations and linked evidence items that is used for evidence synthesis in companion software (Webb et al., 2011), is one such system for which location information is very helpful. However, the manual annotation of such metadata over large quantities of literature is a tedious and time-consuming task.

One possible solution to this issue is to have this information automatically extracted with the aid of natural language processing (NLP) techniques. The abstracts of studies, which are commonly available in bibliographic databases, frequently contain geographic references of various granularities. If identified and resolved, these toponyms provide the potential to make a strong estimation of the overall location of the study. In these experiments, we evaluate the performance of various NLP techniques for automatic classification of the study region in environmental science literature abstracts.

Beyond the aim of being able to quickly assemble a collection of literature from a given area, our motivation in applying NLP to automatically extract information from environmental science literature is driven by our interest in moving towards an evidence-based model of decision-making in the environmental sciences (Sutherland et al., 2004). Similar to evidence-based medicine (Sackett et al., 1996), such a model relies heavily on systematic literature reviews as a means of synthesizing evidence from the literature. The Eco Evidence database (Webb et al., in press) is a compendium of literature citations and linked evidence items that is used for systematic review and evidence synthesis in companion software (Webb et al., 2011). The database is in active use in a number of research projects currently, and evidence therein has also formed the basis of several published systematic reviews (Webb et al., 2012). However, all evidence in the database is currently manually annotated.

2 Background Work

Our motivation in applying NLP to automatically extract information from environmental science literature is driven by our interest in moving towards an evidence-based model of decision-making in the environmental sciences (Sutherland et al., 2004), similar to evidence-based medicine (Sackett et al., 1996). Our work is directly motivated by the possibility of streamlining the population of the Eco Evidence database by automatically extracting location information, but has wider potential application to other bibliographic databases where there is a geospatial dimension to the data.

Comparable work in the biomedical domain has focused on the automatic extraction of Medical Subject Headings (MeSH) terms in abstracts (Gaudinat and Boyer, 2002), labeling documents based on specific terms in the abstract which are to be resolved to more general categories.

The unique opportunities and challenges specific to retrieving geospatial information have been well documented, particularly in the context of geospatial information retrieval where queries and documents have a geospatial dimension (Santos and Chaves, 2006). Aside from finding locations in the text, the disambiguation of what exact location a term in a text is referring to presents a unique challenge in itself, and a variety of approaches have been suggested and demonstrated for this task (Overell and Rüger, 2006).

The methodology described in this work is based on a standard approach to geographic informaton retrieval, which was demonstrated by Stokes et al. (2008) in their study of the performance of individual components of a geographic IR system. In particular, the named entity recognition and toponym resolution (TR) components are the basis for all the main classifiers in this study.

3 Method

3.1 Dataset

The dataset for these experiments consists of the titles and abstracts for 4158 environmental science studies recorded in the Eco Evidence database. One such sample abstract (Fu et al., 2004) can be read below:

> Title: Hydro-climatic trends of the Yellow River basin for the last 50 years
>
> Abstract: Kendall's test was used to analyze the hydro-climatic trends of the Yellow River over the last half century. The results show that: ...[1]

Study regions for these papers have been manually annotated, providing a gold standard for purposes of training and evaluation. The study region can be chosen from ten different options: Europe, Australia, Africa, Antarctica, Asia, North America, South America, Oceania, Multiple and Other. The dataset is not evenly distributed: North America is the most commonly annotated study region, covering 41.5% of the studies, while other classes such as Antarctica and Other were extreme minorities. Oceania represents all countries contained in Australasia, Melanesia, Micronesia and Polynesia, with the exclusion of Australia (which, as a continent, has its own category). 'Multiple' refers to studies done across multiple regions, and 'Other' is used for studies where no particular region is evident or relevant to a work (i.e. a literature review). These two labels present difficulty for methods based on toponym resolution, as studies with toponyms from multiple regions or none at all are often still considered to be located in one continent. However, Multiple and Other are minority labels, comprising only 3.5% and 0.2% of the dataset respectively.

3.2 Named Entity Recognition

The first component of our system involves extracting references to locations contained in the abstract, a task which we approach using named entity recognition (NER). NER is an NLP task in which we seek to automatically extract 'named entities', which refer to any term in a body of text that represents the name of a thing considered an instance of one of a predefined set of categories.

Our first experiments focused on evaluating the performance of the off-the-shelf 3-class model of the Stanford NER system (Finkel et al., 2005) in detecting relevant named entities in the titles and abstracts. The NER system classifies identified entities as people, locations or organizations. For our task, only named entities that are locations are relevant, thus only these entities are extracted and evaluated.

3.3 Toponym Resolution

Once the named entities tagged as locations for each abstract were collected, we experimented with resolving each location to its corresponding continent using two different databases of geospatial entities. Two methods were employed for each database: (1) observing only the top result to resolve the location; and (2) returning the frequency distribution of the top-five results.

In each classifier where tags were resolved to continents, we experimented with using each sys-

[1] The sample abstract has been truncated here, but contains no further toponyms.

tem separately as well as in combination, simply combining together the results from the two databases.

3.3.1 DBpedia

First, we resolve toponyms with DBpedia (http://www.dbpedia.org), a database of structured content extracted from Wikipedia. If the page retrieved for a given toponym has geographic coordinates available, these are extracted and checked against a set of non-overlapping bounding boxes, which were manually constructed by setting one or more ranges of longitude and latitude for each possible label except 'Multiple' and 'Other'. If the extracted coordinates are within the range of one of the bounding boxes, the corresponding label is applied to the term.

For terms with multiple meanings, DBpedia will contain a disambiguation page. For the top-result TR approach, in the event that coordinates are unavailable for the first possibility on the disambiguation page, no resolution is recorded for the term. For the top-5 approach, we continue to look for results until all disambiguations have been exhausted or five resolutions have been found.

3.3.2 GeoNames

Second, we resolve toponyms with GeoNames (http://www.geonames.org), a gazetteer which collects data from a wide variety of sources. A query was done for each toponym using the GeoNames search function, which directly provides a ranked list of results with continent codes.

3.4 Majority Vote

As a baseline, we use only the retrieved continents from either DBpedia, GeoNames or both, and determine the final classification by a simple majority vote. When there is a tie in the top number of resolutions, the continent that appears most frequently in the training data is chosen. If the classifier is unable to resolve any toponyms for a given instance, the majority class label in the training data (which is consistently North America, across all folds of cross-validation) is used as a backoff.

3.5 SVM Classification

All our supervised classifiers are based on support vector machines (SVMs), using LibSVM (Chang and Lin, 2011). With SVMs, instances are represented as points in n-dimensional space, with each dimension representing a different feature, and the classification of test instances is done based on which side of a binary dividing hyperplane the instance falls on. In all our experiments, we use a linear kernel, and all other LibSVM parameters are set to the default. The SVM method is adapted to the multi-class task in LibSVM using the "one-against-one" method, in which binary classification is used between each two candidate labels and the label for which the instance is classified to the highest number of times it is selected. In this section, the features used to construct the vectors are described.

Classifier	F-score
Majority class	0.415
Oracle	0.969
Bag-of-Toponyms (BoT)	0.834
Bag-of-Words (BoW)	0.729
BoT + BoW	0.773

Table 1: Accuracy for classifiers w/o toponym resolution.

3.5.1 Continent Resolutions

The continent-level results from DBpedia and/or GeoNames were represented as frequency distributions over the number of results for each continent returned for a given instance. When both DBpedia and GeoNames are used, the counts are accumulated into a single frequency distribution.

3.5.2 Bag of Words Features

We used a bag-of-words model in two forms. The first only considered the toponyms as tokens, creating features of a count for each toponym over the full dataset. The second type applied the standard bag-of-words model over all words found in the abstracts.

3.6 Evaluation

In order to establish an upper bound for the task, the first author manually performed the study region classification task over 290 randomly-sampled abstracts classified. The accuracy for this "oracle" method was 0.969. In all of cases where the manual annotation was incorrect, there was insufficient data in the abstract to reasonably deter-

Classifier	DBp:1R	Geo:1R	D+G:1R	DBp:MR	Geo:MR	D+G:MR
Majority Vote	0.802	0.830	0.875	0.788	0.822	0.851
SVM	0.829	0.832	0.877	0.813	0.843	0.862
SVM + BoT	0.879	0.877	0.892	0.873	0.879	0.887
SVM + BoW	0.855	0.862	0.889	0.846	0.868	0.884
SVM + BoT + BoW	0.862	0.868	0.891	0.854	0.873	0.886

Table 2: Accuracy for DBpedia/GeoNames classifiers ("1R" = top-1 toponym resolution; "MR" = multiple resolutions)

mine the location of the study.[2]

Our primary evaluation metric for the overall classification task is classification accuracy. For all classifiers except the oracle annotation, the final scores are the result of 10-fold stratified cross-validation over the dataset.

4 Results

First, we evaluated the token-level accuracy of the NER system over our dataset, to determine its performance in the domain of environmental science. 30 abstracts were selected randomly, and all named entity locations were manually identified. Based on these annotations, the off-the-shelf results for the Stanford NER were a respectable 0.875 precision, 0.778 recall, and 0.824 F-score. One of the most common causes of false positive was species names. The knock-on effect of incorrect or missed tags should be considered as one source of error in the overall classification task.

Table 2 shows the results of the classifiers featuring toponym resolution. Overall, the DBpedia and GeoNames classifiers performed at a similar level, with most GeoNames classifiers slightly outperforming their DBpedia counterparts. When the resolutions from DBpedia and GeoNames were combined, accuracy increased for all classifiers. Combining the results basically doubles the confidence of continents where there is agreement between the databases, which can be particularly helpful given the sparsity of tagged locations for each abstract. Including the top-5 results ("MR" in Table 2) consistently decreased the accuracy, suggesting that noise in incorporating additional possible disambiguations outweighs any gains in capturing ambiguity.

Supervised learning is clearly beneficial to the task, as the majority-vote classifier is consistently outperformed by the SVM classifiers, particularly when bag-of-toponyms and/or bag-of-words features are included. The bag-of-toponyms consistently outperforms the unfiltered bag-of-words, especially when isolated from TR frequency features (shown in Table 2), indicating that including other lexical information provides insufficient additional relevance to outweigh the noise, and that explicitly incorporating geospatial features boosts accuracy. Ultimately, the best-performing classifier utilised the top result from both DBpedia and GeoNames, using the bag-of-toponyms and top-result frequency features, achieving an accuracy of 0.892, well above the accuracy of both the majority class baseline at 0.415 and the simple bag-of-words classifier at 0.729, and only slightly below the human-based upper bound of 0.969. The difference between this best-performing SVM classifer and the majority vote classifier of the same toponym resolution approach was found to be statistically significant ($p = .001$) using randomization tests (Yeh, 2000).

5 Conclusion and Future Work

We have demonstrated that NLP approaches paired with toponym resolution are highly successful at identifying the study region from the abstracts of publications within the environmental science domain, with our best classifier achieving an accuracy of 0.892, compared to a human-based upper bound of 0.969.

Possible future work could include weighting of different toponym granularities, exploiting geo-spatial relationships between identified toponyms, and domain-adapting a NER for the environmental sciences.

Acknowledgments

NICTA is funded by the Australian Government as represented by the Department of Broadband, Com-

[2] In many cases, the gold-standard annotation was based on the full-text paper, which we do not make use of in this study.

munications and the Digital Economy and the Australian Research Council through the ICT Centre of Excellence program.

References

C.-C. Chang and C.-J. Lin. 2011. LIBSVM: A library for support vector machines. *ACM Transactions on Intelligent Systems and Technology*, 2:27:1–27:27. Software available at `http://www.csie.ntu.edu.tw/~cjlin/libsvm`.

J.R. Finkel, T. Grenager, and C. Manning. 2005. Incorporating non-local information into information extraction systems by gibbs sampling. In *Proceedings of the 43rd Annual Meeting on Association for Computational Linguistics*, pages 363–370, Ann Arbor, USA.

G. Fu, S. Chen, C. Liu, and D. Shepard. 2004. Hydro-climatic trends of the yellow river basin for the last 50 years. *Climatic Change*, 65(1):149–178.

A. Gaudinat and C. Boyer. 2002. Automatic extraction of MeSH terms from Medline abstracts. In *Workshop on Natural Language Processing in Biomedical Applications*, pages 53–57, Nicosia, Cyprus.

S.E. Overell and S. Rüger. 2006. Identifying and grounding descriptions of places. In *3rd Workshop on Geographic Information Retrieval*, Seattle, USA. SIGIR.

D.L. Sackett, W. Rosenberg, JA Gray, R.B. Haynes, and W.S. Richardson. 1996. Evidence based medicine: what it is and what it isn't. *BMJ*, 312(7023):71–72.

D. Santos and M.S. Chaves. 2006. The place of place in geographical IR. In *3rd Workshop on Geographic Information Retrieval*, Seattle, USA. SIGIR.

N. Stokes, Y. Li, A. Moffat, and J. Rong. 2008. An empirical study of the effects of nlp components on geographic ir performance. *International Journal of Geographical Information Science*, 22(3):247–264.

W.J. Sutherland, A.S. Pullin, P.M. Dolman, and T.M. Knight. 2004. The need for evidence-based conservation. *Trends in Ecology & Evolution*, 19(6):305–308.

J.A. Webb, S.R. Wealands, P. Lea, S.J. Nichols, S.C. de Little, M.J. Stewardson, R.H. Norris, F. Chan, D. Marinova, and R.S. Anderssen. 2011. Eco Evidence: using the scientific literature to inform evidence-based decision making in environmental management. In *MODSIM2011 International Congress on Modelling and Simulation*, pages 2472–2478, Perth, Australia.

J.A. Webb, E.M. Wallis, and M.J. Stewardson. 2012. A systematic review of published evidence linking wetland plants to water regime components. *Aquatic Botany*.

J.A. Webb, S.C. de Little, K.A. Miller, and M.J. Stewardson. in press. Eco evidence database: a distributed modelling resource for systematic literature analysis in environmental science and management. In R. Seppelt, A. A. Voinov, S. Lange, and D. Bankamp, editors, *2012 International Congress on Environmental Modelling and Software*, Leipzig, Germany. International Environmental Modelling and Software Society.

A. Yeh. 2000. More accurate tests for the statistical significance of result differences. In *Proc. of the 18th International Conference on Computational Linguistics (COLING 2000)*, volume 2, pages 947–953, Saarbrücken, Germany. Association for Computational Linguistics.

ALTA Shared Task papers

Overview of the ALTA 2012 Shared Task

Iman Amini* David Martinez[†] Diego Molla‡
***RMIT Dept of Computer Science and NICTA, Australia**
[†]NICTA and the University of Melbourne, CIS Department, Australia
‡Department of Computing, Macquarie University, Australia
iman.amini@rmit.edu.au
david.martinez@nicta.edu.au
diego.molla-aliod@mq.edu.au

Abstract

The ALTA shared task ran for the third time in 2012, with the aim of bringing research students together to work on the same task and data set, and compare their methods in a current research problem. The task was based on a recent study to build classifiers for automatically labeling sentences to a pre-defined set of categories, in the domain of Evidence Based Medicine (EBM). The partaking groups demonstrated strong skills this year, outperforming our proposed benchmark systems. In this overview paper we explain the process of building the benchmark classifiers and data set, and present the submitted systems and their performance.

1 Introduction

Medical research articles are one of the main sources for finding answers to clinical queries, and medical practitioners are advised to base their decisions on the available medical literature. Using the literature for the purpose of medical decision making is known as Evidence Based Medicine (EBM).

According to the EBM guidelines, users are suggested to formulate queries which follow structured settings, and one of the most used systems is known as PICO: Population (P) (i.e., participants in a study); Intervention (I); Comparison (C) (if appropriate); and Outcome (O) (of an Intervention). This system allows for a better classification of articles, and improved search. However curating this kind of information manually is unfeasible, due to the large amount of publications being created on daily basis.

The goal of the ALTA 2012 shared task was to build automatic sentence classifiers to map the content of biomedical abstracts into a set of pre-defined categories. The development of this kind of technology would speed up the curation process, and this has been explored in recent work (Chung, 2009; Kim et al., 2011). One of the aims of this task was to determine whether participants could develop systems that can improve over the state of the art.

2 Dataset

Different variations and extensions of the PICO classification have been proposed and the schema used for this competition is PIBOSO (Kim et al., 2011), which removes the *Comparison* tag, and adds three new tags: *Background* , *Study Design* and *Other*. Thus, the tag-set is defined as follows:

- *Population*: The group of individual persons, objects, or items comprising the study's sample, or from which the sample was taken for statistical measurement;
- *Intervention*: The act of interfering with a condition to modify it or with a process to change its course (includes prevention);
- *Background*: Material that informs and may place the current study in perspective, e.g. work that preceded the current; information about disease prevalence; etc;
- *Outcome*: The sentence(s) that best summarise(s) the consequences of an intervention;
- *Study Design*: The type of study that is described in the abstract;

	All	Struct.	Unstruct.
Total			
- Abstracts	1,000	38.9%	61.1%
- Sentences	11,616	56.2%	43.8%
- Labels	12,211	55.9%	44.1%
% per label			
- Population	7.0%	5.6%	7.9%
- Intervention	5.9%	4.9%	6.6%
- Background	22.0%	10.3%	34.2%
- Outcome	38.9%	34.0%	40.9%
- Study Design	2.0%	2.3%	1.4%
- Other	29.2%	42.9%	9.0%

Table 1: Statistics of the dataset. "% per label" refers to the percentage of sentences that contain the given label (the sum is higher than 100% because of multilabel sentences).

- *Other*: Any sentence not falling into one of the other categories and presumed to provide little help with clinical decision making, i.e. non-key or irrelevant sentences.

We rely on the data manually annotated at sentence level by (Kim et al., 2011), which consists of 1,000 abstracts from diverse topics. Topics of the abstracts refer to various queries relating to traumatic brain injury, spinal cord injury, and diagnosis of sleep apnoea. Over three hundred abstracts are originally structured, that is, they contain rhetorical roles or headings such as *Background*, *Method*, etc. For the competition, however, we do not separate abstracts based on their structuring, rather we leave them interspersed in the training and test data. Nonetheless, we provide participants with the headings extracted from the structured abstracts to be used as a set of structural features.

In order to build classifiers, 800 annotated training abstracts were provided, and the goal was to automatically annotate 200 test abstracts with the relevant labels. Table 1 shows the exact number of sentences and the percentages of the frequency of labels across the data set. We relied on "Kaggle in Class" to manage the submissions and rankings[1], and randomly divided the test data into "public" and "private" evaluation; the former was used to provide preliminary evaluations during the competition, and the latter to define the final classification of systems.

[1]http://www.kaggle.com/

We provided two benchmark systems at the beginning of the competition. The first system is a simple frequency-based approach, and the second system is a variant of the state-of-the-art system presented by (Kim et al., 2011), using a machine learning algorithm for predictions.

2.1 Naive Baseline

For the naive baseline we merely rely on the most frequent label occurring in the training data, given the position of a sentence. For instance, for the first four sentences in the abstract the most frequent label is *Background*, for the fifth it is *Other*, etc.

2.2 Conditional Random Field (CRF) Benchmark

CRFs (Lafferty et al., 2001) were designed to label sequential data, and we chose this approach because it has shown success in sentence-level classification (Hirohata et al., 2008; Chung, 2009; Kim et al., 2011). Thus we tried to replicate the classifier used by (Kim et al., 2011). However our systems differ in the selection of features used for training. We use lexical and structural features:

1. **Lexical features:** bag of words and Part Of Speech (POS) tags for the lexical features; and

2. **Structural features:** position of the sentences and the rhetorical headings from the structured abstracts. If a heading *h1* covered three lines in the abstract, all the three lines will be labeled as *h1*.

We used NLTK (Bird et al., 2009) to produce a list of POS tags and for the CRF classifier we utilized the Mallet (McCallum, 2002) open source software.

Upon completion of the challenge we learned that our input to the CRF Benchmark did not have a separation between abstracts, causing Mallet to underperform. We rectified the training representation and obtained the accurate score which we refer to as CRF_corrected.

3 Evaluation

Previous work has relied on F-score for evaluating this task, but we decided to choose the *receiver operating characteristic* (ROC) curves and corresponding *area under curve* (AUC) value as

Student Category	Open Category
Marco Lui	Macquarie Test
A_MQ	DPMCNA
System_Ict	Dalibor
	Starling
	Mix

Table 2: Team names and categories.

System	Private Test	Public Test	F-score
Marco Lui	**0.96**	**0.97**	**0.82**
A_MQ	0.95	0.96	0.80
Macquarie Test	0.94	0.94	0.78
DPMCNA	0.92	0.93	0.71
System_Ict	0.92	0.93	0.73
Dalibor	0.86	0.92	0.73
Starling	0.86	0.87	0.78
Mix	0.83	0.84	0.74
Benchmarks			
- CRF_corrected	0.86	0.88	0.80
- CRF_official	0.80	0.83	0.70
- Naive	0.70	0.70	0.55

Table 3: AUC and F-scores for public and private tests. The best results per column are given in bold.

the main metric. ROC curves plot the fraction of true positives out of the positives (TPR = true positive rate) vs. the fraction of false positives out of the negatives (FPR = false positive rate), at various threshold settings. The AUC score is the area under this plot, and the main benefit of this metric is that it allows us to compare classification outputs that assign probability distributions to labels, instead of a binary decision. We also provide F-scores for a better comparison with the existing literature.

Table 2 shows the team names and the categories. There were two categories: "student" and "open". Members of the "student" category were exclusively students at any level: undergraduate or postgraduate. None of the members of the "student" category can hold a PhD in a relevant area. Members of the "open" category included those who could not participate in the "student" category. The winner of the student category and winner overall was Marco Lui from NICTA and the University of Melbourne, followed by Team A_MQ (Abeed Sarker) from Macquarie University and Team System_Ict (Spandana Gella and Duong Thanh Long) from the University of Melbourne. The top participants of the open category were Team Macquarie_Test (Diego Mollá, one of the task organisers) from Macquarie University, and Team DPMCNA (Daniel McNamara) from Australia National University and Kaggle. The description of the systems is provided in Section 4.

Table 3 shows the final scores obtained by the 8 participants and the baseline systems. The scores for private and public test data are very similar. We can see that the top system improved over our state-of-the-art baseline, and all the top-3 were close to its performance.

We relied on a non-parametric statistical significance test known as random shuffling (Yeh, 2000) to better compare the F-scores of the participating systems and benchmarks. We present in Table 5 the ranking of systems according to their F-scores, and the p-value when comparing each system with the one immediately below it in the table[2]. The p-values illustrate different clusters of performance, and they show that team "Marco Lui" significantly improves the CRF_corrected state-of-the-art benchmark, and that team "A_MQ" and CRF_corrected perform at the same level.

Table 4 shows the F-scores separately for each class; the best scoring system is superior for most of the 6 classes. We observed that the ranking of the participants as measured by the official AUC score was the same for the top participants, but the ranking at the bottom of the list of participants differed. The *Outcome* and *Intervention* labels have the highest and lowest scores, respectively, which mostly correlates to the amount of available training instances for each.

4 Description of Systems

The top participants in the task kindly provided a short description of their architectures, which is given in the Appendix. All these submissions relied on Machine Learning (ML) methods, namely Support Vector Machines (SVM), Stacked Logistic Regression, Maximum Entropy, Random Forests, and CRF. Only one of the top participants

[2] The p-value gives the probability of obtaining such an F-score difference between the compared systems assuming that the null hypothesis (that the systems are not significantly different from each other) holds.

System	Population	Intervention	Background	Outcome	Study Design	Other
Marco Lui	**0.58**	0.34	**0.80**	**0.89**	0.59	**0.85**
A_MQ	0.51	**0.35**	0.78	0.86	0.58	0.84
Macquarie Test	0.56	0.34	0.75	0.84	0.52	0.80
Starling	0.32	0.20	**0.80**	0.87	0.00	0.82
DPMCNA	0.28	0.12	0.70	0.78	0.48	0.73
Mix	0.45	0.19	0.68	0.82	0.40	0.81
System_Ict	0.30	0.15	0.68	0.84	0.35	0.83
Dalibor	0.30	0.15	0.68	0.84	0.40	0.83
Naive	0.00	0.00	0.59	0.68	0.00	0.15
CRF_official	0.33	0.22	0.55	0.78	0.67	0.81
CRF_corrected	**0.58**	0.18	**0.80**	0.86	**0.68**	0.83
Aggregate	0.38	0.21	0.71	0.83	0.42	0.76

Table 4: F-scores across each individual label class and the aggregate. The best results per column are given in bold.

System	F-score	p-value
Marco Lui	0.82	0.0012
CRF_corrected	0.80	0.482
A_MQ	0.80	0.03
Starling	0.78	0.3615
Macquarie Test	0.78	0.0001
Mix	0.74	0.1646
System_Ict	0.73	0.5028
Dalibor	0.73	0.0041
DPMCNA	0.71	0
Naive	0.55	-

Table 5: Ranking of systems according to F-score, and pairwise statistical significance test between the target row and the one immediately below. The horizontal lines cluster systems according to statistically significant differences.

relied on sequential classifiers (team "System_Ict" applied CRFs).

Two of the top systems (teams "Marco Lui" and "Macquarie Test") used a two-layered architecture, where features are learned through a first pass (supervised for "Marco Lui", unsupervised for "Macquarie Test"). Team "A_MQ" performed parameter optimisation separately for each of the PIBOSO categories, and it was the only team to use Metamap as a source of features. Feature selection was used by teams "Daniel McNamara" and "System_Ict", which also achieved high performances.

5 Conclusions

The third shared task aimed at fostering research on classifying medical sentences into the predefined PIBOSO category to aid the practice of EBM. Participants from Australia and world-wide competed on this task and the winning team obtained better results than state of the art where the difference was shown to be statistically significant. The best performing technique was attributed to the usage of the meta-learner feature stacking approach using three different sets of features.

We will endeavor to identify such important research problems and provide a forum for research students to provide their effective solutions in the forthcoming shared tasks.

6 Acknowledgements

NICTA is funded by the Australian Government as represented by the Department of Broadband, Communications and the Digital Economy and the Australian Research Council through the ICT Centre of Excellence program.

We would like to thank all the sponsors, management of Kaggle in Class and participants. We would also like to congratulate the winners for their fine work.

References

Steven Bird, Ewan Klein, and Edward Loper. 2009. *Natural Language Processing with Python.* O'Reilly Media.

Grace Chung. 2009. Sentence retrieval for abstracts of randomized controlled trials. *BMC Med Inform Decis Mak*, 9:10.

Spandana Gella and Duong Thanh Long. 2012. Automatic sentence classifier for event based medicine: Shared task system description. In *Australasian*

Language Technology Workshop 2012 : ALTA Shared Task.

Kenji Hirohata, Naoaki Okazaki, Sophia Ananiadou, and Mitsuru Ishizuka. 2008. Identifying sections in scientific abstracts using conditional random fields. In *Proc. of 3rd International Joint Conference on Natural Language Processing*, pages 381–388.

Su Nam Kim, David Martinez, Lawrence Cavedon, and Lars Yencken. 2011. Automatic classification of sentences to support evidence based medicine. *BMC bioinformatics*, 12:S5.

John Lafferty, Andrew Kachites McCallum, and Fernando Pereira. 2001. Conditional random fields: Probabilistic models for segmenting and labeling sequence data. In *Proceedings of the Eighteenth International Conference on Machine Learning*, pages 282–289. Morgan Kaufmann Publishers Inc.

Marco Lui. 2012. Feature stacking for sentence classification in evidence-based medicine. In *Australasian Language Technology Workshop 2012 : ALTA Shared Task*.

Andrew Kachites McCallum. 2002. Mallet: A machine learning for language toolkit. http://mallet.cs.umass.edu.

Diego Molla. 2012. Experiments with clustering-based features for sentence classification in medical publications: Macquarie test's participation in the alta 2012 shared task. In *Australasian Language Technology Workshop 2012 : ALTA Shared Task*.

Alexander Yeh. 2000. More accurate tests for the statistical significance of result differences. In *Proceedings of the 18th Conference on Computational Linguistics (COLING)*, pages 947–953, Saarbrücken, Germany.

Appendix: Description of the top systems

The following text is by the team competitors who kindly agreed to send us their system descriptions.

Team Marco (Marco Lui)

A full description of this system is given in (Lui, 2012). We used a stacked logistic regression classifier with a variety of feature sets to attain the highest result. The stacking was carried out using a 10-fold cross-validation on the training data, generating a pseudo-distribution over class labels for each training instance for each feature set. These distribution vectors were concatenated to generate the full feature vector for each instance, which was used to train another logistic regression classifier. The test data was projected into the stacked vector space by logistic regression classifiers trained on each feature set over the entire training collection. No sequential learning algorithms were used; the sequential information is captured entirely in the features. The feature sets we used are an elaboration of the lexical, semantic, structural and sequential features described by Kim et al (Kim et al., 2011). The key differences are: (1) we used part-of-speech (POS) features differently. Instead of POS-tagging individual terms, we represented a document as a sequence of POS-tags (as opposed to a sequence of words), and generated features based on POS-tag n-grams, (2) we added features to describe sentence length, both in absolute (number of bytes) and relative (bytes in sentence / bytes in abstract) terms, (3) we expanded the range of dependency features to cover bag-of-words (BOW) of not just preceding but also subsequent sentences, (4) we considered the distribution of preceding and subsequent POS-tag n-grams, (5) we considered the distribution of preceding and subsequent headings. We also did not investigate some of the techniques of Kim et al, including: (1) we did not use any external resources (e.g. MetaMap) to introduce additional semantic information, (2) we did not use rhetorical roles of headings for structural information, (3) we did not use any direct dependency features.

Team A_MQ (Abeed Sarker)

In our approach, we divide the multi-class classification problem to several binary classification problems, and apply SVMs as the machine learning algorithm. Overall, we use six classifiers, one for each of the six PIBOSO categories. Each sentence, therefore, is classified by each of the six classifiers to indicate whether it belongs to a specific category or not. An advantage of using binary classifiers is that we can customise the features to each classification task. This means that if there are features that are particularly useful for identifying a specific class, we can use those features for the classification task involving that class, and leave them out if they are not useful for other classes. We use RBF kernels for each of our SVM classifiers, and optimise the parameters using 10-fold cross validations over the training data for each class. We use the MetaMap tool box to identify medical concepts (CUIs) and semantic types for all the medical terms in each sentence. We use the MedPost/SKR parts of speech tagger to annotate each word, and further pre-process the text by lowercasing, stemming and removing stopwords. For features, we use n-grams, sentence positions (absolute and relative), sentence lengths, section headings (if available), CUIs and semantic types for each medical concept, and previous sentence n-grams. For the outcome classification task, we use a class-specific feature called 'cue-word-count'. We use a set of key-words that have been shown to occur frequently with sentences representing outcomes, and, for each sentence, we use the number of occurrences of those key-words as a feature. Our experiments, on the training data, showed that such a class-specific feature can improve classifier performance for the associated class.

Team Macquarie Test (Diego Molla)

A full description of this system is given in (Molla, 2012). The system is the result of a series of experiments where we tested the impact of using cluster-based features for the task of sentence classification in medical texts. The rationale is that, presumably, different types of medical texts will have specific types of distributions of sentence types. But since we don't know the document types, we cluster the documents according to their distribution of sentence types and use the resulting clusters as the document types. We first trained a classifier to obtain a first prediction of the sentence types. Then the documents were clustered based on the distribution of sentence types. The resulting cluster information, plus additional features, were used to train the final set of classifiers. Since a sentence may have multiple labels we used binary classifiers, one per sentence type. At the classification stage, the sentences were classified using the first set of classifiers. Then their documents were assigned the closest cluster, and this information was fed to the second set of classifiers. The submission with best results used Maxent classifiers, all classifiers used uni-gram features plus the normalised sentence position, and the second classifiers used, in addition, the cluster information. The number of clusters was 4.

Team DPMCNA (Daniel McNamara)

We got all of the rows in the training set with a 1 in the prediction column and treated each row as series of predictors and a class label corresponding to sentence type ('background', 'population', etc.) We performed pre-processing of the training and test sets using stemming, and removing case, punctuation and extra white space. We then calculated the training set mutual information of each 1-gram with respect to the class labels, recording the top 1000 features. For each sentence, We converted it into a feature vector where the entries were the frequencies of the top features, plus an entry for the sentence number. We then trained a Random Forest (using R's randomForest package with the default settings) using these features and class labels. We used the Random Forest to predict class probabilities for each test response variable. Note that We ignored the multi-label nature of the problem considering most sentences only had a single label.

Team System_Ict (Spandana Gella, Duong Thanh Long)

A full description of this system is given in (Gella and Long, 2012). Our top 5 sentence classifiers use Support Vector Machine (SVM) and Conditional Random Fields (CRFs) for learning algorithm. For SVM we have used libsvm 1 package and for CRF we used CRF++ 2 package. We used 10-fold cross validation to tweak and test the best suitable hyper parameters for our methods. We have observed that our systems performed very well when we do cross validation on train data but suffered over fitting. To avoid this we used train plus labelled test data with one of the best performing systems as our new training data. We observed that this has improved our results by approximately 3%. We trained our classifiers with different set of features which include lexical, structural and sequential features. Lexical features include collocational information, lemmatized bag-of-words features, part-of-speech information (we have used MedPost part-of-speech tagger) and dependency relations. Structural features include position of the sentence in the abstract, normalised sentence position, reverse sentence position, number of content words in the sentence, abstract section headings with and without modification as mentioned in (Kim et al., 2011). Sequential features were implemented the same way as in (Kim et al., 2011) with the direct and indirect features. After having the pool of features from the above defined features, we perform feature selection to ensure that we always have the most informative features. We used the information gain algorithm from R system3 to do feature selection.

Automatic sentence classifier using sentence ordering features for Event Based Medicine: Shared task system description

Spandana Gella
University of Melbourne
sgella@student.unimelb.edu.au

Duong Thanh Long
University of Melbourne
lduong@student.unimelb.edu.au

Abstract

In this paper, we propose an automatic sentence classification model that can map sentences of a given biomedical abstract into set of pre-defined categories which are used for Evidence Based Medicine (EBM). In our model we explored the use of various lexical, structural and sequential features and worked with Conditional Random Fields (CRF) for classification. Results obtained with our proposed method show improvement with respect to current state-of-the-art systems. We have participated in the ALTA shared task 2012 and our best performing model is ranked among top 5 systems.

1 Introduction

Evidence Based Medicine (EBM) or Evidence based practice is "systematically locating, appraising, and using contemporaneous research findings as the basis for clinical decisions" (Rosenberg and Donald, 1995). Considering the huge amounts of literature and millions of clinical articles currently available and continuously being added to databases like PubMed[1], automating the information access or searching scientific evidence for EBM is a crucial task. Currently evidence based practitioners use the PICO criterion which was proposed by Armstrong (1999) to construct queries and search information in EBM tasks. The PICO concepts or tag-sets are: *Population* (P), *Intervention* (I), *Comparison* (C) and *Outcome* (O).

In this paper, we present a method that classifies sentences in the abstract of a clinical article according to PIBOSO criteria which is an extension of PICO. PIBOSO has six tags: *Population* (P), *Intervention* (I), *Background* (B), *Outcome* (O), *Study Design* (SD) and *Other* (Oth). This information could be used in constructing queries or searching relevant articles in the EBM task. A clear description of the PIBOSO tag-set is available in (Kim et al., 2011), who proposed the tag-set. Our system is based on the CRF algorithm which was earlier used by Kim et al. (2011) for a similar task and proven to be useful.

The major contribution of this paper is that we use a simple and large set of features such as lexical, structural and sequential features and show major improvements on the task of sentence classification over earlier attempts. Our classification techniques have shown clear improvement over existing state-of-the art systems especially for unstructured abstracts.

The paper is organised as follows: We present our related work in Section 2, describe the dataset for training and evaluation in Section 3, and our method and experimental setup in Section 4. We present the analysis of our results in Section 5 and conclude in Section 6.

2 Related work

The first attempt to classify abstract sentences based on the PIBOSO schema is made by Kim et al. (2011). They used the Conditional Random Field (CRF) classifier for learning, and their feature set included lexical features (unigram and bigram with part-of-speech), semantic features (using metathesaurus), structural features (sentence positional features) and sequential features (features from previous sentences). They found out that the best features are **unigrams, sentence po-**

[1] http://en.wikipedia.org/wiki/PubMed

sitional attributes, and sequential information. Using this best configuration of features and the same data set as in our experiment, they did 10 fold cross validation. The best microaverage F-score for each class or label for both Structured (S) and Unstructured (U) data are summarised in Table 3.

The other attempt of same 6 way PIBOSO classification on the same dataset is presented by (Verbeke et al., 2012). In this method, the input sentences are pre-processed with a named-entity tagger and dependency parser. They used a statistical relational learning approach in which features are constructed declaratively using intentional relation. Unlike us and Kim et al. (2011) they have used SVM-HMM[2] for learning. Similar to Kim et al. (2011) they did 10 fold cross validation and the best microaverage F-score of their system is also summarised in Table 3.

3 Dataset

To build the EBM classifier we used the 800 expert annotated training abstracts and 200 test abstracts which were given as part of the shared task. Kim et al(2011) annotated this data using abstracts retrieved from MEDLINE. Both the training and test abstracts have two types of abstracts, structured (S) and unstructured (S). In structured abstracts sentences are organised (and labelled) in an orderly fashion such as *Aim, Method, Results, Conclusions and Other* whereas these labels are absent in unstructured abstracts.

Please note that the way we categorised an abstract as structured or unstructured might be a bit different from previous approaches by Kim et al. (2011) and Verbeke et al. 2012. If the first sentence in an abstract is a sentence ordering label then we considered the abstract as structured or else unstructured. There are 1000 abstracts containing 11616 sentences in total. Statistics of the dataset used are presented in Table 1 and Table 2

	All	**S**	**U**
Abstracts	1000	37.4%	62.6%
Sentences	11616	54.4%	45.6%

Table 1: Dataset statistics

[2]http://www.cs.cornell.edu/people/tj/svm_light/svm_hmm.html

	All	**S**	**U**
Labels	12211	6553	5658%
-Background	22%	10.5%	35.7%
-Intervention	5.9%	4.9%	7.1%
-Outcome	38.9%	35.2%	43.3%
-Population	6.9%	5.8%	8.4%
-Study Design	2.0%	2.36%	1.6%
-Other	29.2%	44.7%	10.8%

Table 2: Dataset statistics

4 System Description

In this section we present the details of our feature set, the training (classification) algorithm, the tools used and assumptions made in executing the experiments.

4.1 Features

We have trained our classifier with different set of features which include lexical features, structural features, sequential features and dependency features [3].

- Lexical features include lemmatized bag-of-words, their part-of-speech, collocational information, the number of content words, verbs and nouns in the sentence (we have used the MedPost (Smith et al., 2004) part-of-speech tagger).
- Structural features include position of the sentence in the abstract, normalised sentence position, reverse sentence position (Kim et al., 2011).
- Sequential features include previous sentence label, similar to Kim et al. (2011).

Additionally, for structured abstracts, we use the sentence ordering labels as features: Heading, Aim, Method, Results, Conclusions. These are provided in the data. Since unstructured abstracts do not have these ordering labels, we automatically annotate the training and testing data with ordering labels using simple heuristics. In the unstructured training data, sentences are classified into an ordering label based on its PIBOSO label: *Background* –> Aim, (*Population or Intervention or Study Design*) –> Method, *Outcome* –> Results and *Other* –> Other. In the unstructured testing data, we have divided sentences into four equal groups based on their position and mapped

[3]We have tried using dependency relations as features but found they did not improve the results. The reason for this could be data sparsity.

them to Aim, Method, Results and Conclusions in this order. **Using *sentence ordering labels* for *unstructured abstracts* is the main difference compared to earlier methods (Kim et al., 2011; Verbeke et al., 2012).**

We tried 6 combinations of features which will be discussed in Results section.

Class	Kim et al. S	Kim et al. U	Verbeke et al. S	Verbeke et al. U	Our System S	Our System U
Background	81.84	68.46	86.19	76.90	**95.55**	**95.02**
Intervention	20.25	12.68	26.05	16.14	23.71	**50.79**
Outcome	92.32	72.94	92.99	77.69	**95.24**	**99.04**
Population	56.25	39.8	35.62	21.58	42.11	**60.36**
Study Design	43.95	4.40	45.5	6.67	0.67	3.57
Other	69.98	24.28	87.98	24.42	83.71	**91.76**
Overall	80.9	66.9	84.29	67.14	81.7	**89.2**

Table 3: F-score per class for structured (S) and unstructured (U) abstracts (bold states improvement over other systems)

4.2 Algorithm

Our sentence classifier uses CRF learning algorithm[4]. We have also executed few experiments using SVM and observed CRF performed better over this dataset with our choice of features. Due to space constraints in this paper we are not comparing CRF versus SVM results.

For feature selection, we used Fselector[5] package from R-system[6]. From the pool of features, we select the "meaningful" features based on the selecting criteria. We have tested several criteria including (1) information gain (2) oneR (3) chi-square test (4) spearman test. Among them, information gain outperformed the others. We select the 700 best features from our pool of features based on information gain score.

Other technique we used for this shared task is "bootstrapping". Our system performed very well on training data but did not perform well on test data, perhaps it suffered over-fitting. To overcome this, we ran our current best model on test data (without using gold-standard labels) and then merge the result with train data to get the new train. In that way, under ROC evaluation, we improved our final scores **by 3%**. In addition, we also pre-process the data. Since the heading such as "AIM,OUTCOME,INTRODUCTION etc." are always classified as "other" in train data, when we find sentence which has less than 20 characters and all in upper case (our notion of heading), we directly classify it as "other" in test data.

[4]We used open-source CRF++ tool. http://crfpp.googlecode.com

[5]http://cran.r-project.org/web/packages/FSelector/index.html

[6]http://www.r-project.org/

5 Results

Features	B	I	O	P	SD	Oth	All
BOW	9.1	3.2	68.8	2.9	0	31.7	38.4
+lexical	18.2	7.0	71.6	11.1	0	65.2	55.3
+struct	60.7	8.3	87.7	17.1	0.6	57.4	62.2
+ordering	93.7	**23.7**	**96.6**	41.0	**1.3**	80.9	80.8
All	95.2	23.7	95.2	42.1	0.6	**83.7**	**81.7**
All+seq	**95.5**	23.7	94.9	**44.2**	0.6	82.9	81.4

Table 4: Analysis of structured abstracts: microaverage f-score, best performance per column is given in bold

Features	B	I	O	P	SD	Oth	All
BOW	13.0	0.7	79.1	1.8	0	14.3	38
+lexical	34.2	1.5	68.0	2.2	0	13.3	40.0
+struct	58.1	5.0	72.1	12.3	1.2	26.9	52.6
+ordering	93.7	40.2	**99.2**	52.4	1.2	**96.6**	88.0
All	**95.0**	**50.7**	99.0	**60.3**	**3.5**	91.7	**89.2**
All+seq	94.9	50.7	98.7	60.1	3.5	90.8	89.0

Table 5: Analysis of unstructured abstracts: microaverage f-score, best performance per column is given in bold

In this section we present the analysis of results on structured and unstructured abstracts separately. In all our experiments, we performed 10-fold cross validation on the given dataset. Shared task organisers have used Receiver operating characteristic (ROC) to evaluate the scores. According to ROC our best system scored **93.78%** (public board) and **92.16%** (private board). However, we compare our results with (Kim et al., 2011) and (Verbeke et al., 2012) using the micro-averaged F-scores as in Table 3. Our system **outperformed previous works in unstructured** abstracts (22% higher than state-of-the-art). Our system performed well in classifying Background, Outcome and Other for both structured and un-structured data. However, our system performed poor in classifying study design as very few instances of it is available in both test and train.

We present the results of 6 systems learned using different feature sets: Table 4 for structured abstracts and Table 5 for unstructured abstracts. We choose bag-of-words (BOW) as the base features, *+lexical* includes BOW and lexical features, *+struct* include BOW and structural features, *+ordering* includes BOW and sentence ordering labels, *All* includes BOW, lexical, struct and ordering features. *All+seq* includes all these features and sequential features.

In previous works, F-scores for unstructured data are low (compared to structured data). However, adding the automatic **sentence ordering label** to the unstructured data improved the performance drastically. This is the main difference compared to earlier models. Overall, our system outperformed existing systems in both structured and unstructured in many labels, which are highlighted in Table 3 under our system section.

Finally, combining **BOW, lexical, structure and sentence ordering** features showed the highest performance for both structured and unstructured data. It also showed that adding the sequential feature (i.e. the PIBOSO label of the previous sentence) do not help in our system, in fact the result slightly reduced. (81.7 –> 81.4 for structured and 89.2 –> 89.0 for unstructured).

6 Conclusions

In this paper, we have presented a brief overview of our method to classify sentences to support EBM. We showed that structural and lexical features coupled with a CRF classifier is an effective method for dealing with sentence classification tasks. The best features in our setting are found to be words, lexical features such as part-of-speech information, sentence positional features, collocations and **sentence ordering labels**. Our system outperformed earlier existing state-of-art systems (Kim et al., 2011; Verbeke et al., 2012).

Acknowledgements

This work is funded by Erasmus Mundus European Masters Program in Language and Communication Technologies. We thank Dr. Paul Cook for his valuable suggestions and helpful comments. We also thank the shared task organisers for providing the gold standard data for evaluations.

References

Kim, S. N., Martinez, D., Cavedon, L., and Yencken, L. (2011). Automatic classification of sentences to support evidence based medicine. *BMC Bioinformatics*, 12(Suppl 2):S5.

Rosenberg, W. and Donald, A. (1995). Evidence based medicine: an approach to clinical problem-solving. *Bmj*, 310(6987):1122–1126.

Smith, L., Rindflesch, T., Wilbur, W., et al. (2004). Medpost: a part-of-speech tagger for biomedical text. *Bioinformatics*, 20(14):2320–2321.

Verbeke, M., Asch, V. V., Morante, R., Frasconi, P., Daelemans, W., and Raedt, L. D. (2012). A statistical relational learning approach to identifying evidence based medicine categories. In *EMNLP-CoNLL*, pages 579–589.

Feature Stacking for Sentence Classification in Evidence-Based Medicine

Marco Lui
NICTA VRL
Department of Computing and Information Systems
University of Melbourne
mhlui@unimelb.edu.au

Abstract

We describe the feature sets and methodology that produced the winning entry to the ALTA 2012 Shared Task (sentence classification in evidence-based medicine). Our approach is based on a variety of feature sets, drawn from lexical and structural information at the sentence level, as well as sequential information at the abstract level. We introduce feature stacking, a metalearner to combine multiple feature sets, based on an approach similar to the well-known stacking metalearner. Our system attains a ROC area-under-curve of 0.972 and 0.963 on two subsets of test data.

1 Introduction

The ALTA Shared Task 2012[1] was a sentence-level classification problem in the domain of biomedical abstracts. Given a collection of abstracts pre-segmented into discrete sentences, the task is to label each sentence according to one of 6 pre-defined classes. The dataset used was introduced by Kim et al. (2011), which also give a description of the classes and an analysis of their distribution. In this work, we will describe the winning entry, focusing on the feature sets and machine learning techniques used.

The main contributions of this work are: (1) additional features to describe sentences for automatic classification of sentences to support evidence based medicine beyond those of Kim et al. (2011), (2) a method for performing the task that does not use a sequential learning algorithm, and (3) a method to combine multiple feature sets that outperforms a standard concatenation approach.

[1]http://www.alta.asn.au/events/sharedtask2012

2 Task Description

The dataset of Kim et al. (2011) (hereafter referred to as NICTA-PIBOSO) consists of 11616 sentences (10379 after headings are removed), manually annotated over the 6 PIBOSO classes (Kim et al., 2011). For the shared task, NICTA-PIBOSO was divided by the competition organizers into train and test partitions. Participants were given labels for the training sentences, and asked to produce an automatic system to predict the labels of the test instances. We do not give further details of the task as it will be covered in much greater depth by the shared task organizers in a paper that will appear alongside this paper.

The shared task was hosted on Kaggle,[2] and as part of Kaggle's standard competition structure, the test dataset was further subdivided into "public" and "private" subsets. Participants did not know which test sentence belonged to which subset. Each submission by a participant consisted of predictions over the entire test set, and Kaggle then automatically computed the competition metric broken down over the public and private subsets. Participants were allowed to submit up to 2 entries per day, and upon submission were immediately given a score on the public subset. The score on the private subset was withheld until after the conclusion of the submission period. Final ranking of competitors is based on the private subset of the test data; the breakdown between public and private serves to penalize entries that overfit the test data in the public subset. The method we describe in this work was the top-scoring system on both the public and private subsets.

[2]http://www.kaggle.com

3 Software Used

All experimentation and analysis was implemented using `hydrat`[3], a declarative framework for text categorization developed by the author. Word tokenization was carried out using NLTK (Bird et al., 2009). The learning algorithm used was logistic regression, as implemented in `liblinear` (Fan et al., 2008). For part-of-speech tagging, we used `TreeTagger` (Schmid, 1994).

4 Features

NICTA-PIBOSO contains two different types of abstracts, *structured* and *unstructured*. Unstructured abstracts are free text, as is the common format in NLP literature. Structured abstracts are divided into sections by headings, such as "Background" or "Outcome", and are becoming increasingly common in biomedical literature. For the shared task participants were not given an explicit indication of which abstracts were structured, or which "sentences" were actually headings. In this work, we applied a simple heuristic: any sentence which contained only uppercase letters was considered a heading, and any abstract containing a heading was considered structured. This definition is slightly more simplistic than that used by Kim et al. (2011), but in practice the difference is minimal.

4.1 Lexical Features

Lexical features are features drawn from the text of a sentence. The lexical feature sets we use are: (1) BoW, a standard bag-of-words. We retained the 15,000 most frequent words, and did not apply stopping or stemming. (2) LemmaPOS, bigrams of part-of-speech tagged lemmas. (3) POS, bigrams and trigrams of part-of-speech tags, without the underlying lemma. Whereas BoW and LemmaPOS are fairly standard lexical features, POS is relatively novel. We included POS based on the work of Wong and Dras (2009), which used POS n-grams to capture unlexicalized aspects of grammar in order to profile a document's author by their native language. The intuition behind the use of POS for our task is that sentences from different PIBOSO categories may have systematic differences in their grammatical structure.

Each of BoW, LemmaPOS and POS are extracted for each sentence. We then use these features to define lexico-sequential features, which are simply the summation of the feature vectors of specific sentences in the same abstract as the target sentence. We refer to these other sentences as the *context*. The contexts that we use are: (1) all prior sentences in the same abstract, (2) all subsequent sentences, (3) n-prior sentences ($1 \leq n \leq 6$), (4) n-subsequent sentences ($1 \leq n \leq 6$), (5) n-window (i.e. n-prior and n-subsequent, $1 \leq n \leq 3$). These lexico-sequential features are intended to capture the information that would be utilized by a sequential learner.

4.2 Structural Features

Structural features model characteristics of a sentence not directly tied to the specific lexicalization.[4] In this work, our structural features are: (1) SentLen, the length of the sentence, in both absolute and relative terms, (2) Heading, the heading associated with each sentence, (3) AbstLen, the length of the containing abstract, and (4) IsStruct, a Boolean feature indicating if the abstract is structured.

We treat Heading similarly to BoW, LemmaPOS and POS, and extract the same 5 types of sequential (indirect dependency) features. We also extract Position, a set of sequential features based on the position of the sentence in the abstract, in both absolute and relative terms.

4.3 Differences with Kim et al. (2011)

To summarize, the differences between our sentence features and those of Kim et al. (2011) are: (1) we use POS n-grams in addition to POS-tagged lemmas, (2) we used sentence length as a feature, (3) we expanded indirect dependencies to include sentences both before as well as after the target sentence, and (4) we increased the scope of indirect dependencies to include BoW, POS as well as section heading information. Differently to Kim et al. (2011), we did not use (1) MetaMap (or any thesaurus), (2) rhetorical roles to group headings, and (3) direct dependency features.

[3] `http://hydrat.googlecode.com`

[4] The distinction between lexical and structural is somewhat arbitrary, as for example the length of sentences is obviously dependent on the length of the words contained, but we maintain this distinction for consistency with Kim et al. (2011).

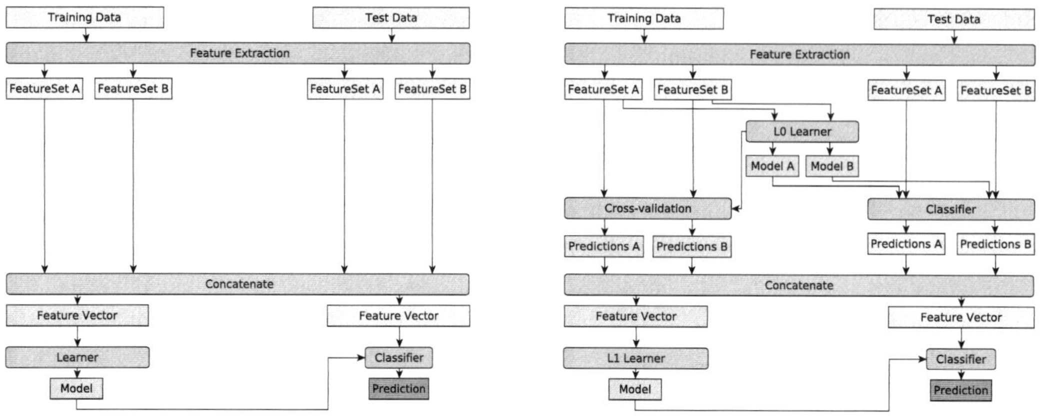

(a) concatenation (b) feature stacking

Figure 1: Comparison of (left) a standard concatenation-based approach to combining feature sets with (right) feature stacking, a metalearning approach.

5 Classifiers

Our main challenge in building a classifier was the need to integrate the large variety of features we extracted. The feature sets are very heterogeneous; some are large and sparse (e.g. BoW), whereas others are small and dense (e.g. structural features). Relative weighting between feature sets is difficult, and simply concatenating the feature vectors often led to situations where adding more features reduced the overall accuracy of the system. Rather than attempt to tune feature weights in an ad-hoc fashion, we opted for a metalearning approach. The intuition behind this is that in principle, the output of "weak" learners can be combined to produce a "strong(-er)" learner (Schapire, 1990).

The metalearner we implemented is closely related to stacking (Wolpert, 1992). We call our approach *feature stacking* in order to highlight the difference, the main difference being that in conventional stacking, a number of different learning algorithms (the *L0* learners) are used on the same training data, and their respective predictions are combined using another learner (the *L1* learner). In our approach, we do not use different algorithms as L0 learners; we always use logistic regression, but instead of training each L0 learner on all the available features, we train a learner on each feature set (e.g. BoW, LEMMAPOS, etc). Hence, we are learning a "weak" learner for each feature set, which are then composed into the final "strong" learner. This approach has two main advantages over simple concatenation of features: (1) it learns the relative importance of each feature set, and (2), it allows learning of non-linear relationships between features.

Figure 1 shows a side-by-side comparison of the two approaches to feature combination. The key difference is that the stacking approach introduces an additional inner (L0) layer, where each instance is projected into the stacked feature space. Given that we have n feature sets and k possible classes, each sentence (training and test) is passed to the L1 learner as a $n \times k$ feature vector. The process for converting L0 features into L1 features is different for the training and the test data, because we only have labels for the training data. For the training data, we use a cross-validation to generate a vector over the k classes for each sentence. We repeat this once for each of the n feature sets, thus yielding the $n \times k$ feature L1 representation. For the test data, we do not have labels and thus for each of the n feature sets we train a classifier over all of the training sentences. We use each of these n classifiers to generate a k-feature vector for each test sentence, which we then concatenate into the final $n \times k$ feature L1 representation.

We chose logistic regression as the learner after initial results indicated it outperformed naive Bayes and SVM in feature stacking on this task. Logistic regression is theoretically well-suited to feature stacking, as stacked logistic regression corresponds to an artificial neural network (Dreiseitl and Ohno-Machado, 2002).

Combination	Output	Public	Private
Concatenation	Boolean	0.885	0.883
Stacking	Boolean	0.893	0.875
Stacking	Probability	0.972	0.963

Table 1: ROC area-under-curve for Public and Private test sets, using (1) feature stacking or concatenation for feature combination, and (2) Boolean or probabilistic output.

6 Results

In this work, we report results that were made available on the Kaggle leaderboard. These results are not directly comparable to previous work (Kim et al., 2011; Verbeke et al., 2012), because the evaluation metric used is fundamentally different. Previously, the task was evaluated using metrics based on precision, recall and F1-score, which is standard for classification tasks. However, in the shared task the metric used was the Receiver Operating Characteristic area under curve (ROC AUC). This metric is common in information retrieval, and it takes into consideration not just a single classification for each sentence, but rather the relative ordering between classes, in order to evaluate a system's ability to trade off precision for recall. This is an easier problem than classification, because classification is all-or-nothing; an instance label is either correct or wrong. Ranking-based metrics such as ROC AUC soften this, by penalizing ranking the correct class second much less than ranking it sixth.

Despite this ranking based metric, there was some initial confusion amongst competitors as to whether classification predictions (i.e. a Boolean value for each possible class) or ranking predictions (i.e. a probability value for each class, which is used to rank the classes) should be submitted. This was clarified by the organizers, and led to all participants seeing substantial increases in score. This difference can be seen in Table 1, where our system improved from 0.893 to 0.972 on the public leaderboard. For Boolean output, we assigned only the most probable label to each sentence, whereas for probabilistic output, we provided the computed probability of each label. Our Boolean output essentially ignored the small proportion of multi-label sentences, treating all sentences as mono-label. This likely accounts for some of the increase in score, though we expect that a good proportion is also due to instances where the correct class was ranked second.

In Table 1, our performance on the public leaderboard suggested that the stacking-based approach to feature combination improved over the concatenation approach (also using logistic regression). On this basis, we focused all further development on using the stacking-based approach. However, the private leaderboard results (which were only released at the conclusion of the competition) tell a different story; here the stacking result is lower than the concatenation result on Boolean output. Unfortunately, we did not submit a run using probabilistic output from concatenation, so we do not have this data point for comparison. Based on just these results, we cannot draw any conclusions on whether the stacking approach outperforms concatenation. We are currently carrying out further evaluation, based on the full dataset (including the goldstandard labels of the test data), which was only made available to participants after the conclusion of the shared task. This evaluation will be based on micro-averaged F1-score, in order to enable direct comparison to the results of Kim et al. (2011) and Verbeke et al. (2012). Our early analysis is highly encouraging, indicating that feature stacking clearly outperforms concatenation, and that our method outperforms the published state-of-the art on this task (Verbeke et al., 2012), with particular improvement on unstructured abstracts. We are currently investigating if this is attributable to our extended features or to feature stacking. We expect to make our full analysis available at a later date.

7 Conclusion

In this work, we presented the features and methodology that were used to produce the winning entry to the ALTA2012 Shared Task. We provided an overview of the feature sets, and a detailed description of feature stacking, a metalearning approach to combining feature sets to produce a high-accuracy classifier for the task. In future work, we will provide a more detailed analysis of the impact of the metalearning approach, as well as the relative impact of the different feature sets, using micro-averaged F1-score as the metric for direct comparability to previous work. We will also compare the use of sequential features with stacked logistic regression to a sequential learning algorithm.

Acknowledgments

NICTA is funded by the Australian Government as represented by the Department of Broadband, Communications and the Digital Economy and the Australian Research Council through the ICT Centre of Excellence program.

References

Steven Bird, Ewan Klein, and Edward Loper. 2009. *Natural Language Processing with Python — Analyzing Text with the Natural Language Toolkit*. O'Reilly Media, Sebastopol, USA.

Stephan Dreiseitl and Lucila Ohno-Machado. 2002. Logistic regression and artificial neural network classification models: a methodology review. *Brain and Cognition*, 35:352–359.

Rong-En Fan, Kai-Wei Chang, Cho-Jui Hsieh, Xiang-Rui Wang, and Chih-Jen Lin. 2008. Liblinear: A library for large linear classification. *J. Mach. Learn. Res.*, 9:1871–1874, June.

Su Nam Kim, David Martinez, Lawrence Cavedon, and Lars Yencken. 2011. Automatic classification of sentences to support evidence based medicine. *BMC Bioinformatics*, 12:1–10.

Robert E. Schapire. 1990. The Strength of Weak Learnability. *Machine Learning*, 5:197–227.

Helmut Schmid. 1994. Probabilistic part-of-speech tagging using decision trees. In *Proceedings of the Conference on New Methods in Natural Language Processing*, Manchester, 1994.

Mathias Verbeke, Vincent Van Asch, Roser Morante, Paolo Frasconi, Walter Daelemans, and Luc De Raedt. 2012. A statistical relational learning approach to identifying evidence based medicine categories. In *Proceedings of the 2012 Joint Conference on Empirical Methods in Natural Language Processing and Computational Natural Language Learning*, pages 579–589, Jeju Island, Korea, July. Association for Computational Linguistics.

David H. Wolpert. 1992. Stacked generalization. *Neural Networks*, 5:241–259.

Sze-Meng Jojo Wong and Mark Dras. 2009. Contrastive analysis and native language identification. In *Proceedings of the Australasian Language Technology Workshop 2009 (ALTW 2009)*, pages 53–61, Sydney, Australia, December.

Experiments with Clustering-based Features for Sentence Classification in Medical Publications: Macquarie Test's participation in the ALTA 2012 shared task.

Diego Mollá
Department of Computing
Macquarie University
Sydney, NSW 2109, Australia
diego.molla-aliod@mq.edu.au

Abstract

In our contribution to the ALTA 2012 shared task we experimented with the use of cluster-based features for sentence classification. In a first stage we cluster the documents according to the distribution of sentence labels. We then use this information as a feature in standard classifiers. We observed that the cluster-based feature improved the results for Naive-Bayes classifiers but not for better-informed classifiers such as MaxEnt or Logistic Regression.

1 Introduction

In this paper we describe the experiments that led to our participation to the ALTA 2012 shared task. The ALTA shared tasks[1] are programming competitions where all participants attempt to solve a problem based on the same data. The participants are given annotated sample data that can be used to develop their systems, and unannotated test data that is used to submit the results of their runs. There are no constraints about what techniques of information are used to produce the final results, other than that the process should be fully automatic.

The 2012 task was about classifying sentences of medical publications according to the PIBOSO taxonomy. PIBOSO (Kim et al., 2011) is an alternative to PICO for the specification of the main types of information useful for evidence-based medicine. The taxonomy specifies the following types: **P**opulation, **I**ntervention, **B**ackground, **O**utcome, **S**tudy design, and **O**ther. The dataset was provided by NICTA[2] and consisted of 1,000 medical abstracts extracted from PubMed split into an annotated training set of 800 abstracts and an unannotated test set of 200 abstracts. The competition was hosted by "Kaggle in Class"[3].

Each sentence of each abstract can have multiple labels, one per sentence type. The "other" label is special in that it applies only to sentences that cannot be categorised into any of the other categories. The "other" label is therefore disjoint from the other labels. Every sentence has at least one label.

2 Approach

The task can be approached as a multi-label sequence classification problem. As a sequence classification problem, one can attempt to train a sequence classifier such as Conditional Random Fields (CRF), as was done by Kim et al. (2011). As a multi-label classification problem, one can attempt to train multiple binary classifiers, one per target label. We followed the latter approach.

It has been observed that the abstracts of different publication types present different characteristics that can be exploited. This lead Sarker and Mollá (2010) to the implementation simple but effective rule-based classifiers that determine some of the key publication types for evidence based medicine. In our contribution to the ALTA shared task, we want to use information about different publication types to determine the actual sentence labels of the abstract.

To recover the publication types one can attempt to use the meta-data available in PubMed. However, as mentioned by Sarker and Mollá (2010), only a percentage of the PubMed abstracts is annotated with the publication type. Also,

[1] http://alta.asn.au/events/sharedtask2012/

[2] http://www.nicta.com.au/

[3] http://inclass.kaggle.com/c/alta-nicta-challenge2

time limitations did not let us attempt to recover the PubMed information before the competition deadline. Alternatively, one can attempt to use a classifier to determine the abstract type, as done by Sarker and Mollá (2010).

Our approach was based on a third option. We use the sentence distribution present in the abstract to determine the abstract type. In other words, we frame the task of determining the abstract type as a task of clustering. We attempt to determine natural clusters of abstracts according to the actual sentence distributions in the abstracts, and then use this information to determine the labels of the abstract sentences.

Our approach runs into a chicken-and-egg problem: to cluster the abstracts we need to know the distribution of their sentence labels. But to determine the sentence labels we need to know the cluster to which the abstract belongs. To break this cycle we use the following procedure:

At the training stage:

1. Use the annotated data to train a set of classifiers (one per target label) to determine a first guess of the sentence labels.

2. Replace the annotated information with the information predicted by these classifiers, and cluster the abstracts according to the distribution of predicted sentence labels (more on this below).

3. Train a new set of classifiers to determine the final prediction of the sentence labels. The classifier features include, among other features, information about the cluster ID of the abstract to which the sentence belongs.

Then, at the prediction stage:

1. Use the first set of classifiers to obtain a first guess of the sentence labels.

2. Use the clusters calculated during the training stage to determine the cluster ID of the abstracts of the test set.

3. Feed the cluster ID to the second set of classifiers to obtain the final sentence type prediction.

2.1 Clustering the abstracts

The clustering phase clusters the abstracts according the distribution of sentence labels. In particular, each abstract is represented as a vector, where each vector element represents the relative frequency of a sentence label. For example, if abstract A contains 10 sentences such that there are 2 with label "background", 1 with label "population", 2 with label "study design", 3 with label "intervention", 3 with label "outcome", and 1 with label "other", then A is represented as $(0.2, 0.1, 0.2, 0.3, 0.3, 0.2, 0.1)$. Note that a sentence may have several labels, so the sum of all features of the vector is greater than or equal to 1.

We use K-means to cluster the abstracts. We then use the cluster centroid information to determine the cluster ID of unseen abstracts at the prediction stage. In particular, at prediction type an abstract is assigned the cluster ID whose centroid is closest according to the clustering algorithm inherent distance measure.

In preliminary experiments we divided the abstracts into different zones and computed the label distributions in each zone. The rationale is that different parts of the abstract are expected to feature different label distributions. For example, the beginning of the abstract would have a relatively larger proportion of "background" sentences, and the end would have a relatively larger proportion of "outcome" sentences. However, our preliminary experiments did not show significant differences in the results with respect to the number of zones. Therefore, in the final experiments we used the complete sentence distribution of the as one unique zone, as described at the beginning of this section.

Our preliminary experiments gave best results for a cluster size of $K = 4$ and we used that number in the final experiments. We initially used NLTK's implementation of K-Means and submitted our results to Kaggle using this implementation. However, in subsequent experiments we replaced NLTK's implementation with our own implementation because NLTK's implementation was not stable and would often crash, especially for values of $K >= 4$. In our final implementation of K-Means we run 100 instances of the cluster algorithm with different initialisation values and choose the run with lower final cost. The chosen distance measure is $\sum_i (x_i - c_i)^2$, where x_i is feature i of the abstract, and c_i is feature i of the centroid of the cluster candidate.

3 Results

For the initial experiments we used NLTK's Naive Bayes classifiers. We experimented with the following features:

p Sentence position in the abstract.

np Normalised sentence position. The position is normalised by dividing the value of p with the total number of sentences in the abstract.

w Word unigrams.

s Stem unigrams.

c Cluster ID as returned by the clustering algorithm.

The results of the intial experiments are shown in Table 1. Rows in the table indicate the first classifier, and columns indicate the second classifier. Thus, the best results (in boldface) are obtained with a first set of classifiers that use word unigrams plus the normalised sentence position, and a second set of classifiers that use the cluster information and the normalised sentence position.

Due to time constraints we were not able to try all combinations of features, but we can observe that the cluster information generally improves the $F1$ scores. We can also observe that the word information is not very useful, presumably because the correlation between some of the features degrades the performance of the Naive Bayes classifiers.

In the second round of experiments we used NLTK's MaxEnt classifier. We decided to use MaxEnt because it handles correlated features and therefore better results are expected. As Table 1 shows, the results are considerably better. Now, word unigram features are decidedly better, but the impact of the cluster information is reduced. MaxEnt with cluster information is only marginally better than the run without cluster information, and in fact the difference was not greater than the variation of values that were produced among repeated runs of the algorithms.

We performed very few experiments with the MaxEnt classifier because of a practical problem: shortly after running the experiments and submitting to Kaggle, NLTK's MaxEnt classifier stopped working. We attributed this to an upgrade of our system to a newer release of Ubuntu, which presumably carried a less stable version of NLTK. We subsequently implemented a Logistic Regression classifier from scratch and carried a few further experiments. The most relevant ones are included in Table 1. We only tested the impact using all features due to time constraints, and to the presumption that using only sentence positions would likely produce results very similar to those of the Naive Bayes classifiers, as was observed with the MaxEnt method.

The Logistic Regression classifier used a simple gradient descent optimisation algorithm. Due to time constraints, however, we forced it to stop after 50 iterations. We observed that the runs that did not use the cluster information reached closer to convergence than those that used the cluster information, and we attribute to this the fact that the runs with cluster information had slightly worse $F1$. Overall the results were slightly worse than with NLTK's MaxEnt classifiers, presumably due to the fact that the optimisation algorithm was stopped before convergence.

The value in boldface in the MaxEnt component of Table 1 shows the best result. This corresponds to a first and second set of classifiers that use all the available features. This set up of classifiers was used for the run submitted to Kaggle which achieved best results, with an AUC of 0.943. That placed us in third position in the overall ranking.

Table 2 shows the results of several of the runs submitted to Kaggle. Note that, whereas in Table 1 we used a partition of 70% of the training set for training and 30% for testing, in Table 2 we used the complete training set for training and the unannotated test set for the submission to Kaggle. Note also that Kaggle used AUC as the evaluation measure. Column *prob* shows the results when we submitted class probabilities. Column *theshold* shows the results when we submitted labels 0 and 1 according to the classifier threshold. We observe the expected degradation of results due to the ties. Overall, $F1$ and *AUC (prob)* preserved the same order, but *AUC (threshold)* presented discrepancies, again presumably because of the presence of ties.

4 Summary and Conclusions

We tested the use of cluster-based features for the prediction of sentence labels of medical abstracts. We used multiple binary classifiers, one per sentence label, in two stages. The first stage used

With Naive Bayes classifiers

	–	$c+p$	$c+np$	$c+w$	$c+w+np$	$c+s+np$
p	0.440	0.572				
np	0.555		0.577			
w	0.448		0.610	0.442		
$w+np$	0.471		**0.611**		0.468	
$s+np$						0.485

With MaxEnt classifiers

	–	$c+p$	$c+np$	$c+w$	$c+w+np$	$c+s+np$
p						
np			0.574			
w		0.646		0.704		
$w+np$	0.740				**0.759**	
$ws+np$						0.758

With Logistic Regression classifiers

	–	$c+p$	$c+np$	$c+w$	$c+w+np$	$c+s+np$
$w+np$	**0.757**				0.747	

Table 1: $F1$ scores with a Naive Bayes classifiers.

	$F1$	AUC *(prob)*	AUC *(threshold)*
MaxEnt $w+np-c+w+np$	0.759	0.943	
NB $w-c+np$	0.610	0.896	
NB $np-c+np$	0.577	0.888	
NB $p-c+p$	0.572	0.873	0.673
NB w	0.448		0.727
NB $w-c+w$	0.442	0.793	
NB p	0.440		0.654

Table 2: Comparison between $F1$ in our results and AUC in the results submitted to Kaggle.

standard features, and the second stage incorporated cluster-based information.

We observed that, whereas cluster-based information improved results in Naive Bayes classifiers, it did not improve results in better informed classifiers such as MaxEnt or Logistic Regression. Time constraints did not allow us to perform comprehensive tests, but it appears that cluster-based information as derived in this study is not sufficiently informative. So, after all, a simple set of features based on word unigrams and sentence positions fed to multiple MaxEnt or Logistic Regression classifiers were enough to obtain reasonably good results for this task.

Further work on this line includes the incorporation of additional features at the clustering stage. It is also worth testing the impact of publication types as annotated by MetaMap or as generated by Sarker and Mollá (2010).

References

Su Nam Kim, David Martinez, Lawrence Cavedon, and Lars Yencken. 2011. Automatic classification of sentences to support Evidence Based Medicine. *BMC bioinformatics*, 12 Suppl 2:S5, January.

Abeed Sarker and Diego Mollá. 2010. A Rule-based Approach for Automatic Identification of Publication Types of Medical Papers. In *Proceedings of the Fifteenth Australasian Document Computing Symposium*.